REBIRTHING
A NATION

RACE
RHETORIC
& MEDIA

Race, Rhetoric, and Media Series
Davis W. Houck, General Editor

REBIRTHING A NATION

White Women, Identity Politics, and the Internet

Wendy K. Z. Anderson

University Press of Mississippi / Jackson

The University Press of Mississippi is the scholarly publishing agency of
the Mississippi Institutions of Higher Learning: Alcorn State University,
Delta State University, Jackson State University, Mississippi State University,
Mississippi University for Women, Mississippi Valley State University,
University of Mississippi, and University of Southern Mississippi.

www.upress.state.ms.us

The University Press of Mississippi is a member
of the Association of University Presses.

First printing 2021
∞

Library of Congress Cataloging-in-Publication Data

Names: Anderson, Wendy K. Z., author.
Title: Rebirthing a nation : white women, identity politics, and the
   internet / Wendy K. Z. Anderson.
Other titles: Race, rhetoric, and media series.
Description: Jackson : University Press of Mississippi, 2021. | Series:
   Race, rhetoric, and media series | Includes bibliographical references
   and index.
Identifiers: LCCN 2021006485 (print) | LCCN 2021006486 (ebook) | ISBN
   9781496832771 (hardback) | ISBN 9781496832764 (trade paperback) | ISBN
   9781496832788 (epub) | ISBN 9781496832795 (epub) | ISBN 9781496832801
   (pdf) | ISBN 9781496832818 (pdf)
Subjects: LCSH: White nationalism—United States. | Racism—United States.
   | Racism in the press.
Classification: LCC HS1703 .A54 2021 (print) | LCC HS1703 (ebook) | DDC
   322.4/20973—dc23
LC record available at https://lccn.loc.gov/2021006485
LC ebook record available at https://lccn.loc.gov/2021006486

British Library Cataloging-in-Publication Data available

I dedicate this book to everyone working together to foster ethical and equitable social change through coalitional community labor.

Contents

Section One: Collective Voices of White Nationalist Women

Section Two: Individual Women's Voices as Institutional Coding of White Supremacy

    Disassembling "Contained Agency" of the Alt-Right 97

6   Responsibility of a White "Privilege Filter": Dismantling Conservative
    White Women as Color-Blind Maiden Shields................................. 121

    Epilogue: Amplifying Intersectionality as an Ethical Response 148

    Appendix: Values 173

    Notes 175

    Bibliography.. 217

    Index..243

Acknowledgments

I find myself grateful for the support of so many scholars, friends, and family that it is difficult to know where to begin my thanks.

First, I want to thank my partner, Matthew, who has supported this project from its inception, especially when I felt exhausted through the revision process. Thank you for all the insight, work time, and space I've needed to complete this book. I appreciate that you understood the value of the work that I do and continue to teach me about necessary personal acceptance and humility that comes with a growth mindset. Without you pushing me out the door on those days that I did not feel like working, this project would never have been completed. I also want to thank my children, Jackson and Jakodi, who gave up many family days and found Legos to play with as I finished my book. Our family is stronger because of our reliance on both parents and independence of both children. Additionally, I want to thank my mother, Virginia Zeitz, who knew that moving to Minnesota, an ideologically progressive, but racially discriminatory state, would require conscientious work to ensure her children critically engaged racial discrimination. My mom taught me to value my voice, but also encouraged me to educate myself by listening to and being responsive to others concerning respect and injustice. My mom always said that she learned more from her kids than anything else in the world and I continue to learn from my mom's responsive and vocal example. Mom, thank you for supporting our hard conversations about the content of this book and challenging others, especially family members, to do the same. Also, I would like to thank my Uncle Dick. Although he never saw this work become the book that it is, his presence during my earlier research and ability to have critical conversations about racism helped me feel supported to ensure I would continue down the path that felt right to me without being held back by other white people's assumptions.

Next, I want to thank my academic advisors, mentors, and peers. My advisor from Purdue University, Dr. Charles Stewart, not only challenged me to study something I did not agree with, but also questioned the validity of what I was studying. Without his counterarguments, I would have not researched how white women are at the apex of racism within the United States. Additionally, I thank Dr. Samantha Blackmon, who not only supported my work, but also offered critical race theory as a means to ethically engage in my research. Dr. Blackmon provided the impetus for me to continue developing my work while engaging in necessary self-reflection of my own coded white privilege. During a time when I wanted to walk away from the academy, Dr. Blackmon listened to me and challenged me to keep valuing myself and my work. I don't doubt that my naivety ranged from eyeroll-worthy to infuriating for her, but I am grateful for our continued dialogue about antiracist work.

I also want to thank Dr. Karma Chávez, who has supported my graduate-level work since my master's degree. Words will not suffice to clarify the value of her continued support. Every time I have asked to meet and chat about my work, she made time. Dr. Chávez stands as the epitome of ethical, engaged scholarship and mentorship within the field of Communication Studies. She never pushed me to do anything, yet, similar to Dr. Blackmon, the critical questions she asked and the braveness she models through her work continue to inspire me today.

Additionally, I feel fortunate for the insight offered by Dr. Kate Lockwood Harris, Dr. Lisa Corrigan, Dr. Catherine Squires, Dr. Maegan Parker Brooks, Dr. Scott Makstenieks, Sara Anderson, Dr. Sue Zaeske, and Dr. Angela Ray on this work. Lisa, Maegan, Scott, and Sara offered feedback on early drafts and the book publication process, which helped me transition this work to publication. Dr. Catherine Squires listened, bought me lunch, chatted with me about how to develop the project, and shared exceptional publication outlets in which to place an early chapter. Further, I am grateful for Dr. Kate Harris, who offered insight during writing group, which led to the conceptual development of agency and intersectionality as foundations to my theory of contained agency. I am grateful for our continued conversations about how to humbly engage our white privilege through responsiveness. Both Dr. Zaeske and Dr. Ray offered mentoring and support at different stages of this book that helped me continue to develop the work and honor the accomplishment. I thank them both for helping me see how outside mentors in the field can help us understand the meaning of our work.

As I worked to finalize revisions, my writing group, which included Dr. Attila Hallsby, Dr. Michael Lechuga, Dr. Emily Winderman, Dr. Kate Harris, and Dr. Zorniza Kornminechev, as well as my department chair, Dr. Ron Greene, provided structural advice concerning how to organize the chapters and reframe the macro argument, which elucidated the rhetorical connection between white nationalism and conservative white women. I thank them for their time, attention, and insight.

In addition to my immediate colleagues, throughout this entire research process Kittie Grace, Aimee Dobbs, LaShara Davis, and Alda Norris have engaged my work and sent along relevant articles. Kittie, thank you for making sure I did not leave the academy and for connecting me with students who valued my work. Our conversations reminded me that I am engaged in significant work and kept me moving forward on this project. Aimee, the baked goods and critical conversations we shared allowed me to keep moving even when I was exhausted. LaShara, your continued support, collegiality, and friendship allowed me to continue my work even when I wanted to walk away from the academy. Alda, I am grateful that you read my research and that we engage the far reaches of white conservativism together. Family members such as Austin Klein, Genevieve Klein, Alex Zeitz, Ben Zeitz, and David Zeitz provided familial responsiveness and support that allowed me to perform my best through their friendship. I am also indebted to Andrew Boge and Alyssa Benson for their dialectic about this work and for reading early drafts. Andrew's persistence, collegiality, insight, and kindness illustrated a continued value of my work for the larger field of Communication Studies. I am grateful for his engaged discussions. My advisor at Kansas State University, Charles Griffin, once said that he used to put his thesis in the freezer just in case his apartment caught on fire; I am grateful for Andrew's willingness to function as my metaphoric freezer for early drafts of the book. I was also grateful that he, and Michael Lechuga, offered me a space to be humbled without feeling humiliated through my work to ensure the ethical foundation of my analytic, antiracist approach. Thank you for being willing to listen and for offering constructive advice about how to ensure I offered meaningful work while "staying in my lane."

The institutional support in the form of lecture series presentations at Hastings College and Winona State University allowed me to keep developing this book. I am grateful for Hastings College's support as I developed the first chapters of the book. As I neared the end of its development I was grateful for Winona State University, in particular Dr. MaryJo Klinger, Dr. Emilie Falc, the History, Communication Studies, and Women, Gender, and Sexuality Studies departments, as well as the Krueger Library for bringing me in to speak about my research. Those presentations helped me tighten my analysis as well as prepare myself to respond to critical concerns about the white supremacy and the alt-right.

Much of this work was written and revised within public libraries, my home, and one public business, the Workhorse Coffee Bar. To its owner, Ty, thank you for letting me order hot chocolates and your glorious red pepper and tomato soup with a grilled cheese croissant and sit to work for hours on end. Your space helped me move this work when a library would not do. I appreciate your independent business that felt like home.

Another group of people for whom I am grateful is our children's care workers. I know this may seem unusual, but I am grateful for the teachers at the University of Minnesota Child Development Center and S'more Fun who took such amazing care of our children, which allowed me to have the mental security to spend less time in their classroom and more time writing. Without having strong programs like the UMCDC and S'more Fun, scholars who are also parents, particularly mothers who are typically the default parent when it comes to organizing childcare, would not complete the work we do. Additionally, without the support of Diane Odash when it came to scheduling my classes to ensure I could be home for my fair share of the sick kid child care and research days, this book would have never been finished.

Certainly not least, I want to thank my closest friends, the LKAs—Alma Mendez, Illiana Cantu, Nicole Bates, Stephanie Zeitz, Sue Brennan, Neal Rasmussen, Luis Puga, and others who come to play at game night. Our time together professionally and personally is why I always felt value in this project. I hope to always preserve the community we have; I hope that our children will have similar communities in the future. You are my sisters and family and my community for life. You have been there when I struggled the most with this project and my life. Thank you for supporting every step that I have made and helping me learn to be more critical of my privilege while supporting me for who I am so I could grow. I feel honored to have you in my life.

For all those other friends and family members who asked about the book project, like my dad, Al Zeitz, or offered support concerning my safety, like my brother, Mark Zeitz, I am grateful for your continued support and kindness. I have appreciated your inspiring words throughout the process.

I am grateful to the University Press of Mississippi, for their editors who sought me out at NCA because they saw the promise of my work and who supported its development by connecting me with reviewers who gave concrete and engaging feedback. Folks like Vijay Shah, who continue to offer me articles and insightful notes, and Emily Bandy, who actively listened and responded to my concerns, made the book revising process more accessible for me. I am grateful for their willingness to work around my instructor and parenting schedule, to ensure that I could produce the best possible work. I am also grateful to my copyeditor, Will Rigby, for his insightful comments and to journal editorial staff for copyright permissions to publish later versions of those manuscripts:

Material from Anderson, Wendy K. Z., "Classifying Whiteness: Unmasking White Nationalist Women's Digital Design through an Intersectional Analysis of Contained Agency." Special Issue on Media and the Extreme Right in *Communication, Culture, and Critique* 11, no. 1: 116–32 (March 2018), is used by permission of Oxford University Press.

An earlier version of chapter 1, "(De)coding Whiteness: Appropriations of White Nationalist Women's Inferential Racism as Coded Rhetoric in US Politics," was published in Rhetoric, Race, and Resentment: Whiteness and the New Days of Rage [Symposium], *Rhetoric Review* 36, no.4 (2017): 255–347, DOI: 0.1080/07350198.2017.135519110.1080/07350198.2017.1355191. The material is used by permission of Taylor & Francis Group, https://www.tandfonline.com/.

Finally, I want to thank all the reviewers, students, colleagues, and staff who made my research possible. Every time I was asked to visit an institution, I sent out the manuscript, and I had to schedule classes, a cadre of people (students, staff, faculty, activists, parents) showed up, offered support, organized meetings, asked and answered questions, and encouraged me to continue this work. Without their continued interest and kindness, I would have never finished this book. Thank you for being interested in developing ethical and equitable antiracist communities.

REBIRTHING
A NATION

Introduction

Last fall when I returned home from a conference, my partner took me aside and asked if I had seen a recent Facebook post he had made about a Diwali lamp our oldest child brought home from school. After my partner posted a picture of the lit lamp and a description of the excitement he and the kids shared, a seventy-two-year-old white woman (who would identify herself as a progressive Democrat) who is a close family member commented, "It looks like an ashtray." When my partner responded that he and the kids planned on decorating it, she retorted that she was "Just making fun." I felt devastated that someone, a family member, responded so capriciously on something they did not know much about. After a quick Google search, I added an NPR article that explained Diwali to the thread, encouraging the relative to seek more information online about this part of Hindu culture. I still felt stymied and conflicted by this display of ethnocentrism, so I texted a cousin, who encouraged me to call my relative. During the phone call the relative was receptive to the concern and apologized to my spouse and me, asking me how she could take her comments down. She then rationalized that she grew up around white people, raised her kids around white people, and had been socialized that Black people would hurt her. She noted the continued effort it takes for her to intervene when faced with those coded racial cues and how she tried to break them with her own kids by encouraging friendships with children of color. However, as she has gotten older, she "chooses to be around white people" and has to force herself to quiet the

3

discomfort she feels around Black, Indigenous, and People of Color (BIPOC) in connection to her safety.

My example embodies a tension with white people concerning race and racism we see on a larger scale today. From Brexit to right-wing nationalism in Norway, Hungary, Austria, France, Germany, and Greece, to the US Republican presidential primary election of Donald Trump, whiteness as "identity politics"[1] became a salient rhetorical strategy to forward white supremacy on a transnational scope. We witnessed what *New York Times* reporter Amanda Taub called a global "crisis of whiteness," as Donald Trump frames his and other white people's insecurity as a lost "greatness" of the United States. Through a rhetorical style of "white rage,"[2] Trump continues to scapegoat members of underrepresented groups as America's downfall, playing into coded fears about safety, igniting what CNN commentator Van Jones calls a cultural "whitelash."[3]

Whiteness is a "membership in an 'ethno-national' majority,"[4] where white identity becomes a socially accepted perspective from which to engage white power and grievance.[5] In a conversation between white nationalist and Stormfront leader Don Black and his son, Derek Black (who had recently walked away from the white nationalist movement), about Donald Trump's rhetoric, Derek mused, "'Who would have thought he'd be the one to take it mainstream?' Don said, and in a moment of so much division, it was the one point on which they agreed."[6] When two people with an extensive history of forwarding white nationalism, one who leads Stormfront and the other who walked away from white nationalism, identify that Donald Trump validates the white nationalist movement, further scrutiny of a white supremacist rhetoric is warranted.

Although Donald Trump amplifies and validates white supremacist rhetoric, the refinement of his racist rhetoric occurred well before his campaign. Within digital spaces, white nationalists' overt racism provide a guide as to how implied racialized rhetoric signals white audiences. Although some scholars believe that racism is easily identified, by reducing or relabeling white nationalist ideologies and assuming that other "rational" people will identify racism, scholars miss the "genius" (or effectiveness) of unethical, inferential, even unwitting racialized rhetoric (racism).[7] As Reni Eddo-Lodge articulates:

> If all racism was as easy to spot, grasp and denounce as white extremism is, the task of the anti-racist would be simple. People feel that if a racist attack has not

occurred, if the word "nigger" has not been uttered, an action can't be racist. . . . We tell ourselves that good people can't be racist. We seem to think that true racism only exists in the hearts of evil people. We tell ourselves that racism is about moral values, when instead it is about the survival strategy of systemic power. When swathes of the population vote for politicians and political efforts that explicitly use racism as a campaigning tool, we tell ourselves that huge sections of the electorate simply cannot be racist, as that would render them heartless monsters. But this isn't about good and bad people.[8]

People code "covert"[9] racism into institutional and organizational structures (education, politics, government, workplaces, housing, etc.) within the United States to sustain racial power and inequity. I define structures using Bonilla-Silva's definition, which highlights the "totality of the social relations and practices that reinforce white privilege."[10] Using a more nuanced form and style than white nationalist men's rhetoric, white nationalist women rhetorically refine coded racism through color-blind values, ideologies, and classifications to validate white identity politics, which alt-right and conservative white women structurally employ to sustain white supremacy within US institutions. As a form of social movement rhetoric, white nationalist arguments become rhetorical resources, which conservative white women and men, who do not explicitly identify as white nationalists, appropriate to forward white supremacy.

Rhetorical Refinement within Social Movements

Social movements are generative spaces for the rhetorical refinement of cultural meaning through language. According to rhetorical scholar Charles Wilkinson, social movements embody "[l]anguaging strategies by which a significantly vocal part of an established society, experiencing together a sustained dialectical tension growing out of moral (ethical) conflict, agitate to induce cooperation in others, either directly or indirectly, thereby affecting the status quo."[11] Due to their place at the margins of communities, social movement actors must use rhetoric to redefine their identities and context to frame conflict in a way that implicates mainstream audiences. Power over the symbols people use to create identity provides legitimacy for any movement. Typically, the power of identification "accrues to the institutions because they are the keepers, protectors, and proselytizers of the sacred symbols, emblems, places, offices, documents, codes, values, and myths of the social order."[12] Organizations have significant influence over interpretation and amplification via media outlets to influence cultural meaning. The power of identity politics lies in media access and amplification. Social movement actors must adapt their rhetoric, both in content and mediated form, to meet the needs and values of mainstream audiences, or the movement dies. Rhetorical refinement of language and medium keep social movements viable.

Rhetorical refinement encompasses how social actors express, revise, and retest rhetoric in a social movement context to influence exigency for audiences. As a required legitimation task, rhetorical refinement ensures code palatability in a larger political arena. As Michael McGee notes, social actors use symbols (or codes) to identify specific values that mediate ideologies. Rhetorical refinement of a *"rhetoric of* [racism]*"*[13] can code (justify and preserve racial social construction and classification) for social control. For example, by identifying outgroups such as "Mexicans" and "Muslims" as threats, racialized boundaries or classifications are set that privilege and empower certain racialized groups (white) over others. Rhetorical refinement calls attention to shared values between audience members as an epideictic display, while it exposes and undermines outsiders of that group.[14] Due to their refinement, rhetorical codes become resources mainstream politicians can appropriate and, in this case, signal whiteness to mainstream audiences while not explicitly associating with the overt racism of white nationalism. As Eduardo Bonilla-Silva states, "Since the central racial debates and the language used to debate those matters have changed, our analytical focus ought to be dedicated to the analysis of the new racial issues,"[15] like those forwarded by political actors in mainstream arenas. Although political rhetors like Donald Trump may have never directly read white nationalist women's web or social media sites, the use of rhetorically refined values, ideologies, and classifications (like Sarah Palin's use of "14 Words"[16]) still signals or symbolizes whiteness in similar ways.

Yet, symbols (values, ideologies, and classifications) function differently based on medium and representation of the rhetorics of content and form. By rhetorics I mean not only traditional "content" such as language and symbols (values, ideologies, classifications), but also digital forms of rhetoric, in which the medium makes an argument by the way its users engage in dissemination of information and interact with other users/audiences. Language is something we are taught in a rote, utilitarian form, yet "[t]o speak a language is to take on a world, a culture."[17] Linguistic symbols are embedded with bias, or a perspective. People socialize by listening to words without knowledge of historic context of terms; they use the "coded" symbol systems within their communities and organizations to reinforce and discipline people through rhetorical utility and consistency, or by getting adequate or inadequate responses.[18] Symbols become rhetoric when social actors use them strategically to wield power or influence.

In addition to rhetorical content, we are taught rhetorical form—from smiles and hugs to memes and tweets—of communication. The communicative "flow" of a platform, or medium, illustrates a responsiveness (or lack thereof) to particular actors and perspectives within a community. Context influences the meaning of our rhetoric,[19] yet shifts in locality of meaning by digital platform and, by consequence, "the affective and embodied experiences that circulate" within those communities.[20] In order to understand and dismantle codes of identity politics within particular platforms, we must critically interrogate, or decode, how social actors rhetorically refine identity rhetorics, in both content and form, as a means to amplify or constrain voice.

Coding and Decoding a Rhetorical and Institutional Legacy of Gendered Racism

In hopes of decoding racialized rhetoric, popular media outlets continue to create segments unmasking the US cultural legacy of racism. On MTV's *Decoded*, for example, television personality Franchesca Ramsey decodes systematic racialization by historicizing uses of terms, stereotypes, and events that privilege white people while undermining BIPOC. In her April 27, 2016, episode entitled "The surprisingly racist history of 'Caucasian,'" Ramsey historicizes the use of the term "Caucasian" by recognizing how scientists developed terminology like Caucasian to socially construct race based on beauty standards.[21] Although it is based primarily on skin color, Caucasian continues to be used today when legally defining and classifying identity. Similar to binaries noted between men/women and white/black, the term "Caucasian" serves to privilege white people as a standard of race. Using "Caucasian" as a classification places whiteness at the top of a racial hierarchy. However, rather than a culture, "whiteness" is a set of discursive, ideological, economic, and political systems that foster, maintain, and naturalize racial inequality."[22] As noted by Charles Mills, "*[w]hiteness is not really a color at all, but a set of power relations.*"[23]

In a political arena, political actors use whiteness performatively as a reactive identity to insecurity to solidify a social organization to bond white people together through a political identity. According to feminist theorist and cultural critic bell hooks, "whiteness is a unifying feature—not culture,"[24] meaning that when white people use "white" identifiers like "Caucasian," we are identifying a common skin color rather than a set of common traditions, mores, or experiences. Whiteness becomes a means to justify value over others. The legacy of colonialism has roots in other-self constructions, where the "Western self is itself produced as *an effect* of the Western discursive production of its Others."[25] White is a responsive identity term that people use in an attempt to separate and distinguish themselves from otherness—a response to socially constructing BIPOC as having a "race" or difference. As professor of philosophy George Yancy clarifies, "whiteness is secured through marking what it is not."[26] Creating a classification involves division,[27] yet through a racialized classification of "others," those in power (e.g., white people) identify deviants (e.g., black and brown people) who *will* constrain the invisible "whiteness" that serves as the expectation of normalcy.[28] Classification is "biopolitical" in that it serves as a "technology"[29] to sort based on a specific framework, and, in the case of people, that sorting has dire consequences.

By differentiating from "other," "white" is validated as "a political system, a particular power structure of formal or informal rule, socioeconomic privilege, and forms for the differential distribution of material wealth and opportunities, benefits and burdens, rights and duties" of global white supremacy.[30] Instead of struggling for the economic wages they may desire, working-class white people are offered a "psychological wage" of whiteness (a feeling of being better than "others") by white people with economic or political power in order to enforce the racialized separation.[31] A perceived difference becomes a justification or defense against the other, or, "in other words, to personify The Other."[32] Personifying a Black, Indigenous, or Person of Color (BIPOC) as "other" hierarchically situates a racial classification—white identity as better than "others." BIPOC are framed as the negative, or in a "role with regard to unfulfilled [white] expectations."[33]

From an ethnocentric perspective, white people define "Other"[34] (e.g., Black and Brown people) by their inability to measure up, or be engaged as "normal" (read: white) people, using rules and guidelines established by white people, from a white perspective. As clarified by legal critical race scholar Kimberlé Crenshaw,

> Throughout American history, racism has identified the interests of subordinated whites with those of society's white elite. Racism does not support the dominant order simply because all whites want to maintain their privilege at the expense of blacks, or because blacks sometimes serve as convenient political scapegoats; rather the very existence of a clearly subordinated Other group is contrasted with the norm in a way that reinforces identification with the dominant group.[35]

By creating an Other, identity characteristics people share with a dominant group define in and out groups. In US culture, race and ethnicity are synonymous with "nonwhite people" or those considered "other" than white.[36] Race becomes the normative rule by which people are measured. On a global scale, white European people develop and reinforce racialized constructs through a desire to measure their identity with BIPOC to justify their continuing conquest and oppression of "others."[37]

By oppression, I mean "any unjust situation where, systematically and over a long period of time, one group denies another group access to the resources of society."[38] Institutions and organizations use race rhetorically to sustain the objectification and separation of BIPOC (as "other") rather than engage the term as a social construction to understand how people code and are coded through classifications. Ethnocentrism becomes the equivalent of "race prejudice."[39] Through a corresponding ideology of white nationalism, white people code whiteness into our institutions, both political, organizational, and cultural systems.

"Coding whiteness," then, is a rhetorical process of altering symbolic strategies into condensed arguments that signal, rather than overtly state, whiteness. Although the signal may be similar to that of a dog whistle because the impact is the same, my interest is not in deciding whether or not the signaling is purposeful or unwitting racism. Instead, my focus is that the signal as a shibboleth is significant because it is a marker of a racist speech act. By coding whiteness, people normalize and invisibilize a white perspective through linguistic and symbolic choices to reinforce white privilege, while avoiding the subsequent social consequences of overtly racist language. For example, the "okay" hand gesture, which has come under discussion as a white nationalist symbol, has a history within white nationalist (KKK) and conservative organizations.[40] When used by a US National Guardsman on a briefing on MSNBC,[41] regardless if he meant it as such, an impact is that his sign *infers* a support of white nationalism. The discussion itself raises the symbol to become a speech act, which can infer a type of meaning for some audience members. Unlike "referential" racism (cross burning and racial epithets), "inferential racism"[42] stems from unexamined, underlying racial bias and is rhetorically coding culture. Inferential racism is powerful due to the "unquestioned assumptions"[43] that naturalize racism through color-blind linguistic choices and organizational form. An impact is that racism is alive and well and the symbols serve as means to perpetuate fear through reminders of racial hierarchy.

Scholars have considered the slipperiness of "color-blind" ideologies found in statements such as "some of my best friends are black"[44] or "I am not racist, but . . . ," which separate rhetorical meaning from rhetorical accountability and responsibility. Symbols socially construct the world in which we live and what lens filters our identities, perspectives, and subsequent meaning and decisions. However, we need to shift decoding whiteness into the heart of whiteness studies. As feminist writer and independent scholar Sara Ahmed notes, "Whiteness studies should instead be about attending to forms of white racism and white privilege that are not undone, and may even be repeated and intensified, through declarations of whiteness, or through the recognition of privilege as privilege . . ."[45]—what I call decoding whiteness.

Rhetorically decoding whiteness becomes challenging when audiences want to believe they and their communities are not racist. In an attempt to deny personal responsibility for addressing racism and to retain white privilege, people may claim that "everyone is equal" or "I do not see color." By white privilege I mean not only the "absence of consequences of racism" like "structural discrimination," but also our ability to gain advantages based on having white skin, white sounding names, etc.[46] By preempting the statistical and narrative realities of systemic racism with their desire for equality, people retain their privilege, while rhetorically sidestepping an argument about race. The argumentative sidestep is especially effective by white women to separate themselves from another oppressed group.

White nationalists co-opt terms like "marginal" and "multicultural" within new contexts to signal "oppressive" environments. When facing the realities of institutionalized and systemic racial oppression, white people appropriate "oppressed" language to claim an identity attack and recenter themselves in the discourse. For example, the term "reverse racism" appropriates the term "racism" yet asserts a more personal identity discrimination that does not account for the systemic discrimination BIPOC experience. By framing themselves as victims, white nationalists appropriate the feeling of being oppressed without the systemic, racialized oppression. As noted by Lisa Nakamura, a leading scholar of digital studies, due to a comfort with and desire to reject the existence of white privilege, a "lack of white privilege can be experienced as oppression."[47] However, by appropriating descriptive terms like "reverse racism" or "marginalization" without contextual or historical recognition of a term's etymology, a person does not account for the institutional and historical depth of systemic racism. Instead, victim claims recenter the issue on white people's discomfort.

Although racism continues, the field of Communication Studies has been slow to question and challenge these color-blind politics. Professor Lisa Flores notes, "it is only relatively recently that rhetorical critics have paid consistent attention to race."[48] Many white people research as though race does not influence the rhetorics of what we study, as though somehow our language and study exist as a set of objective tools. I amplify Flores's call for racial rhetorical criticism to engage "the persistence of racial oppression, logics, voices, and bodies,"[49] which comprises rhetorics of race, particularly at the intersection of race and gender, to better understand how "social contracts" continue to influence even our fields of study.

Historically, social contracts, which function as racialized and gendered codes, constrain voices of people identified as "different." Social contracts function as reasoning (white, male right to establish facts, false dichotomies of women/men, white/black binaries, inherent dependency of women and slaves as evidence of inadequacy, scientific observation of "facts" laden with expectancy bias, entitlement to control "deficient souls" of women and slaves)[50] to the inferiority of women and BIPOC. Professor of women and gender studies Sally Kitch clarifies that the cultural development of gender and racial ideologies "evolved together as the Gender Contract supporting patriarchal rule in Western cultures inspired the Racial Contract that promotes the global dominance of European males, especially over black Africans."[51] Similar gendered and racialized contracts illustrate today how people clarify or code their values. "Race and gender are thus at the heart of identity construction in relation to nationalist and religious discourse,"[52] making an intersectional analysis of race and sex necessary to unpack nationalist rhetoric; yet how that racist rhetorical content becomes built into social structures requires an analysis of the racially coded infrastructure as well.

Transmediating Coded Identity within Digital Contexts

Although prominent media and technology scholars take techno-optimistic stances of digital spheres becoming an "interdependent . . . global village"[53] where "[o]ur children are not going to know what nationalism is,"[54] media historian Lisa Gitelman acknowledges that "modern forms of mediation are in part defined by normative constructions of difference, whether gender, racial, or other versions of difference."[55] Within digital spheres, content is often de- and recontextualized from the context in which communication happens. Digital space lends itself to the (re)coding of oppression, when part of a dominant group is not held accountable for the cultural and historical context from which the term originated. The extremity and the explicitness of white nationalists' racism makes digital constraints on community very obvious, thus offering scholars a roadmap for how less obvious inferential[56] racism and sexism are embedded in physical and digital realities. Through masked white "privilege filters" as well as promises of "contained agency" (see chapters 2 and 3), white women rhetorically refine the white supremacy Donald Trump espouses, which allows him to gain and retain power in the US political system.

As I allude to in my title, reinstating power dynamics can guide technological development. By using rebirthing as a metaphor for white women's role in white supremacy, I hope to invoke DJ Spooky's "Rebirth of a Nation" as a remix of D. W. Griffith's film *Birth of a Nation*. White women can be framed as the victim, the object of desire, the vessel as a means to advocate for their support of white supremacy.

Yet, digital protocols influence how a digital public sphere is coded to function, how a frame is made. By "protocols" I mean the flexible rules that guide programming languages (such as those found at the W3 consortium that dictate HTML, CSS, the modding options defining specific gaming arenas, algorithms[57]) as well as informal cultural expectations and formalized rules that people interpret and negotiate to coexist within digital spaces (such as social expectations and terms of service agreements and rules that govern engagement). HTML, CSS, and the modding options are the design rules that influence the form or shape of digital rhetoric. Building on the metaphor of "code as law,"[58] protocols guide the design and development of the language of code.[59] Understanding the flexibility of protocol involves recognizing agency within institutional and organizational recommendations, or how people design their websites and can gate their communities through their coded argument of whiteness. As associate professor in the Department of Information Studies Safiya Noble notes in her book *Algorithms of Oppression*, classification systems inherent in algorithm-based programs like Google's search engine systematize white bias.[60] Web users and web designers filter our Facebook social media and Google search sites to privilege [white], [male], [other dominant group] content.

Privilege filters classify all social spaces in our lives—including digital spaces. Instead of helping us find people based solely on demographics, digital technology allows us to find and isolate ourselves with other people who share our personality or perspective on the world; to surround ourselves with people who think like us. Similar to what Vox author David Roberts calls a "tribal epistemology,"[61] we gravitate toward others whom we see as similar to us. Social, filtered digital media allow us to isolate ourselves with those like-minded people, as seen through the *Wall Street Journal's* Blue Feed Red Feed application, which illustrates how social media sites filter content by political party affiliation.[62] Further, Lisa Nakamura calls for media scholars to critically engage how "digital platforms support fatally racist media, how they ought to be regulated, and how this media exploits and remediates earlier forms."[63] Through this book, I clarify how white supremacists design and exploit digital protocols within different digital platforms to code racism into various communities. By reflecting on the affordances of these particular platforms, I offer suggestions to decode and regulate racism within online communities. By understanding digital protocols, I illustrate how an ideological foundation and praxis of code allow white women to code whiteness into digital spaces (see chapter 3) and use similar protocols to signal whiteness within our communities (see chapters 4, 5, and 6).

Since white women have historically been excluded "from official political participation precisely on the basis of ascribed gender status,"[64] online spaces become access points for white nationalist women to influence the political arena. Due to its reductive form, digital media can facilitate white supremacy through values, ideologies, and classifications that signal and distribute whiteness within a digital processes. In order to unpack how people code white supremacy through online content and form, throughout this book I consider the following questions:

- What is the state of white supremacy in the present moment in the United States? How have digital media enabled the spread of white supremacy?
- Why is a digital context conducive to forms of empowerment for white women?
- How can we respond ethically as white scholars to engage whiteness within our research practices to break racialized protocols?

By engaging these questions, I hope this text extends knowledge on contemporary white women's conservative rhetorics[65] as agency to decode and dismantle oppressive racialized rhetorics and ensure a more equitable and deliberative path toward coalitional politics. Studying white nationalist, conservative, and alt-right[66] women within digital spaces unmasks how even liberal white feminists may simulate the "right" work rhetorically, yet undermine addressing structural and political oppression. As Education Studies scholar Zeus Leonardo notes, "the conditions of white supremacy make white privilege possible,"[67] making it imperative that we address the conditions of white supremacy to analyze white privilege.

Radically Engaging the Privilege of Whiteness

Some scholars may fear, as I did, that in focusing on white nationalists and alt-right members I was forwarding their agenda. At times I wondered, should I be amplifying the words of BIPOC activists and scholars rather than analyzing overt racism? However, over time I realized that, similar to how the term "white fragility" jars white people to decode rationales we use to defend our white privilege, well-researched, ethical scholarship required both. This research not only amplifies the work of critical race scholars, but also holds white social actors accountable for the identity politics they, ironically, accuse BIPOC of using when describing the impact of racism on their lives. Robin DiAngelo identifies "white fragility" as "a state in which even a minimum amount of racial stress becomes intolerable, triggering a range of defensive moves."[68] When faced with the impact of white privilege on other people, to preserve an emotional equilibrium (e.g., feeling good about themselves), many white people engage in apologia or a defense/ rationalization of their privilege rather than addressing the impact of white privilege. Addressing white fragility becomes a means to critically confront our racialized insecurity, which Judith Butler calls precarity, or focusing on "conditions that threaten life in ways that appear to be outside of one's control,"[69] which is standing in the way of our epistemological humility. Without epistemological humility, we struggle with our ability to be humble enough to hear our accountability for the impact of racism. Too many white scholars and well-intentioned white people act to retain their white privilege filter, and too many people internalize racism and sexism to avoid how oppression functions rhetorically.

Additionally, some may ask what insight a white woman may offer a conversation concerning racism. When I was nine, my family moved from a working-class neighborhood to one with higher incomes on the other side of a Saint Paul, Minnesota suburb. I was a vocal middle child and grew up with cousins from multiple religious and racial backgrounds and identities. My cousins lived in Chicago and we visited them frequently, yet proximity to BIPOC did not decode my white privilege. In many ways, my childhood illustrates a potentially diverse, yet experientially sheltered upbringing. However, while developing friendships, taking and designing graduate-level classes, and engaging in critical race theory research,[70] I started hearing a multitude of voices challenged me to reconcile my underrepresented female, working-class roots with my privileged white, financially stable status.

I recall both an invisibility of race (color-blind ideology) and witnessing brief, but grating experiences of overt racism directed at my cousins and friends: a phone call on New Year's Eve that contained a barrage of racial slurs, nonverbal hesitations from my peers about the difference between me and my family ("you are different," "who is adopted?," pauses and glances), and even a botched investigation by the Chicago area police (a racial hate assault experienced by one of my cousins). The investigation brought with it a salient example of institutional racism. My cousin, one of six men of color, was physically harassed and then verbally assaulted one night in a bar in a suburb of Chicago. The instigators' use of what are legally determined as "fighting words"[71] and attempt at physical assault prompted my cousin to physically defend himself; in fear of being hurt, he hit the aggressor. The investigators on the scene charged my cousin with a felony (along with another unfounded claim about gang affiliation) and, after eighteen months in court, he agreed to a misdemeanor. My uncle, a white man from a working-class background, began by letting the judicial system handle the situation. I watched as my uncle became dismayed by the police through the process and then as he told me that he recognized his misplaced faith in a broken system. The felony charge has followed my cousin throughout his life and career. This event became a turning point for me as I begin to see how institutions treat my family members differently, and I wanted to understand why. I hope this text serves to contribute to "a particular atmosphere in which progressive scholars who identify as BIPOC struggled to piece together an intellectual identity and a political practice that would take the form both of *a left intervention into race discourse* and a race intervention into left discourse" (italics mine).[72]

Through my initial values of an equal society and desire for a voice, I found myself wanting to separate my woman self from my white privileged self. However, as standpoint theory and situated knowledge theorists note,[73] we cannot separate from ourselves to embody another's identities. For example, Rachel Dolezal "signaled" or engaged in "blackfishing" a Black identity by identifying as African American, having a weave and having a substantial skin tone change over time.[74] Yet the Netflix documentary and her interviews tend to focus on the abuse and personal childhood trauma she experienced. Dolezal's focus on her history of trauma and description of herself as a white savior mutes how her fluid identity is a part of her white privilege within systemic oppression.[75] To dismantle the many layers and intersections of oppression (see chapter 3), rather than objectifying, consuming,[76] and punishing others, we must make space for humility, compassion, accountability, and equitability concerning political and structural oppression and on how we treat difference. We need to listen to voices from underrepresented people and create democratic spaces where those voices can be listened to and influence the development of more equitable communities. Further, we need to understand how identity differences influence oppression by listening[77] ethically and "metonymically"[78] to those at the intersections of those different oppressions. Through this research, I hope to be responsive to Lisa Corrigan's call for "ethical racial politics"[79] by listening to, amplifying, and engaging critical race theorists' work to hold people accountable for their privilege in forwarding coded white supremacist rhetoric.

Boundaries of a White "Privilege Filter" as a Rhetorical Shibboleth

Our rhetorical codes give audiences and networks permission or direction to act in certain ways, especially when we hold positions of power. However, it is not always easy to engage one's privilege filter when other identity filters disempower us and mark us as a part of an underrepresented group. A privilege filter is an affinity-based dominant language and cultural perspective that frames observations and meaning of experiences through a blindness to difference. For example, as Jona Olsson notes:

> As a white person, an anti-racist, I am required now to cross the line that separates my experience as target (women) to my place of privilege (white). Here I must uncover what I have internalized about people of color, myself, other white people and being white. Then I have to identify how those internalized attitudes have been actualized into racist behavior. Like with the head-hitting, it is the behavior that signals the problem area. The behaviors will vary for each white person. I recognize that no two white people share exactly the same experiences and societal moldings. We learned racism in our unique and personal ways from different teachers and at different times. But we all learned the lessons well.[80]

In learning about feminism, I found my voice, but I also came to realize that my ethical understanding of and use of my voice stem from a white perspective. Due to insolation from race-based communicative stress, a competitive, all-or-nothing mindset for dealing with intellectual insecurity, no growth mindset when it comes to race-based heuristics, and apologia-based color-blind politics, white people are less receptive and willing target audiences for critical conversations about race. Vocal competition may trump human compassion.

By amplifying underrepresented critical BIPOC scholars and critically analyzing white identity politics, I push back on the oppressive constraints imposed when a majority of white voices seemingly equal a consensus of our democracy. Only when people in positions of privilege (race, class, gender, sexuality, abilities, etc.) choose to be humble enough to listen and be responsive to the impact of oppression on people from differing perspectives do we use our privilege to become accomplices with people from underrepresented groups to strengthen equitable access to our democracy. Like many other disempowered groups, white women[81] can disengage defensive, victim status when it is used to recenter racialized discussions about oppression on ourselves. By not using one's protected victim status as a racial shield, we have the potential to build coalitions with other oppressed groups based on political and structural oppression.

When asked by my major professor to study something I disagreed with for an Extremist Rhetoric on the Internet course, racism seemed a likely choice. Only later in life and after rigorous study could I better conceptualize how "inferential racism," or "naturalized representations of events and situations relating to race, whether 'factual' or 'fictional,' have racist premises and propositions inscribed in them as a set of *unquestioned* assumptions,"[82] and experiences of institutional bias that had intersectional implications. By understanding whiteness as coded, not only in its rhetorical, symbolic content, but also in its digital, organizational form, I validate the impact of racism by understanding how terms and procedures could seamlessly perpetuate systemic racial inequity within different cultural contexts and institutions. In their continued fight against feminism, white nationalist women refine white identity politics of contained agency for white women, palatable to conservative white people and silencing to liberal white people, to support white supremacy on a transnational scale. By critically analyzing our decisions from an intersectional perspective (see chapter 3),[83] we avoid using the master's tools to unsuccessfully dismantle the master's house[84] and refrain from using "contained agency" as a means to justify the oppression of others.

Institutionalization of Whiteness through White Women's "Contained Agency"

When activists are "unwilling to subsume their contestation of multiple oppressions under a single axis of marginalization,"[85] intersectional concerns become silenced and scholars fall prey to the possibilities of "black racialism"[86] or "contained agency." As a counterpoint to intersectionality,[87] *contained agency* consists of the boundaries, limits, or restrictions placed on transcending historical, biological, and cultural oppression when systematic, political, and institutional foundations for oppression are not addressed.[88] I contribute to "discursive debates about the scope of intersectionality as a theoretical perspective"[89] by clarifying a boundary with white feminism to disrupt or "disturb the politics of knowledge production,"[90] which facilitates white supremacy through the guise of "feminism." As Chávez and Griffin note, "conversations about what our feminisms are, how we define them, and how they move us forward in the world are among the most important feminist conversations that we could have."[91] A critical investigation of feminisms helps us understand the constraints or boundaries or affordances of those feminisms. Through the guise of "feminism," offers of contained agency by people in power extend protection to members of oppressed groups, which functions a like carrot on a stick of selective benevolence for token people of that oppressed group. Lin et al. identify this carrot as "single issue politics."[92] For example, when politicians appeal to "white women," white women seemingly get the choice to be oppressed. Specific, individual white women are chosen as models who accept structural or legal discrimination as token "maiden shields" (see chapter 6) that white men protect. Yet, by accepting the offer of "protection," we reinforce the hierarchy and hegemony of white women because social, political, historical, or legal discrimination goes unaddressed. White skin provides white people with the privilege to connect with other white people, to seemingly remove ourselves from an oppressed state, because a knight in shining armor protects us. But that protection creates another gilded cage, making this iteration of agency so troubling, yet powerful for recentering whiteness. In a racial rhetorical criticism, we unmask a "mythical notion of 'whiteness'"[93] through a necessary consideration of institutional and systemic oppression, yet, without intersectional consideration of oppression, dialectical tension is contained, as Crenshaw notes:

> By accepting the bounds of law and ordering their lives according to its categories and relations, people think that they are confirming reality—the way things must be. Yet by accepting the worldview implicit in the law, people are also bound by its conceptual limitations. Thus, conflict and antagonism are contained: the legitimacy of the entire order is never seriously questioned.[94]

Institutions and systems seek to perpetuate themselves without regard for dialectically engaging conversations concerning equity, fairness, or justice, and through organizational rules institutions positively reinforce people who go along with the flow.

Due to institutional and systemic power dynamics that pressure people to internalize their oppression, critical awareness of underrepresented status takes deliberate and continued work to recognize and maintain. Similar to Foucault's notion of the panopticon,[95] oppressed people can undermine their and others' epistemological agency, or their ability to learn how they understand the world differently, by rationalizing power differentials. By accepting a contained agency by which they individually receive or deserve empowerment based on their identity, oppressed people accept a contained potential for revolutionary change. Individualism places oppression on a case-by-case basis rather than as a systemic social structure.[96]

Contained agency is most restrictive when people internalize oppression (see chapter 3). For example, similar to Hunt, Benford, and Snow's notion of "boundary framing,"[97] contained agency accounts for context by recognizing long-term implications of boundaries or commitments. Due to privileged access by one identity politic (e.g., white), but unequal status in another (e.g., women), members of underrepresented groups end up comparing and combating against one another rather than against oppressive institutions and systems.[98] Working-class rhetorical coding of "picking yourself up by your bootstraps" or "working harder" amplify when facing women's rhetorics of a "lean in" philosophy. White, affluent women such as Sheryl Sandberg locate oppressive blame in women, stating "We [women] hold ourselves back in ways both big and small, by lacking self-confidence, by not raising our hands, and by pulling back when we should be leaning in."[99] In both cases, people blame oppressed groups for oppression and, if a person identifies with multiple descriptors, non-summative blaming and implications occur. The problematic pairing of a value of equal opportunity with the ideal of American meritocracy[100] has led some white people to cries of reverse discrimination and the potential questioning and elimination of diversity and equity policies like Title IX or funding of Historically Black Colleges and Universities.[101] From altering protections in Title IX processing to protect victims of sexual assault, to limiting investigations of civil rights compliance of public school bathroom equity for transgender students, to supporting the privatization of education, to blocking the Obama administration's protections "for students attending for-profit colleges" and for "racial discrimination in school discipline,"[102] DeVos procedurally reverts US educational focus from gender, racial, and class equity back to seemingly color-blind "equality." DeVos strengthens a white privilege filter within educational processes to protect and perpetuate male, cisgendered, abled, wealthy white men who have historically dominated these educational institutions, while dramatically shifting how students, specifically, women, trans, working-class, and BIPOC, can succeed in education. The dominant privilege filter from which the institutional and systemic expectations originate treat difference similarly (deregulating equity policy), yet experiences of oppression for people excluded are significantly different, making it imperative that we understand how racist oppression functions institutionally, especially at the intersections of gender and class.

Chapter Development

Responding to Carrie Crenshaw's call that "rhetoricians must do the critical and radical ideological work necessary to make whiteness visible and over-turn its silences for the purpose of resisting racism,"[103] I begin each chapter using a narrative vignette to illustrate how white people embody[104] *and can respond to* racism through "everyday actions"[105] to encourage critical reflection of ethical communicative processes and foster dialectical engagement[106] of whiteness. In the narratives, most of the people with whom I spoke or wrote with will identify themselves as "liberal," "progressive," and/or "democratic." Yet, even from liberal circles, racist assumptions contribute to the institutionalization of oppressive structures within institutional mechanizations of values, ideologies, and classifications through our digital systems. Further, through use of these systems people internalize classifications and identities—even the way white women who identify as "liberal" classify and embody our identities. I hope my intervention does not recenter this conversation on whiteness, similar to when white people place emotional labor on BIPOC through their "confessions" of their family's racist past or as stories where white people are glorified as the saviors of BIPOC. Instead my narratives at the beginning of each chapter serve as a critical whiteness: an intervention of racism to decode and recode a communicative cycle. Critical intervention requires a reflection, deliberation, revelation, and break from the silence that preserves white privilege. These steps help us understand what future areas of antiracist scholarship lie ahead as we continue to dismantle white supremacy.

Although the analytical part of each chapter focuses on conservative white women's texts, decoding heuristics of racism, even for "liberal" or "progressive" white people, requires a recognition of structural connections with one another and white peoples' receptiveness and responsiveness in critically and practically challenging our white privilege in our everyday actions. Despite white people's best intentions, the coded privilege of race pervades the values, ideologies, and classifications we protect. Values become the building blocks (such as HTML) social actors use to connect with people to solidify cultural meaning. The meaning then becomes styled, like CSS, through an ideographic lens. Once a rhetorical refinement from a value to an ideology resonates with a particular population, people can begin to shape environments through mechanization of classifications as identity heuristics that become internalized within institutions.

To understand the relationship between content and form, I developed this book in two sections: my first three chapters establish the rhetorical white nationalist–laden digital environment as a foundation for white identity politics primarily using white nationalist women's collective voices via their webspaces,[107] whereas my fourth, fifth, and sixth chapters illustrate how individual conservative and alt-right women are core political actors in the coding of white supremacy through various forms of digital, rhetorical environments. Rhetorical value, ideological, and classificatory similarities that exist between white nationalist, Tea Party, alt-right women and those Donald Trump appointed, as well as Donald Trump himself, illustrate how racist cultural codes permeate digital environments. In the following chapters, I offer concepts of contained agency and privilege filter as means to understand the status of white supremacy today.

In chapter 1, through a comparative analysis of white nationalist women's websites and spaces in 2007 with Donald Trump's 2016 campaign rhetoric as well as past articulations of his daughter, Ivanka, I identify how white nationalist women's rhetorical refinement of survival, social, and independence values mirror coded values rhetoric Donald Trump used in the 2016 election cycle. Chapter 1 establishes how white nationalist women and Donald Trump vocalize and prioritize safety and security and social values over independence values to create a foundation for the conservative platform. Economic hardship, desires for a postracial community, immigration-focused efforts,[108] and historic and legal racism (slavery and the prison system[109]) sharpen a cultural zeitgeist of insecurity for people in the United States to become targets for a populist,[110] unifying frame of whiteness. By rhetorically refining American independence values into narrowly defined [white][111] survival and social values, white nationalist women construct a palatable white identity foundationally similar to the populist rhetoric Donald Trump uses.

Based on the values established in chapter 1, in chapter 2, starting with Carr's[112] and Bonilla-Silva's notions of "color-blind" ideology,[113] I contextualize how, through online rhetoric, white nationalist women coopt 1960 civil rights rhetoric to advance their concerns into one palatable for a conservative audience. By naming their "oppression" using ideologies they link to ideographs[114] such as <American>,[115] <diversity>, and <freedom of speech>, white nationalist women code their experience within a "color-blind" ideology to forward a [white] politic. Through an analysis of how white nationalist women use ideographs, I unmask how ideographs keep white privilege filters intact by decontextualizing, appropriating, and relativizing marginalization to justify white identity politics. Value and ideologies offer rhetorical content white nationalist women code into the communicative protocol within the websites themselves.

In chapter 3, I clarify how white nationalist women code whiteness into the epistemological foundations of digitally mediated communication protocols and communities to reify oppression through digital systems. For example, white nationalist women code gateway pages that require enthymematic agreement (via clicking links) to gain access to the site. Through an intersectional analysis of white nationalist women's webspaces, I illustrate how white nationalist women perpetuate "contained agency" through white feminism within white nationalist digital design (classifications and architecture) to clarify the architecture of gated digital communities. Scholars such as Anna Zacejik call for an effort to help understand white feminism's hesitations toward furthering antiracist efforts.[116] In this chapter I show that, without engaging critical race theory, neoliberal, class-situated, white feminism reifies rather than engages multidimensional systems of oppression. Due to a lack of intersectional engagement, white women contain their empowerment through a narrow conception of "antagonists,"[117] limiting political and structural implications for revolutionary change.

In chapter 4, using excerpts from speeches by and interviews with Sarah Palin during and after campaigning for vice president as she talks about the classificatory terms of motherhood and feminism (as defined in chapters 2 and 3), I show how the Tea Party's rhetoric functions as early public testing grounds for identity politics of white <American> outsiderism, naturalizing matriarchy and [white] maternal feminism. Although unsuccessful in influencing political office seats, Tea Party campaigns serve as a rhetorical testing ground of white identity politics on the mainstream political stage. Using ideographs such as <America> and <freedom of speech> and classification of womanhood based on motherhood and "maternal feminism," Tea Party figureheads like Sarah Palin use white nationalist arguments to target conservative white women. However, after limited public success, the Republican Party supports white women like Sarah Palin and Michelle Bachmann as shield maidens for white political agendas by simulating unrealistic ideals of "having it all," while not articulating systemic oppression. Affluent white motherhood, where white women exist as primary and default parent,[118] serves as a performance of contained agency.

In chapter 5, I disassemble rhetoric of the alt-right women as they validate their white privilege through a motherhood-based rhetoric of "contained agency" to justify their attack on independent, feminist women. However, DiAngelo notes that multiple factors "inculcate" white fragility to preserve white privilege: segregation, universalism and individualism, racial arrogance, entitlement to racial comfort, racial belonging, psychic freedom, and hierarchical value.[119] An analysis of the rhetoric of four alt-right women's rhetoric connected with the "identitarian movement" (on their Twitter accounts and vlogs[120] from 2018) illustrates the severity of a rhetoric of classification and apologia of white fragility. Alt-right women create barriers between groups of people who are similarly oppressed by trying to center white women's concerns. Further, their attack on feminist women to broaden their membership illustrates implications of the biological extension of "individual feminism" I introduce in chapter 6. Through their vlogs, alt-right women illustrate what Miller identifies as a loss of agency due to the lack of "*immediate*" relationship between white audiences and speakers.[121] Yet, their lack of epistemological agency, or altering how they or others understand how they produce knowledge, contains their frameset.

In chapter 6, I dismantle the white identity politics of conservative white women placed in positions of communicative power by Trump (Kellyanne Conway, Ivanka Trump, Sarah Huckabee) as affluent white women who serve as shield maidens against outside critique. Written texts, such as books and speeches with women as a primary audience, as well as press briefings during and after the presidential campaign—manifested as a Sandberg-style "lean in" philosophy white women use in support of Trump—illustrate the intimate tie between white privilege and male privilege. Through their classification of motherhood, individual "feminism," and color-blind merit-based claims, conservative white women use a white privilege filter to shield Donald Trump from the impact of his oppressive rhetoric. These conservative white women simulate, but do not actually engage in, feminism that dismantles power structures; instead, they strategically use their white privilege filters of motherhood, "individual feminism," and internalized misogyny (similar to classifications, values, and ideologies white nationalist and alt-right women use) as disarming argumentative shields to keep political, historical, and structural responsibility away from Donald Trump as a means to sustain white supremacy.

By elucidating how coding theory illustrates white supremacist power dynamics that manifest within digital contexts, these chapters provide a foundation for my concluding chapter, where I clarify the state of white supremacy within the United States, how a digital medium enables its continuation through white women, and how we can respond in ethical, antiracist ways as white scholars to whiteness within our research practices. Only through continuing to engage in critical intervention can we use our white privilege to curate more equitable institutions and communities. As I note through the narrative above, I critique and confront whiteness as a means to illustrate a need to engage critical race theory when unmasking whiteness. By unmasking privilege filters, we develop "stamina"[122] for sustaining dialectical tension to recognize and respond to white privilege through anti-racist coalitional politics and form a more equitable democracy. By amplifying and as a counterpoint to the concept of intersectionality, I develop "contained agency" and "privilege filters" as analytical tools and ethically engage white identity politics in our communities. Only through our deliberate, collective, and continual responses can we ethically heal and curate healthy communities.

By interrogating their most overt forms, we can see how whiteness seeps even into "progressive" communities to institutionalize racism. This text offers a means to listen, critically engage, and ethically respond to white nationalism, offering bridges to where we can heal and move deliberately and collectively in the twenty-first century. To preserve and embody the democracy we value, I provide insight concerning the form and function of privilege and how it shapes the "villages" we hope to foster. Recognizing privilege is not about punishment or hating others or ourselves—it is about sustaining dialectical tensions to recognize impacts of racism in our communities and ensure our collective, democratic future. Without a willingness to center difference,[123] we are unable to break the institutionalized heuristic of racism to make connections with other people who we may perceive as different from ourselves. Justice is found in ethically engaging, reprioritizing, and redesigning values, ideologies, and digital constructions to ensure democratic access for underrepresented groups. White coding is a site of intervention. By showing the parallels between overt racism and covert racism, I illustrate how we need to challenge the way we code difference to continue to unmask whiteness. Through our rhetoric we can move closer to the democracy we idealize. Through our knowledge we can redesign equitable systems, rather than succumb to a designer's default through a white liberal culpability of silence and coded acceptance. We can act more wisely than our digital programs are arguably "smart" to ensure that human agency within technological systems is not undermined by contained agency given to token people by those in control of those spaces.

As seen by the Facebook example about the Diwali lamp at the beginning of the introduction, white folks have the privilege to critically engage (in dialogues that may involve discomfort) or remain silent (preserve their privilege) on the issue of racism. Writing within a Facebook feed or other online social medium, people do not see other people's nonverbal feedback, which means that we rely on our individually coded cultural frames to interpret what we see. As a smoker (e.g., ashtray) who was socialized to be afraid of BIPOC, this white woman wrote without critical reflection of her audience, primarily the white man who assessed racist implications of her comments. However, that meant that I also had to be willing to engage a communicative argument, which took not only a conversation with my partner, as he was concerned about potential conflict, but also encouragement from a family member for me to call her. When rhetorically refined as a value, whiteness becomes part of the building blocks of our community makeup and, when whiteness continues without response, cultural meaning codes our community perspective through an acceptance of white privilege.

COLLECTIVE VOICES OF WHITE NATIONALIST WOMEN

1

Safety for White People Only through Nationalism

Decoding Rhetorical Refinement of White Supremacist Values

Following the 2016 US presidential election, and the shock that many people continue to experience after its results, media outlets implicated various groups of people believed responsible for the election outcome. Some journalists criticized millennials not voting or voting for third-party candidates.[1] Other correspondents castigated voters with religious affiliations like evangelicals[2] or even working-class white voters[3] for the outcome, yet evidence showed that a majority of working-class voters cast ballots for Hillary Clinton.[4] However, based on exit poll data, many organizations statically located white women as the source or turning point for the 2016 election.[5] Of all the different groups of people Donald Trump specifically targeted during the 2016 election (Black people, Latino people, Muslim people, women), more white women (53 percent) voted for Donald Trump than any other group of explicitly marginalized people polled: Black men (13 percent), Black women (4), Latino men (33), and Latino women (6).[6] Further, news outlets like NBC made claims that "Alabama's women wrote the verdict on Roy Moore,"[7] even though an astounding 63 percent of white women cast a vote for Roy Moore.[8] As shown by exit poll statistics from the 2016 presidential election, US white women have become a force we must reckon with. And, when it comes to identity politics, white women are at the forefront of racial politics. While studying white nationalism and racism in digital space in the United States over the last fifteen years, I found that white nationalist women refined a rhetoric of whiteness, which was a foundation for coded white identity politics specifically in the 2016 election cycle. The process came full circle as conservative white women became a tipping point in the 2016 election. White nationalist women's rhetorics of privileged values, appropriated ideographs, and contained classifications served to refine white identity politics for the Tea Party. By offering rhetorical means to frame a cultural acceptance of racism, classism, and sexism, they provided rationales similar to those found within Donald Trump's campaign. Value, ideological, and classificatory efforts provided a foundation to reframe whiteness in US culture.

Due to fear of BIPOC, during the 2016 presidential election Trump's assertions about the values of safety and security (codes) dramatically influenced the results. Trump linked values of safety and security with BIPOC to institutionalize overt racism within our political systems. Trump's coded rhetoric, which he directed at people[9] who share his white privilege filter (see chapter 2), mainstreamed racist rhetoric into US politics. Independent, Republican, and even Green Party candidates (such as David Duke, Tony Harvater, and Rick Tyler) followed his lead using "pro-White" campaign slogans such as "Make America White Again" and "White Lives Matter."[10] While staggering racial discrepancies exist regarding legal enforcement (police), drug laws, mass incarceration, criminal justice, education, employment, economic security, career advancement, civil rights, media access, and housing,[11] claims of "political correctness" and "reverse racism" infused US political discourse during the 2016 presidential campaign.[12] Through his campaign promise to "Make America Great Again," Donald Trump harnessed values central to the white nationalist movement. At the height of white nationalist growth online in 2007, white nationalist women's websites became places of rhetorical refinement of survival over independence values to code rhetorics of whiteness within political discourse.[13] The similarities between terminology and classifications[14] of white nationalist women's online rhetoric in 2007 and Trump's presidential campaign rhetoric in 2016 illustrated how whiteness could be rhetorically refined into US politics by privileging survival values to perpetuate racist ideologies. By unmasking[15] coded rhetorical refinement of values we can understand how white nationalist women and Donald Trump[16] signal white people's potentially unwitting[17] whiteness ideologies that codify white privilege in US cultural and political institutions.

White Nationalist Women as Advocates for a Whiteness Ideology

Although never absent from American social and political culture, over the last twenty years white nationalism has proliferated online.[18] Klan chapters more than doubled in 2016, from 72 to 190 offshoots.[19] When covering white nationalism, most media outlets have identified figureheads of white nationalist organizations such as Don Black and David Duke, or lone wolf bombers such as Eric Robert Rudolph, Buford O. Furrow, and Timothy McVeigh, all of whom are white and male. Not surprisingly, most research on white nationalism is focused on white men and their organizations.[20] Further, people who amplify the movement, like Donald Trump, tend to be white and male. Since white men usually made headlines as agents of change in white nationalism, this book steps in to fill a necessary gap in the literature that is itself expressive of a masculinist bias in criticism of white nationalism: white nationalist women. White nationalist men's rhetoric is less stylistically nuanced than concerns that are "rhetorically refined" in digital spaces of white nationalist women.

White nationalist women have made palatable white supremacist rhetoric and orchestrated organizational and recruitment efforts for the white nationalist movement. However, few studies on conservative and white nationalist white women's rhetoric exist.[21] Sociologist Kathleen Blee clarifies, "[e]xtremist right-wing and reactionary women are nearly absent from studies on women in political movements, which have focused on progressive and women's rights movements or, to a lesser degree, on antifeminist movements."[22] Yet, many white nationalist men see white women as the cornerstone of their households, guiding their families', including their husbands', long-term involvement in the movement.[23] Women are the child bearers, organizers of the household, and in some cases office managers of white nationalist organizations, roles similar to those white men attributed to republican women by philosophers of the Enlightenment era.[24] As American Studies professor Linda Kerber notes, "[t]he model republican woman was to be self-reliant (with limits): literate, untempted by the frivolities of fashion. She has a responsibility in the public scene, though not to act on it" as a form of "self relian[ce]," and to preserve "virtue."[25] White nationalist women and republican women alike have the expectation of understanding and supporting white men's politics as a form of citizenship. Since women have historically been excluded from "citizenship" classifications within a "public" context, women in the political sphere function as a *counter-public*.[26] Being more educated and capable than many people assume (many hold associate or even more advanced degrees), through unique support roles, white nationalist women have facilitated the growth of the social movement,[27] even at the expense of their agency.

Although white nationalists historically have portrayed women as idealized goddesses and in subservient roles such as mothers and wives,[28] to improve "the image of white racial activism and advocacy,"[29] white nationalists are increasingly portraying white women in strong female roles such as Valkyries and Amazons[30] to reach white women disaffected with racially and gender-inclusive and intersectional feminism. Through both portrayals of white mothers and activist classifications, white nationalists subsumed "anti-" racialized "other" messages with "pro-white" ones, idealizing how white women who embodied the traditional roles or forecast intentions to be wives and mothers served as activists for white nationalist organizations. Yet, these white women offered more to the white nationalist movement. White nationalist women rhetorically refined coded whiteness to appear "more conversational and reasonable in tone" to attract more economically or culturally aggrieved audiences, specifically "women who might not want to consider themselves racists."[31] The websites white nationalists created included "pro-social" identities that balanced nurturing with instrumental qualities to assert community an underlying value of the movement. As women increasingly use the World Wide Web as a means to find social support, empowerment, and stable forms of identity through community affinity,[32] women online have become a vulnerable audience to coded white nationalist women's recruitment efforts.

Refining "Pro-White" as "Pro-Social" Rhetoric

Communication and sociology scholars describe the white nationalist movement as stemming from "hate," "racist," "separatist," "extreme," "radical right," or "white power" groups, reducing its complexity. By analyzing their "pro-white" stance, scholars acknowledge the negative[33] or othering perspective white nationalists forward. As I noted in the introductory chapter, white is a responsive identity term, only created after attempting to separate oneself from an out-group. By implying an out-group, the "pro-white" terms allowed white nationalists to rhetorically sidestep claims of overt, hate-focused racism,[34] reducing structural racism to only prejudice. The pro-white label evoked the [non-white] Other, coding colonialism into a cultural context. Social acceptance of white nationalism and an increase in racial discord and violence[35] have continued to fuel the Trump campaign and presidency.[36] White nationalists cloaked their racism[37] by changing the values in which they classify (see chapter 3) their content (as seen with martinlutherking. org) to forward white supremacy.

Instead of explicitly naming or blaming their enemies, white nationalists have increasingly used pro-social racist rhetoric or positive messages that focus on surviving as a community. Through a rhetoric of "new racism"[38] ideologically founded in "Kultural Pluralism," white nationalists blurred cultural pluralism and white supremacy into emotional appeals directed at conservative whites.[39] White nationalists have conveyed feelings of love and pride for white racial heritage in an "idealized traditional family" to build community.[40] According to Patricia Hill Collins, an "idealized traditional family" included focusing on 1) naturalized hierarchies, 2) home(land), 3) blood ties, 4) rights with responsibilities, 5) socioeconomic class, and 6) family planning.[41] Even by naming one's progeny and family pets after prominent white nationalist figures, such as figures of Nordic mythology, white nationalists attempted to perpetuate a "white history" within their families.[42] To better understand how white nationalist women rhetorically refined white nationalist values in public arenas, I studied white nationalist value-laden rhetoric in informal spaces of the digital sphere. Studying white nationalist women online provided clarification as to how values circulated around networks of communities.

Political Avenues for White Nationalism in the United States

Instead of ethnocentric arguments about white supremacy over other cultures, white nationalists appropriated reparation policies to address historic and systematic racial discrimination of BIPOC. In 2002, professor of Political Science and Law Carol Swain articulated:

> [The movement] seeks to expand its influence mainly through argument and ratio-
> nal discourse aimed at its target audience of white Americans who have become
> embittered or aggrieved over what they perceive to be a host of racial double stan-
> dards in the areas of affirmative action policy and crime reporting, as well as over
> the continuance of large-scale immigration from third world countries.[43]

By targeting affirmative action policies, which use universal or neutral race terminology, white nationalists socially constructed and validated white identity politics.

Further, the relationship becomes tautological as conservative government agents provided nationalist groundwork for white nationalist claims about safety. For example, past presidents exploited highly charged catalytic events for government action and policy (like 9/11 and the Iraq War by George W. Bush, as well as the Patriot Act, which was renewed under Barack Obama[44]) in relation to foreign relations and cultural differences in the public sphere. Following 9/11, the US government attempted to reestablish control of domestic and economic agencies through increased security efforts made within airports (not allowing objects such as scissors and liquids on planes or visitors past the baggage areas), at border stations (needing a passport to travel into Canada), and through controversial laws such as the USA Patriot Act (Uniting and Strengthening America by Providing Appropriate Tools Required to Intercept and Obstruct Terrorism Act of 2001). These policies perpetuated rhetoric about "terrorist" actions taken against "America" by people not originally from the United States and justified an increase in border security, especially at the border between the United States and Mexico, to preserve a sense of "safety."[45]

In addition to historic events, arguments about perceived censorship of language constrained dialogue about independence values. Due to a fear of being labeled as racist, many white people were afraid to speak about race.[46] Censorship-type enforcement of "politically correct" language by fearful administrators and assumed or actual problematic application of affirmative action policies also bred resentment of opportunity based on racial makeup. In some cases, the adoption or forced adherence to politically correct language only masked racial tensions and differences in socially appropriate language (e.g., extreme "we are all the same" philosophy). Rather than discussing perspectives, white people's perception of censorship prompted white people to use language that covered up how language culturally perpetuated prejudice and stereotypes. However, "politically incorrect" language problematically enacted colonial racial structures as well as debased and retraumatized people through hate speech.

Without productive critical dialogue, white people do not recognize or understand racial disparities. Although the civil rights movement earned some recognition and rights for BIPOC, white people still express a post–civil rights attitude concerning race, or an attitude that racial disparities no longer exist in US society. Opinion polls show "favorable assessments of black chances for success often accompanied extremely negative judgments about the abilities, work habits, and character of black people,"[47] illustrating post–civil rights or "post-racial"[48] attitudes concerning equality and potential for making BIPOC a scapegoat for the litany of concerns I note above.[49] Favorable assessments of success with negative assessments of personal character illustrate external loci of control for BIPOC—that external influences, not a person of color's abilities, are responsible for their success, while their efforts or existence become the limitation on or downfall of our "greatness." Token examples (e.g., Obama as president)[50] serve as the rule rather than the exception that BIPOC have "succeeded" in the United States. Statistical discrepancies of racial discrimination and discriminatory enforcement of civil rights laws tell another story.[51]

White people may deny the existence of racial injustice because they may be "embarrassed by the benefits they receive from white supremacy, and others are inconvenienced or even threatened by the resentment it creates."[52] Recognizing oppressive structures may complicate or otherwise implicate the lives and choices of white people. Instead of engaging the insecurity they feel in race-based conversations, to retain a sense of white, male privilege and authority, "right populism fuels a 'know nothing' culture in response: one that disparages not only expert knowledge, but also deliberative processes of public judgment, in favor of more immediate forms of knowledge based parochially in 'community and personal experiences.'"[53] White men focus on what "their gut" tells them rather than listening to research BIPOC's experiences, because it maintains their privilege.

During his successful 2016 presidential campaign, Trump gained public support by appropriating coded racist rhetoric to fuel a white populism. By populism, I mean "both academic and public discourse" characterized "by its symbolic and affectively charged practices of identification, which arouse the people on behalf of a common vision of collective identity and political life and either unsettle or shore up the borders of politics and democracy."[54] By not addressing white privilege or equitable independence, white people reduce BIPOC to socially and culturally dependent terms within US politics. As Lipsitz clarifies, "by generating an ever repeating cycle of 'moral panics' about the family, crime, welfare, race, and terrorism, politicians are able to distance concerns from economic and social policy."[55] Fears of identity (authority and privilege) safety successfully distract people from addressing social problems.

Due to the potential for white people to feel sympathetic toward white nationalist concerns due to shared values, a comparative analysis of how white nationalist women used US values with mainstream political rhetoric illustrated how rhetorical refinement of whiteness is built into US politics. US value systems[56] provided common ground to identify inferentially racist rhetoric that would connect with US audiences. White nationalist women and Donald Trump connected safety values to immigration, security values with rising expectations of racial and ethnic minorities and the global structure of the economy, independence values with a perception of unfair racial policies and a growing resistance to acceptance of multiculturalism and its emphasis on promoting racial and ethnic group pride and identity politics, and progressive values with the exponential growth of the Internet to justify white identity politics in the United States. Noting boundaries for safety and security values, critiquing pro-social values, and contextualizing independence values of political correctness as more than "being rude"[57] illustrated how rhetorical refinement of whiteness "codes" racism.

Exposing White Privilege Coded through Survival Values

To justify their white privilege, white nationalists and Donald Trump identified survival values of health, safety, and security through biological and physical boundaries. White nationalists simulated whiteness through bodily "material referents"[58] of white, young, innocent, fertile, and technologically empowered women and girls.[59] For example, on the National Alliance main page, a poster for *RESISTANCE* magazine depicted a young, large-breasted, partially naked female in a bikini and halter top.[60] Similarly, the kirkwomen's website featured a black and white poster of a woman with long blonde hair in a tight black shirt and skirt or pants. The image revealed much of her white skin and large breasts as she holds a semi-automatic assault rifle—all referents of white, female sexual vivacity and power. Next to the woman was the text: "GIVE UP MY RIFLE? NEVER! I am blonde, not stupid."[61] With her hand on her hip, the unsmiling woman stared directly into the camera/audience, appearing empowered and attractive due to her ability to be independent (see independence value section below). White nationalists' images created simulacra of sexualized white warrior women as the ideal embodiment of health.

Similarly, Donald Trump asserted the biological, sexual "perfection" of his daughter Ivanka and wife Melania.[62] When asked on television show *The View* whether he would be okay if his daughter was put on the cover of *Playboy*, he responded, "Although she does have a very nice figure. I've said that if Ivanka weren't my daughter, perhaps, I would be dating her."[63] Even recently Trump defined Ivanka by her "beauty" in comparison to US Secretary of State Mike Pompeo, who he refers to as "beast."[64] By calling attention to the physical prowess of his daughter and how she came from himself, Trump gestured to her biological "perfection" and desirability (vivacity via her figure), focusing not on her white skin but the value of health her attractiveness (whiteness) illustrated. Further examples of Melania Trump's ability to retain her physique after childbirth and even a hypothetical car accident[65] illustrated the reduction of Melania to her sexual viability. Both illustrations highlighted the value of sexual vivacity as "healthy" perfection and the reduction of women to mates, which validated attractiveness as deserving privilege (attention). The implied whiteness stemmed from the physical (beauty) focus of health. In both the white nationalists' and Trump's identity reductions of women, whiteness was implied by focusing on the body, or physical signs of health of women. Although the technology was not guns for Ivanka Trump, liberation came in the form of digital technology. In 2019 Ivanka Trump was awarded the Internet Association's[66] Internet Freedom Award,[67] yet the timeliness of the award following her father's continued accusations of media bias seemed auspicious,[68] allowing Ivanka Trump to become a corrective, or "maiden shield" (see chapter 6) for her father.

In addition to valuing attractiveness as representative of individual white health, white nationalists identified physical boundaries as indicative of [white] American safety and security values. For example, in their photo gallery webpage, the National Socialists Movement (NSM) Women's Division provided images of anti-immigration signs with the words "Protect our Border" and "Close the Border!"[69] By using the term "border," the NSM Women's Division defined the nation by physical borders, specifically with Mexico. White nationalists provided physical boundaries as indicative of cultural boundaries to assert their white privilege as Americans as separate from "others."

Similarly, Trump capitalized on increasing fear of not having safety and security from "others." During his presidential campaign, Donald Trump argued for identification and surveillance of people of the Muslim faith[70] and identified people of Mexican descent as criminals.[71] In his campaign announcement, Trump asserted, "When Mexico sends its people, they're not sending their best. They're not sending you. They're sending people that have lots of problems, and they're bringing those problems with us. They're bringing drugs. They're bringing crime. They're rapists. And some, I assume, are good people. . . . I'll bring back our jobs from China, from Mexico, from Japan."[72] By identifying people of Muslim faith and Mexican descent as well as from non-Western or nonwhite backgrounds, he created an out-group of others based on non-"American"[73] origins that is to be blamed.[74] Trump asserted white identity politics by implying that physical boundaries determine whiteness, illustrating how "constructions of citizenship in America are tied to racial hierarchies."[75] Trump justified racialized assertions and poor treatment of a nonwhite other to preserve American values of safety and security through examples like how Trump articulated the identity of people from Mexico through programs such as DACA (Deferred Action for Childhood Arrivals).[76]

Both white nationalists and Trump highlighted the same values of health and safety and security by idolizing [white] biological health and demonizing [racial other] identities, a white identity which deserved privilege and a non-American other that threatens privilege.[77] Although it was not surprising that citizenship was tied with racial identities, the values of safety and security are uniquely coded through personal and community health. Arguments of superior biology and physical boundaries become reasoning for white privilege.

Revealing White Community Boundaries by Coding [White] Identity as Social Values

Once the safety and security of white people were established, white nationalist women and Trump used social values to situate boundaries of their historic, patriotic identity of white privilege. White nationalists asserted "white" as synonymous with American by locating patriotism in "European heritage" and negating "non-western ways."[78] White nationalist Snow White identified pride in multiple European heritages: "I am Scottish-Irish-German-Dutch and I get cranky if you make me fess up to that little bit of French in there!"[79] A blogger, Snow White proudly asserts her European roots, using European roots as synonymous with white American. These argumentative forms retained warrants of credibility through defining race through biological roots, which reinforce problematic arguments about defining race. Unfortunately, as seen by Elizabeth Warren's use of a DNA test to react to Trump's questioning of her tribal heritage,[80] when responding (rather than reacting) to biological race arguments, a change in definitional frame was necessary to shift from a frameset that embodies whiteness.

Similarly, white nationalist women connected European heritage with a historic American legacy ("first generation") to validate and situate their white dominance. For example, UC Berkeley graduate Elena Haskins and author of her site "A One Woman Site by Elena Haskins" identified herself as a "first generation American of Icelandic descent" and her father as a "Nebraska-born descendent [sic] of colonists and pioneers."[81] By identifying as multi-ethnic, yet with implied white European roots, Haskins's white heritage becomes "an anchoring point for an American identity," as noted by Nakayama and Krizek.[82] Due to a heritage of superior white identity, connecting an American identity with white European roots facilitated Americanness as white "property."[83]

Similarly, during his campaign rallies and debates, Donald Trump coded [white] patriotic identity as "hardworking" [white] midwestern "Americans." At the Iowa Freedom Summit, Trump stated, "I have great respect for Steve King and have great respect likewise for Citizens United, David and everybody, and tremendous respect for the Tea Party. Also, the people of Iowa. They have something in common. Hard-working people."[84] Due to the dominance of white people in these groups, Trump coded white American identity in descriptors hardworking, midwestern, and Tea Party. Further, Trump solidified a racial bifurcation between white and BIPOC as he contrasted his implied whiteness with racialized others. In his June 16, 2015, presidential announcement speech, Trump described the "other" as criminal people from Mexico and "South and Latin America" and "probably from the Middle East" who are "criminals," "bringing drugs," and "rapists." Although Trump had not indicated that everyone from these countries was a "criminal,"[85] through his focus and racial reduction Trump constructed a non-American racialized other as dangerous, undeserving people, harkening stereotypes used by former President George W. Bush,[86] nineteenth-century white US journalists, and others when justifying national economic and political boundaries.[87] Trump's definition of [white] Americans not only justified white identity and validated white privilege, but also validated a white birthright for greatness. In his speech on foreign policy, Trump stated, "We will not apologize for becoming successful again, but will instead embrace the unique heritage that makes us who we are."[88] By calling attention to "heritage" and negating people of immigrant status, Trump signaled to [white] people that patriotism is found within [white, European] American heritage with him as our "medicine man"[89] to bring us to that greatness.

Unmasking Cultural Appropriation and [White] Domination through Independence Values

By valuing white privilege and a white American patriotic identity, white nationalist women and Trump appropriated rhetorics of domination in arguing for white independence by power over "others." White nationalist women desired independence from political correctness or multiculturalism, which they viewed as a restriction on their free speech. For example, VDare author Brenda Walker argued that the government supports political correctness toward people of immigrant status "rather than law enforcement."[90] White nationalists claimed that programs for "others" infringe on their right to speak their perspective. White nationalists used rhetorics of domination to describe the racial discrimination they have experienced. For example, white nationalist blogger Angry White Female[91] argued, "I, contrary to White 'lemmings,' refuse to act as a member of a conquered race. I will not learn the languages of the conquerors, nor teach them to my children. I am an upstanding White woman, and will not be forcefully assimilated into my own country."[92] By using the terms "conquered" and "assimilated," Angry White Female framed her victimhood as "reverse racism," an impossible occurrence in the United States where white culture is dominant. However, as Eddo explained, "[r]acism does not go both ways. There are unique forms of discrimination that are backed up by entitlement, assertion and, most importantly, supported by a structural power strong enough to scare you into complying with the demands of the status quo."[93] White nationalist women did not acknowledge continuing structural racism that can be verified by statistical discrepancies, which illustrate discrimination within institutions and contexts such as law enforcement, criminal justice prosecution, education, employment, economics, workplace, voting, and housing BIPOC experience.[94] Instead, through the construction of oppressive inevitability, white nationalists illustrated independence values of power and authority of property through claims of Americanness to justify their coercive acts. As expressions of white fragility,[95] white people coded themselves as victims, instead of a dominant group, in conversations about racial inequity to regain competitive control within conversation of identity politics.

Similarly, during his campaign Trump nostalgically reminisced on a past time when violence toward others would gain independence from political correctness.[96] For example, when heckled during his rally speech in Nevada, Trump asserted, "We're not allowed. You know. The guards are very gentle with him. He's walking out, big high fives, smiling, laughing. I'd like to punch him in the face."[97] Trump further claimed that he would pay the legal fees for someone who did engage in violence against another protester in Iowa. Trump stated, "Knock the crap out of him, would you? Seriously, OK just knock the hell—I promise you I will pay for the legal fees. I promise, I prom- ise."[98] Trump identified the lengths he will go to retain white dominance, including encouraging violent actions against others, like young Black men or women protesting his rallies, when his speech is interrupted, or financially supporting those [white] people who engage in violence against "others." His justification of violence fueled future aggression and violence, as seen by the increase in widespread hateful harassment, intimidation, hate crimes, and racist graffiti, most commonly happening in schools after his election.[99] However, color-blind responses, like questioning the mental sanity of per- petrators of hate crimes, seemed to dull the focus on systemic racism.[100] Through his assertion of independence values, Trump incited the violent roots of the white nationalist movement, justifying aggressive actions toward non-conforming others. For rhetors like Trump, white fragility validated the oppression of others through a nostalgia for authoritarian power and control.

Dismantling Rhetorical Refinement

More palatable than blatantly racist rhetoric, white nationalist women's online sites became rhetorical resources as to how racism was coded in US politics. White nationalist women's websites were spaces for rhetorical refinement, where vivid examples exist of how coded whiteness was expressed, revised, and retested for mainstream audiences. The comparative value application provided justification as to how these values were codified into identity classifications of whiteness. Narrow definitions of [white] European "American" patriotism or nationalism created a foundation for safety, security, and health values to code white privilege. White nationalists and Trump both used cultural appropriation of white fragility and victim rhetoric to justify violence toward others as a means to secure one's independence. The rhetorical refinement of racism by white nationalist women came full circle as US mainstream politicians like Donald Trump used it as coded rhetoric, justifying white supremacist values even if they lost,[101] but more so when they won. Continuing support of Trump's coded rhetoric validated racism, many white people were receptive to criticism of Trump's assertions, without critically contemplating white frames of privilege many would not reconsider and challenge the implications of our coded cultural frames. White folks may not have engaged in the conversation in fear of being wrong, hurting their white networks, feeling as though another issue was more salient, or having to be brave in the face of fear.

2

\<Freedom of Speech\> without Responsibility

Unmasking a Privilege Filter of Color-Blind Racism as a White Supremacist Ideograph

In the fall of 2017, a white, sixty-year-old male student auditing the course came in for an office visit. During the visit the student noted an interest in how taboo speech is "more taboo now," using the N-word as an example. I found myself surprised that a student who recognized that a word was "taboo" would use it. After the session I emailed him to tell him to not use the N-word in class because it would create a hostile environment. He responded that he assumed I understood he was having an intellectual discussion on the word and knew not to use it in class. The exchange offered me insight as to what white people, including those who might identify as "liberal," feel entitled to do under a guise of "free speech" with other white people. Through his rationalization of a color-blind intellectual engagement, the n-word seemed to offer him a sense of power through white privilege to access a dialogue about BIPOC while avoiding the responsibility of his speech. However, what he did not realize was how his claim of \<freedom of speech\> coded a color-blind ideology of racism as an "intellectual exercise."

Similar to my former student, over the last twenty years white nationalists have continued to refine their rhetoric to become more "pro-social," in
messages that focus on community building rather than explicitly naming
or blaming their enemies, to mask the white ideological foundations behind
their arguments. Just like HTML, institutional ideologies structure and style
value rhetoric to form and justify cultural meaning, all of which solidifies
interpretations into cognitive heuristics. White nationalists' use of "inferential,"[1] "facially neutral,"[2] or color-blind[3] racism allowed them to retain racial
perspectives on situations and events due to a set of unquestioned assumptions. As coercive and damaging to communities as other referential racism, or "the snarling, sneering, cross-burning displays of antipathy toward
minorities,"[4] less conspicuous inferential racism was easy to agree upon and,
therefore, dismiss their abhorrent nature within moral politics. In response
to the "hate" label scholars and organizations place on them, white supremacists targeted a more nuanced rhetoric of positively toned and styled messages[5] at white women. White nationalist women significantly fueled white
supremacy by using ideographs such as [white] \<American\>, \<diversity\>,
and \<freedom of speech\> to solidify a white victim identity. By classifying
a white victim identity through ideographs, white nationalist women coded
their racism by decontextualizing and appropriating the critical vernacular
to relativize white marginalization to keep privilege filters intact and justify
white identity politics. By understanding how white nationalists use ideographs to forward white supremacy, I unmasked how they preserve white
privilege within a mainstream political institution.

Color-Blind Ideology as Protection for a White "Privilege Filter"

Ideologies present a picture or perspective of the world. An ideology is a
clarification, rationale, or inference for motives and actions. For example,
people may use terms such as neoliberalism, feminism, or libertarianism to
represent a set a beliefs and assumptions. As Hall notes:

> Largely the [ideological] processes work unconsciously, rather than being pro-
> duced by them. They work most effectively when we are not aware that how
> we formulate and construct a statement about the world is underpinned by

ideological premises—when our formations seem to be simply descriptive statements about how things are (i.e. must be), or of what we can "take-for-granted."[6]

An ideology naturalizes understanding and allows for acceptance of meaning
without conscious cognitive engagement. Ideology provides a framework to
understand a given situation; by framing or reframing a situation, the use
and acceptance of ideological words become "social change" in themselves
because we accept the reasoning behind the ideology as common sense.[7]

People may employ an ideology without recognizing it as an ideology and
believe they are offering factual information. According to Michael McGee,
an ideology "warrants the use of power, excuses behavior and belief which
might otherwise be perceived as eccentric or antisocial, and guides behavior and belief into channels easily recognized by a community as acceptable
and laudable."[8] As an uncontemplated classificatory system or heuristic that
guides people's behavior, an ideology can prompt people to accept traditionally unacceptable behaviors. Ideologies are appealing because they allow for
heuristic rather than central processing.

As a cluster of ideas working together to build meaning, social actors
produce and reproduce ideologies in social settings to transform meaning in
society. Ideologies are powerful because they "are taken-for-granted frameworks that *naturalize* our descriptions of the way the world is."[9] As people
debate how to understand their lives, multiple ideologies come into dialectical engagement with one another in the public sphere, and people illustrate a
"capacity to control 'power' through the manipulation of symbols."[10] Through
symbolic and materialist rhetorical efforts, ideologies shape mass consciousness. Since language influences meaning and interpretation, the dialectical
engagement of ideologies "like any other form of struggle . . . represents an
intervention in an existing field of practices and institutions; those which
sustain the dominant discourse of meaning of society."[11] Ideological negotia-
tions establish or alter cultural commitments.

Ideologies are tricky to identify and engage when classifications are not
clear. For example, a color-blind ideology can preserve a value of equality
through an assumption that an equal distribution of resources by ensuring
race (and subsequent racism) is not a factor is possible. However, "equal
opportunity" embodies a problematic discourse. As law scholar Kimberlé
Crenshaw noted:

In sum, the very terms used to proclaim victory contain within them the seeds of defeat. To demand "equality of opportunity" is to demand nothing specific because "equality of opportunity" has assimilated both the demand and the object against which the demand is made—it is to participate in an abstracted discourse that carries the moral force of the movement as well as the stability of the institutions and interests that the movement opposed.[12]

The "abstracted" discourse preserves institutional stability through abstract, yet seemingly enforceable rules by inconsistent and biased judges. Although this concept may sound good on surface value, "equality of opportunity" does not account for historic and continuing systemic and institutional racism.[13] Bonilla-Silva argues, "[i]f the myth of color blind racism is going to stick, whites need to have tools to repair mistakes (or the appearance of mistakes) rhetorically"[14]—meaning strategic linguistic devices preserve racism by facilitating a myth of merit-based equality. White people rhetorically employ a color-blind ideology through "(1) avoidance of direct racial language, (2) the central rhetorical strategies or 'semantic moves' used by whites to safely express their racial views, (3) the role of projection, (4) the role of diminutives, and (5) how incursions into forbidden issues produce almost total incoherence among many whites."[15]

Instead of responding to inequality, to sidestep being labeled racist white people avoid referentially racist terminology, use their network as qualifiers, blame other people for being more racist in comparison, qualify the extent of their racism, or respond incoherently due to discomfort or avoidance of commitment to an argument. Slipperiness exists in a "color-blind" ideology in statements such as "some of my best friends are Black" or "I am not racist, but . . ."[16] As an epistemological approach to understanding race, a color-blind ideology naturalizes racism by invisibilizing race, separating the rhetorical context and meaning of race from the accountability or politics of racism, making it necessary that we study how people rhetorically employ the color-blind concept.[17]

Without knowing it, many people are socialized through a white perspective and corresponding ideology of whiteness that filters the way they see the world and process their experiences. The split of the discourse of race from the politics of racism is found within many arenas, even academic ones, as hooks notes,[18] when scholarship may be self-reflexive but fails to be radical in the academy. As Carol Lynne D'Arcangelis argues, in contrast to researcher self-reflexivity, which constrains the ability to address scholarly white privilege when attempting to unmask structural oppression, radical reflexivity "must be explicitly vigilant about the ways in which our individual and collective subjectivities are tightly bound up in one another."[19] As white scholars, not only listening and continuing to sustain tension when facing the realities of white privilege and racial discrimination, but also by reflexively sitting in tension of recognizing our white privilege, being uncomfortable through the ambiguity and conflict of racial discord rather than seeking immediate relief or apologia within whiteness, become ways we must be vigilant.

Raising and socializing people within predominantly white communities influences how they learn how to see, understand, and explain "others" from their white perspective, which manifests within the language they use. As Lucaites, Condit, and Caudill note, "If a mass consciousness exists at all, it must be empirically 'present,' itself a thing obvious to those who participate in it, or, at least, empirically manifested in the language which communicates it."[20] For example, my parents raised me to believe in and encourage equality. They argue, "everyone is equal," yet they do not want to talk about it or to engage in anti-racist ideologies or behaviors; so I was raised to treat race as invisible. Although well-intentioned, in their hopes to recognize their community as the equal place their constitution promised, my parents socialized me to filter out alternative voices when it came to explaining discrimination.

A filter provides boundaries on our vision through selective linguistic assessment. A privilege filter is how language of dominance frames observations and the meaning of experiences based on how members of a dominant identity group understand the world. As Franz Fanon clarifies, "the problem of language" is linguistic colonization, or how language functions as a means to teach hierarchy through translation as well as linguistic purity.[21] In other words, BIPOC are forced to translate their experiences into white words to be heard. When "[o]ppressed groups are frequently placed in the situation of being listened to only if we frame our ideas in the language that is familiar to and comfortable for a dominant group,"[22] meaning is lost. Language, or the disciplining of language based on usage and meaning, establishes an epistemological and ontological hierarchy. Word choice frames how the world is understood—what is seen and what is filtered. A privilege filter frames how a dominant group views an event based on linguistic interpretations connected to value and ideological classifications.

Building on Feagin's notion of a "white racial frame,"[23] a privilege filter becomes a disposition toward agency and epistemology. When one filter is dominant, others are muted. A "white privilege filter" functions to decontextualize and appropriate oppression narratives and construct relativist notions of conflict and context to retain white privilege. When people use comparisons like being "treated like a slave" or "raped" in commonplace situations, they decontextualize the systemic experience of marginalization to argue for similar victimization, allowing for the appropriation of marginalization without the implications or depth of oppression. When white people take a relativist stance concerning racial discrimination, they refuse "to recognize how the legacy of the past, as well as ongoing practices in the present, continue to handicap people of color now granted nominal juridical and social justice."[24] Instead, through a color-blind reaction, a white privilege filter allows people to relativize hardship or struggle with oppression. A relativist approach to dealing with systemic oppression (e.g., "we all go through hard times") allows for a willful ignorance of context. By claiming one is taking an objective stance when conflict occurs in a given moment in which we have limited knowledge, we undermine people from oppressed groups to articulate their experiences, and in doing so we deny that discrimination exists.

Ideographs of Whiteness

For white people, and explicitly for white nationalists, color-blind ideology, through ideographs, provides an orientation and corresponding rule structure (privilege filter) to explain the world in a way to keep a white perspective dominant. A color-blind ideology creates an epistemological foundation to perpetuate a white privilege filter. Ideographs, or ordinary-language terms that represent a collective commitment to an abstract or vague normative goal, offer insight into justifications of power and privilege. McGee defines an ideograph as "a high-order abstraction representing collective commitment to a particular but equivocal and ill-defined normative goal."[25] The power of an ideograph lies in its ability to represent fundamental logic without forcing a community to think through the logic of the ideology it represents. Social change requires a rhetor to "speak *against* the dominant ideology, but from *within* its own vocabulary."[26] White nationalists freely express their ideology

of whiteness to perpetuate racial inequality by structuring racial expectations. Burke notes that through a "basis of *expectancy*," we form "judgments
as to how things were, how they are, and how they may be,"[27] a system for
understanding our social environment. Whiteness as a racial ideology frames
white people as unraced or unmarked, creating a racial hierarchy based on
stereotypical expectations.

Whiteness functions ideographically by depicting white people as the
(default) norm and anything/anyone else as abnormal. An ideology of whiteness returns BIPOC to an invisible state, "being present and yet not visible,
being visible and yet not present."[28] BIPOC are clearly present in society;
however, when white people assert racial victimhood, it denies the structural foundation of oppression. When white people employ a victim classification, white identity politics is a means to forward an epistemologically
based privilege filter to retain white supremacy because it flattens oppression. As an ideology, whiteness becomes the norm for humanity, structuring
individuals who are raced through an "other" identity to be dehumanized
through their outsider status as they are treated as Other. BIPOC may find
it easier to conform or assimilate identity pressure to fit into white, middle-
class expectations for behavior.

Similar to other ideological frameworks that guide individuals, people
may employ an ideology of whiteness consciously or unconsciously to clarify
or justify meaning; people may believe they are asserting "common knowledge" because "[w]hite people do not have to talk about whiteness or question
personal dimensions of racism very often."[29] The malleability and adaptability
of whiteness as a race gives it power to move freely between moments, all
while reifying a dominant white privilege filter at the expense of the Other.
By analyzing how white nationalists use and refine (see chapter 1) ideographs
of implied whiteness, we can see how a color-blind ideology further institu-
tionalizes white supremacy.

An Approach to Ideographic Analysis of a Color-Blind Ideology

To analyze ideographs[30] within white nationalist artifacts, I analyze white
nationalist women's webspaces from 2007 (see introduction) to understand
the historical and contextual uses of a whiteness ideology. A diachronic analysis focuses on the grammar of ideology, or the historical use and meaning

of particular ideographs. As Cloud notes, ideologies emerge from historic events and should be analyzed from a historical perspective.[31] Studying the etymology of a term (in the *OED*, other historical dictionaries, or past studies of ideographs) allows me to scrutinize comparative uses of terms. For example, Condit's study of ideographs employed in American public discourse in magazines between 1939–59 compared the use of ideographs by advocates of white-black equality and white southern racists. Advocates pursued the move from an ideograph highlighting <separate but equal> facilities to ideographs of <equality> and <fairness> to end discrimination present in segregationist facilities.

While diachronic analysis focused on historical meaning, my use of a synchronic analysis is focused on the current contextual use and meaning of ideographs. To understand the categorical meaning of an ideograph, I assess the dynamism of a term, or the diversity of contexts in which a term is utilized. Scholars acknowledge ideographs such as <freedom>, <family values>, and <equality> within US culture.[32] Cloud's study illustrates constraints that particular ideographs have placed on different groups of people, such as the use of <family values> to point at problems associated with race, class, and gender. Politicians use examples without race or class labels to illustrate the antithesis of <family values>, although they identify generic black or brown-skinned males who left their families, rioted, or protested in the streets of Los Angeles. In summary, as an ideograph, <family values> reinforces racial stereotypes and gender roles. Through synchronic confrontations, I assess clashes with other ideographs that reveal points of white nationalist ideographic slippage or where inconsistencies lie due to contextual shifts of usage.

Appropriation of Color-Blind Politics through Critical Ideographs

In 2007 white nationalist women online used ideographs diachronically (historical) and synchronically (use and meaning) to shift mass consciousness concerning race and culture. Some white nationalist women identify as libertarian rather than white nationalist, which reinforces a color-blind ideology while mainstreaming whiteness into US politics. Although not all white nationalist women identify themselves as such, they share white nationalist values (see chapter 1) and ideologies, which is why I include them in this analytic subset. White nationalist women utilize ideographs to situate their claims of victimhood within color-blind frames to code their ideology of whiteness to retain a white privilege filter. Specifically, white nationalist women utilize <American>, <diversity>, and <freedom of speech> as color-blind ideographs to recode whiteness as viable identity politics.

<American> as [White] American First, Then Citizen

Through a color-blind ideology, white nationalists use <American> to create white boundaries on and ownership of the American identity and argue race and racial discrimination as relative to identity rather than systemic. Diachronically, white nationalists use the ideograph <American> to imply white Americans means people with citizenship and European heritage to decontextualize racial discrimination.

Implied whiteness creates a clear division between white <Americans> and "others" based on heritage or ethnicity, yet makes the experience of racism relative, defining "disrespect" or disagreement of white privilege filter as discrimination. On the VDare blog, a group who define themselves as "a non-profit journalistic enterprise . . . [who] . . . inform the fight to keep America *American*," blogger Bryanna Bevens argues, "Americans defending their heritage is *racism*."[33] Bevens's use of <American> not only implies a white American identity, but also defined the experience of racism as individual rather than systemic, similar to claims of reverse racism. Similarly, Brenda Walker, an independent blogger, wrote, "'Straight Eye'? If I were to address an Asian as 'Slant' I would be accused of racism, but when Hmong treat <Americans> disrespectfully, it's accepted."[34] Assertion of <American> implies European white identity, which decontextualizes what they then argue is racially based oppression. Further, white nationalist women solidified a color-blind ideology by moving from claims of supremacy to separation. As Angry White Female argued, "part of being an 'American' is 'self-determining' our future through racial separation."[35] Angry White Female used <American> to harken freedom of white privilege over equality. Arguments for racial separation (separate but equal) pervade US history, yet racial equality is not what occurs in those contexts. Similar to arguments made by Brown, implied whiteness reinforces racial hierarchy as well as "superlative references"[36] to make their whiteness synonymous with not nation, but Americanness. Although the *OED* defines American as "[o]f or relating to (any part of) the Americas,"[37] the definition of European American highlights "citizenship."[38] Only over time has usage changed to distinguish early colonists from later people of immigrant status. As Herbst notes, terms such as "Real American, good American, true American, all-American, and 100 percent American have been equated with white, native-born, English-speaking residents, excluding others."[39] The change from defining <American> as inhabitant to citizen reinforces a color-blind ideology by having familial inhabitation or birthright as well as a process-based rule system (citizenship) define the identity.

The implications of <American> racial hierarchy became further evident as white nationalist women appealed to "black Americans" through citizenship. As another VDare blogger Athena Kerry articulated, "if you're a tax-paying <American>, especially a black one, you should be wondering why we're subsidizing the advancement of immigrants at the detriment to the American blacks who are suffering here."[40] Although a clear appeal was made to exclude people of immigrant status from <American>, which appeared color-blind, by separating people with black skin with the <American> ideograph, they set a hierarchy of inclusion based on race. White nationalists articulated the cost of becoming <American> as enforcement of racial hierarchy, a familiar charge when considering how racial assignments began in the United States as a means to separate out "weak" people.[41]

<Diversity> as Difference, Marginalized, and Reclaimed Whiteness

In addition to implying whiteness and citizenship through an <American> ideograph, white nationalist women appropriated the ideograph of <diversity> as a means to relativize oppression based on "difference" and validate white marginalization. White nationalist women framed <diversity> primarily as an identifier of a person of color based on skin color. For example, Angry White Female emphasized how the "exposure to the loving embrace of diversity simply forced me to re-evaluate what my family and society had taught me. I am a reformed leftist who saw the hypocrisy after seeking out the facts and taking an objective look at things. I feel absolutely no shame for being White, or pro-White."[42] By identifying her skin color, Angry White Female framed <diversity> through racial othering or difference. Further, <diversity> was defined as a reason for racial defensiveness. Elena Haskins provided the following title to a section of her website "Answer: Identity

Theft, Murder Threats, Hackers, & <Diversity> in Hatemail. Question: What to Expect if You Are a White 'Gentile' Woman Who Proclaims That She Loves Her Race."[43] Through her question-and-answer sequence, Haskins framed <diversity> as a racial and religious issue. She defined herself not only as white, but also as a "Gentile" whom <diversity> attacks.

White nationalists also code <Diversity> as an ideograph to place BIPOC as a dangerous embodiment of cultural differences, which could control or overpower white people. White nationalists use the terms "cult" and "propaganda" to describe people supporting <diversity>.[44] Elena Haskins argued if people (white Americans) did not "wake up" to the threat of <diversity>, white people would become the minority[45] and, therefore, "victims" of <diversity>. By articulating <diversity> as an aggressive term, Haskins articulated white people as the "the Endangered World Minority."[46] Through her use of the term "endangered," Haskins tied cultural and biological racial existence of white people to the white people's exclusion of <diversity>.

White nationalist women used <diversity> to explain their frustration with perceived exclusive special treatment of BIPOC as well as people of immigrant status. <Diversity> functioned ideographically by allowing white nationalists to identify BIPOC and people of immigrant status by skin color difference rather than by human similarity. As she related her struggle to work her way through college, Haskins stated, "There were all those affirmative action and foreign students who had to be given a free ride."[47] Haskins grouped together BIPOC whom she considered "affirmative action . . . students," and "foreign students" into people who were eligible to receive educational aid. Although Haskins noted that she and other family members had to work hard to pay for their educational degrees, she viewed <diversity> as unfair means to acquire funds for an education.

Similar to the use of <American>, white nationalist women, especially those who identified as libertarian, appealed to Black people to question people from "other" cultures.[48] On her website Brenda Walker wrote, "The next time you are accosted with the idea that you should 'celebrate <diversity>' please remember that some cultures accept despicable practices, including slavery even today."[49] By focusing on "some cultures" as representative of <diversity>, Walker defined <diversity> as an outsider from another country while aligning herself with people against slavery. Rather than recognizing a value in difference, white nationalists positioned <diversity> as recognition of surface differences, such as skin color or "immigrant" status, to demonize them and the "unfair" advantages or celebration they received.

However, white nationalist women did not always use <diversity> in connection to BIPOC or people of immigrant status. White nationalist women attempted to reclaim <diversity> by making racial discrimination relative. For example, Angry White Female argued, "I am proud of my European heritage, and I am tired of the Whitebashing. So, I have left the equality cult, and have finally learned that real <diversity> is about maintaining yours and passing it down to your children."[50] Rather than being only a representation of BIPOC or immigrant status, white nationalist women appropriated <diversity> to identify marginalized people seeking equality, like themselves. Through their white privilege filter, white nationalist women equated the experience of "diversity" and systemic racial discrimination with confronting their white privilege, which feels "oppressive" to them.[51]

The inconsistency of their usage and efforts to redefine <diversity> provided credence to the lost meaning of the ideograph. The *OED* defines diversity as "[t]he condition or quality of being diverse, different, or varied; difference, unlikeness," and as having an origin in "difference, oddness, wickedness, perversity."[52] Due to the historical origins of the term, anything someone defines by a classification of "diversity" would be diachronically "othered." Similar to Kenneth Burke's argument that humans define by difference,[53] without noting diversity we have no categories for classification. However, classification may lead to hierarchical ordering, or arguing that one classification is preferred over another. As Herbst clarifies, "[w]hile abstractly it includes white males, diversity most often today describes situations involving 'non-white' ethnic groups, women, lesbians and gay men, the aged, and the disabled, especially as they relate to each other and to the dominant white male ethos in the workplace."[54] Current synchronic usage of the term <diversity> signals marginalized or underrepresented groups, yet the shibboleth also serve as a reduction of an identity. As Hélène Cixous notes:

> There is, at this time, no general woman, no one typical woman. What they have in common I will say. But what strikes me is the infinite richness of their individual constitutions; you can't talk about a female sexuality, uniform, homogeneous, classifiable into codes—any more than you can talk about one unconscious resembling another. Women's imaginary is inexhaustible, like music, painting, writing: their stream of phantasms is incredible.[55]

When called into action, "diversity" manifest as token representation of someone from a particular classification, yet that reduction allows for the discrediting of their very existence. For example, job postings use the statement that they "encourage minorities to apply" to increase "diversity" in the workplace. In mainstream culture, diversity has become synonymous with "the marginalized," even to the point where those groups are perceived as exclusive or having special rights because of their subordinate or even submissive status rather than recognizing their credibility for the difference of perspective they provide to reach a similar institutional goal. Mimicking the same problematic reduction, white nationalist women used <diversity> synchronically as an identity signifier for BIPOC, an identity reduction, rather than a value of difference of perspective or disposition.

Through their conversion narratives, white nationalists attempt to transform the ideograph, where, due to their choice of critical theory terminology, they assert individual white victimhood rather than mortify themselves through recognition of white privilege. By associating generalized <diversity> with BIPOC and anti-racist allies as controlling "others," white nationalists construct their individual <diversity> as more acceptable and important than BIPOC or immigrant status, making <diversity> appear color-blind while serving a white ideology. As scholars like Vidhya Shanker clarify, it is important to challenge the use of terms like "diversity" and "culture" because of how they sidestep recognizing historic and systemic discrimination and anti-racist action.[56] Further research into institutional use of how those terms allow white people to remain dominant in a conversation without addressing systemic oppression, as an anti-racist stance, will enhance how we disrupt a white privilege filter.

<Freedom of Speech> as a Decontextualized White Right

White nationalist women used <American> and <diversity> to decontextualize oppression and create space for white identity politics, whereas color-blind assertions of freedom of speech implied legal (institutional) grounding. White nationalist women articulated their desire for unfettered allowance of all speech or <free speech> through <freedom of speech> as a form of color-blind ideology to illustrate the assumption of relative access to civil liberties. Specifically, white nationalist women used <free speech> to sidestep racist associations of white nationalist organizations and protect white privilege in unconstrained and unconscionable expression. For example, as Snow White noted on her blog, "HISTORICAL REVISIONISM—DAVID IRVING'S SITE—LOTS of info here . . . including many traditional enemies of free speech, like the ADL."[57] By identifying the ADL (Anti-Defamation League), which works to protect people concerning defamation laws, Snow White called into question the purpose of the organization and <free speech> as equally accessible. Similarly, Carol A. Valentine argued that her organization, Public Action, "sent letters to these self-proclaimed champions of free speech, concerning attempts to shut down Ernst Zundel's free speech on the Internet. No answers have been received. Letters sent in October, 1998."[58] Valentine used <free speech> to decontextualize the work done by organizations like the ADL and internet freedom groups to illustrate how white people, specifically people like Valentine, experience injustice and marginalization.

Further, white nationalists argued their speech should not be "censored," even when they might be engaging in "worthless speech," or "words that by their very utterance inflict injury"[59] by dehumanizing others. For example, Bryanna Bevens claimed, "What I care about is the latest infringement on the very basic, very necessary <freedom of speech> that is (or used to be) guaranteed by the US Constitution. By eliminating the 'N-Word' from social discourse, Councilman Comrie is hoping to send a message to the next generation of Americans . . . Unfortunately, that message may end up being something like: Bye-Bye First Amendment, Hello Censorship!"[60] By focusing on the <freedom of speech>, Bevens attempted to ideologically sidestep the identity reduction and dehumanization inherent in the "N-word" to decontextualize the "N-word." She worked to retain her and other white people's comfort in using terms rather than thinking of how that term dehumanizes Black people. The *OED* defines the freedom of speech as "unrestricted use of something," "the power or right to act, speak, or think freely," and "permitted to take a specified action."[61] The restrictions white nationalists and other white people note and feel may be due to their conception of being white. As Steve Martinot clarifies, "White identity loses its freedom through its identity-dependency on the other. But this dependence is then disguised by means of a standard inversion. The ethics of whiteness and white supremacy determines that it is the other (a black person, for instance) who is perceived as the source of one's felt unfreedom."[62] White nationalism, or even conceiving oneself as "white," is definitionally bound to the conception of others as a variation of "non-white." Through identifying themselves as white, white people tie themselves to a framework of race and racism.

The lack of speaking "freedom" or complete communicative comfort (the ability to feel completely unrestricted) is an indication of privilege in any given context. As communication ethics scholars Arnett et al. argue, "the public arena is not our home. We should never feel totally comfortable in such a place; if we do, there is a good chance that we have excluded others."[63] White nationalist women synchronically defined the <freedom of speech> as a form of white comfort with expressing anything that comes to mind regardless of how that speech excludes the existence of BIPOC. White nationalist women preserved a white privilege filter through how they used <freedom of speech> to sustain their comfort and disposition of speech as privileged over a person of color's humanity or existence.

Akin to using the ideograph, some white nationalists implied the ideograph when they describe themselves as speaking up. For example, on their band's website, Prussian Blue asserted, "In a day and age when most bands are working hard to remain within self-imposed limits of Politically Correct Thought Prussian Blue pushes the envelope,"[64] pairing <freedom of speech> with breaking political correctness. Through the <freedom of speech>, white nationalists sought to have no responsibility or accountability for the words they used, as though words are just words or tools, making their use a relative, color-blind act. Similar to arguments made by Kelly concerning how conservatives appropriated liberal ideographs,[65] white nationalist women reframed their "freedom" as engaging critical thought as a revolutionary act (freedom to express themselves).

Decontextualizing Oppression Makes "Discrimination" a Relative Experience

White nationalist women co-opted critical terminology to rationalize their perspective, using ideographs to justify their right to speech. As a part of their white perspective filter, white nationalist women appropriated terms of marginalization to decontextualize systemic oppression. The use of <American> implied whiteness as it is paired to citizenship. Although Kerry's viewpoint was not the norm for white nationalists in the study, she represented a redefinition of <American> identity or nationalism to include Black people who were born in the United States. Similar to the changing definition of who is considered "white,"[66] some white nationalists included Black people in their definitions of nationalism because they made convenient citizen-based allies against people with immigrant status.

White nationalist women redefined <diversity> from a perspective of whiteness by highlighting their personal diversity (heritage, individuality) to argue how white people did not require a <diverse> racial community. White nationalists appropriated, rather than illustrated, a genuine critical understanding of racial marginalization. Although critical theory does not have a copyright on them, these words developed from a specific context or from a particular viewpoint in social structures. White nationalists appropriated terms like feminism, misogyny, sexism, marginalization, revisionist, and alternative voice to ironically offer credence to their claims of white marginalization as they fight or compete against people who spoke from situations that generated critical theory terms. Since "[u]nity does not exclude diversity any more, without diversity there can be no true and perfect unity."[67] Further research on how white people juxtapose <diversity> with <unity> and <inclusion> may offer additional understanding as to how an implied whiteness is signaled through <unity>. We cannot walk in someone else's shoes or experience the world (e.g., oppression) the way they do. As Rachel Dolezal's example demonstrates,[68] white people cannot separate our white identity to embody another's identity and experience the "situational contingency"[69] of intersectional oppression because white people can always walk away from an oppressed identity. Antiracist action includes listening to, standing with, and amplifying voices of disempowered groups to ensure everyone has access to their civil liberties and the democratic process. However, by recognizing a white privilege filter, we begin the process of "detouring" our responses[70] to recode how we process values and ideographic meaning. The loss of authority an oppressor experiences may create new tensions, illustrating how "a lack of white privilege can be experienced as oppression" by white people[71] and providing an additional barrier to altering social structures or cultural codes.

Finally, assertions by white nationalist women of <freedom of speech> validated relativist, apologia-based statements stemming from a color-blind ideology. White people may feel "oppressed" or censored when they have to critically consider not using certain words because of how it dehumanizes others. However, arguing that everything is subjective and therefore relative equates racial oppression with cultural and community accountability. People who speak in relative terms about "the human" experience may not recognize their own privilege and, therefore, problematically assert a generalized "human" voice or perspective because they may not account for systemic oppression based on institutions unable to change to recognize equity difference in sex, sexuality, class, religion and other differences in US culture. White nationalists felt marginalized due to their racist perspective, yet restored their privilege filter by calling to white <freedom of speech>. White people are heard when they evoke the <freedom of speech>, which is not usually the case for BIPOC. As more white nationalists were accused of being racist, they felt marginalized and, as a result, appropriated more terminology historically associated with critical theory or found ways to articulate an oppressed identity, yet the fact that it was simulation was clear as the actual experience of racial oppression was not occurring.

White nationalist women are not the only people who have found power in using <free speech> to sustain a white privilege filter. Following the University of California, Berkeley's cancellation of Milo Yiannopoulos's speaking engagement during "Free Speech Week," President Trump tweeted, "If U.C. Berkeley does not allow free speech and practices violence on innocent people with a different point of view—NO FEDERAL FUNDS?"[72] Statements that sidestep cultural context to argue for <free speech> connect with audiences who were taught a color-blind politic. Further research is needed in the area of communication ethics concerning public discourse and the <free speech> ideograph. <Free speech> becomes a form of apologia, or defense, of what is ethically suspect, such as questioning and elimination of diversity and equity policies like Title IX or funding to Historically Black Colleges and Universities.[73] The experiences of oppression are different, yet tied based on their origin in a dominant privilege filter (For further clarification on how the alt-right uses <free speech>, see chapter 5.)

Instead of personalizing racism as an identity attack, the term privilege filter creates space for people to recognize that ignoring the difference in forms of oppression equates to relativizing oppression, or to classifying oppression as all the same. Although people cannot change their biological makeup, they can influence their rhetorical (re)construction and (re)production of problematic racial reductions as a communication ethic, as well as critically examining their privilege filters and the institutions that systematically sustain oppression, to rhetorically engage systemic racism rather than sidestep racial conversations.

Conclusion

Ideographs function to reinforce white privilege filters. As the foundation of how we classify meaning and rhetorically refine values in the United States, ideologies perpetuate racial ideologies. An ideographic analysis showed how white nationalist women utilize ideographs such as <American>, <diversity>, and the <freedom of speech> to connect with their audiences through white identity politics. White nationalist women's rhetoric illustrated how white people appropriated critical terminology as color-blind ideology to decon-textualize and relativize oppression to sidestep accountability and sustain a white privilege filter. The willful act of color-blind politics is not surprising by white nationalists, but it becomes quite significant as similar values, ide-ologies, and classifications are used in US politics (see chapters 1, 5, and 6) to sustain white supremacy within our mainstream institutions.

A white privilege filter epistemologically embodies a feigned objectivity, an emotional distance from racism because white people are invisible when it comes to "race," allowing us to argue for an "objectivity" to retain privi-lege and power. However, difference is not the cause of racism; insecurity in the face of difference is the cause of racism. People unwilling to listen to others and critically engage their privilege preserve their privilege by feign-ing objectivity. However, in order for multiple cultural identities to coexist, Herbst argues that individuals must have "equal access to power (pluralism)," allowing various cultures to "enrich one another"[74] by recognizing how privi-lege filters influence us to challenge our ideological assumptions. Without a continued center within communication ethics, white people in pursuit of their "freedom" to be comfortable speaking to any public, at any time, saying anything, will continue to constrain civil liberties and voices of traditionally underrepresented groups. Similar to my student situation at the University of Minnesota, his assertion of "objectivity" in using the N-word as an academic pursuit sustained a white privilege filter only as long as I did not question his usage. His comfort with using any words or language he desired preserved his privilege rather than the communicative ethic of all of my students. Due to the context of a freedom of speech class, white students may feel justified in using language that retains their privilege filter, regardless of the ethical impacts or implications. However, considering how those words reinforce white supremacy, challenging their ideological foundation of whiteness, may offer agency to unmask color-blind assumptions.

3

Classifying Whiteness as "Contained Agency"

Decrypting White Nationalist Women's Digital Design through Understanding Intersectional Analysis

I recall having conversations as a child with my mom about my grandmother's (my dad's mom) choices of "gifts" for my sister and me (eyelet-topped white Cuddleduds long underwear) and how they seemed markedly different from the "gifts" for my younger brother (remote control cars). During one of our conversations, my mom recalled the first birthday card my younger brother received from my grandmother, in which my grandmother wrote "Happy birthday to my first natural born grandson." My aunt and uncle had adopted five boys of color who were older than my brother. When recalling this conversation recently with my mom, she noted that the gift discrepancies between not only my sister and me and my brother, but also between him and my cousins, was why we stopped opening holiday gifts at my cousins' home. At that time, through her words and actions my grandmother made her preference clear, although the "preferencing" was experienced differently for each of us. The coding of "male" and "white" hidden within the classifications of preferential gendered and raced gifting and "natural born" racialized value illustrates how the prejudice is not always about explicit racism—it can be illustrated through preference and privilege, a gate to a community. Privileging of people we revere is a primary way we classify who we value.

White privilege is culturally transcoded into our digital environments. Neoliberal media and technology scholars hope that "[a] common bond reached through electronic proximity may help stave off future flare ups of ethnic hatred and national breakups by giving people another major channel for communication and cooperation, beyond trade and diplomacy,"[1] yet we have found the opposite to occur. We are not an "entire human family" functioning as "a single global tribe."[2] Instead of being the equally accessible *Isegoria* that techno-optimistic scholars envisioned it would become,[3] online life mimics offline cultural stratification.[4] Studies concerning race and diffusion of digital media technologies illustrate a continued discrepancy of media access and development[5]—the one exception being cell phone technologies. Digital culture is primarily produced by and directed at "white producers and consumers"[6]—white is default, the center, the point of reference.[7] Racial exclusion online further essentializes and reifies racial classification within digital environments. Technological development has always directly impacted a social movement's ability to create societal change by influencing how audiences are reached,[8] which is why the Westernized World Wide Web became a space[9] or property[10] of whiteness, ripe for white nationalism.[11] On Twitter alone, American white nationalist movement followers grew "by more than 600% since 2012,"[12] more than organizations like ISIS worldwide. Research on white nationalism has primarily focused on white men and their organizations;[13] however, white women are at the apex of white identity politics due to their organizational work within the white nationalist movement. Detailed accounts of white nationalist men's efforts, which is more "referential"[14] and lone-wolf-focused, differ significantly from more nuanced work "rhetorically refined" by white nationalist women.[15] In decrypting white nationalist women's identity classifications and web architecture, I have identified how white nationalist women code whiteness, as a preferential and privileged classification, into the epistemological foundations of digitally mediated communication systems to provide preliminary designs for gated infrastructures of whiteness. When considering the influence white women had on the 2016 US presidential election—53 percent of white women voted for Donald Trump, more than any other underrepresented group polled[16]—white women's methods of political engagement required additional study. Through an intersectional lens, I clarified how white nationalist women used white feminism as a form of "contained agency" to circumvent defining oppression as structural and political. Decrypting how classifications gate white communities allow scholars to "develop literacies of racism, anti-racism, and social justice"[17] necessary for declassifying oppressive structures.

Intersectionality as Recognition of Political and Structural Oppression

Legal and critical race scholar Kimberlé Crenshaw introduces intersectionality as a means to clarify how Black women were excluded from both sex and race identity politics and discrimination recognition. Intersectionality is defined as structural and political oppression toward people who experience multiple forms of intersecting oppression based on singular identity reductions. Crenshaw writes: "The focus on the most privileged group members marginalizes those who are multiply-burdened and obscures claims that cannot be understood as resulting from discrete sources of discrimination."[18] For example, following the Civil Rights Act of 1964, companies like General Motors were legally responsible to hire people from underrepresented communities. General Motors hired white women and Black men, but when faced with claims of discrimination against Black women, the courts decided to argue that GM was compliant with sex and race representation as separate discriminatory concerns. The court reasoned that, being identified with both identity categories, Black women should have more opportunities to gain employment, yet due to structural discrimination, the opposite is true due to their distinct experience of oppression.[19] Critical white women may identify with structural and political oppression they experience as women; Black men do so with similar racial discrimination. Yet the nonsummative experiences of intersectional oppression of Black women go unaddressed. Politically, Black women are forced "to choose between specifically articulating the intersectional aspects of their subordination, thereby risking their ability to represent Black men, or ignoring intersectionality in order to stake a claim."[20] Being forced to choose a dominant identity characteristic for a claim of discrimination, rather than focusing on the multidimensionality of "situationally contingent"[21] systemic oppression, limits the issue of discrimination to identity rather than the power built into institutional systems. Without engaging a multidimensionality of identity, people reduce discrimination to a single characteristic of an individual's experience.[22] However, the wider the scope of discrimination, the greater the potential for people to recognize they experience not the same, but similar structural and political oppression. By taking an intersectional perspective, I unmasked "the centrality of white female experiences in the conceptualization of gender discrimination."[23] Intersectionality offered a distinct lens to assess the difference between identity politics and systematic, structural oppression. The containment of a white female frame became apparent when interrogating groups that forward their white identity as racial politics.

Whiteness as a Classification for Contained Agency

As I discuss in chapter 2, whiteness is a foundation to construct white identity politics, or a means to voice and articulate roots of grievance; white women embodied white identity politics through using specific values and ideologies to preserve their white privilege. At the root of preserving white privilege is retaining separate classification of self versus other. The legacy of colonialism provided roots for other/self constructions, where the "Western self is itself produced as *an effect* of the Western discursive production of its Others."[24] Racial classifications people use to identify blackness or otherness involve division from whiteness,[25] where "whiteness" becomes the expectation of normalcy and "others" are identified as deviants.[26] However, "[t]he process of classification itself is a demarcation of power, an organization of knowledge and life that frames the condition of possibilities of those who are classified."[27] As a reactive political identity, whiteness bonds people together against others who are not classified within the white "norm." Identifying US economic hardship, desires for a post-racial community, and immigration-focused policies,[28] without considering continued legalized racism (policing, the war on drugs, the prison system, criminal justice, education, employment, wealth, the workplace, voting, media, housing),[29] emboldens white people to use white classification systems to blame "other" people (BIPOC, people with immigrant status, etc.) for societal challenges. Whiteness becomes a platform to articulate oppression at the hands of others through a rhetoric of contained agency.

Social change scholars have identified a need for collective agency by transcending individual experiences of discrimination to recognize structural or political oppression to forward transformative efforts toward social change.[30]

Yet, agency is necessary for social change to occur. Miller notes agency as a recognition of a type of relationship or perspective shared between people,[31] while Cooper focuses on "emergent rhetorical agency" as "a response to a perturbation that is shaped by the rhetor's current goals and past experiences."[32] Cooper's focus on a disposition that prompts self-organizing action provides further explanation on how "organisms create meanings through acting into the world and changing their structure in response to the perceived consequences of their actions."[33] Agency stems from how a person sees the world—their disposition and filter based on their experiences—and how they respond to particular exigencies. White women who recognize gendered oppression may be disposed toward an empowering agency, yet struggle to assess how individual empowerment does not further social change of systemic oppression. A contained form of agency occurs when people localize oppression to an individual's situation rather than from a dispositional recognition of systemic, historical, and institutional frameworks for oppression, and epistemological agency is ignored or resisted. For white women who have received extensive benefits from feminism, personal agency of white men hearing their concerns or including them may feel individually empowering enough, especially since they do not experience systemic racism. Contained agency offers a way to navigate one particular situation, to retain a white privilege frame, but the larger context of oppression is actively denied.

The privileged access of one identity politic (e.g., white), but inequitable status of another (e.g., woman, or when one identity is denied, or unacknowledged members of underrepresented groups), creates a context where people can seemingly remove themselves from an oppressed identity. Whiteness allows white people, in this case white women, the privilege to remove ourselves from an oppressed state (to a certain extent) because white people in power protect other white people. When considering post-feminist politics, white women seemingly get the choice to be oppressed or not. However, people in positions of power over women limit women's agency based on situational contingencies (e.g., is it perceived as beneficial to retaining the hierarchy of power?) rather than unmasking and revolutionizing problematic hierarchies of oppression. Without intellectual humility to change one's epistemological agency, oppressive systems remain intact. By humility I mean "the attention to the limitations of knowing and a willingness to stay within the space of uncertainty, the ongoing need for accountability, and the inescapability of the interconnection of all things."[34] For example, within an intellectual realm, recognizing that "feminism" or "woman" are not all-encompassing terms for all oppression or people who face gendered or intersectional oppression reframes oppression by difference rather than sameness.

Accepting that we do not and may not ever fully understand a topic seems contrary to an academic goal, yet isn't the *pursuit* (not acquisition) of knowledge our actual goal? White people become accountable by understanding how our actions and color-blind correctives sustain white supremacy. Similarly, academic accountability develops from our ability to engage in epistemological flexibility based on evidence and to serve our research areas rather than our individual selves (through promotion, etc.). Further, by working to recognize the privilege we experience, we push ourselves to challenge how white people are preferred based on our community's perceived sameness with those in positions of power. Without creating connections between the seeming randomness of being white with the institutional processes of white supremacy, we will struggle to understand how white supremacy is culturally internalized.

When researching social movement texts where activists privilege one identity politic, an intersectional analysis offers agency in understanding how an overlying identity classification contains epistemological humility. As Hancock notes, "While much of feminist theory has engaged in decades of fraught conversations about the role of identity and experiences grounded in identity, intersectionality theory instead relies on situational contingency to acknowledge and incorporate the permeability of the binary between oppressed and oppressor."[35] In "intersectional" critique, or recognizing non-summative engagement of apexes of oppression,[36] scholars engage different experiences of oppression. Unless discrimination is intersectionally engaged, an oppressed group gets pitted against another oppressed group in a hierarchy or "Oppression Olympics,"[37] and offers of contained agency become an incentive for tokenly identified people of a singular oppressed status to reinforce oppressive structures rather than utilizing revolutionary approaches to address systemic, institutional oppression.

Classifying White Identity to Organize an Epistemology of Whiteness

To critically contemplate contained agency requires an intersectional engagement of classifications. Classification is a process of naming reality based on similarities or differences for categorization within an organizational system. Classifications provide organizational schemas and categorical boundaries to structure and standardize a system of understanding, leading to evaluative judgments.[38] When considering white supremacy, classification functions as a means to "imprisoning . . . , primitivizing . . . , [and] decivilizing"[39] BIPOC based on a racialized identity reduction. Classifications function as symbolic representations of material referents, which reduce difference procedurally to fuel white identity politics.

For example, within the digital spheres, identity classifications influence how web designers structure website usability and community members' interactions. As Cheney-Lippold notes in his text *We Are Data*, "[t]he process of classification itself is a demarcation of power, an organization of knowledge and life that frames the condition of possibilities of those who are classified."[40] For example, specific terms dictate our classificatory options, or more specifically, identity options in digital spaces. Based on a designer's definitions of identity data, a system classifies an individual as a composite of data to be "transcoded" into an organizational system;[41] a user can only control whether they participate in a community or complete the research or a task or play with a given digital mechanic. Yet, these classifications only provide data chosen by the designer as salient. The data does not provide true information but instead allows an identity reduction based on the designers' and dominant users' perspective. In the case of algorithm-based search engines like Google, Noble argues, "what rises to the top of the information pile is *strictly* what is most popular as indicated by hyperlinking . . . what is most popular is not necessarily what is *most true*."[42] Classifications serve as "pure" interpretational information (e.g., how people organize reality) rather than a fragment of selected reality by a select group of designers or users.

As "a fragment of reality,"[43] classifications serve as foundational components of arguments. Bogost articulates that digital mechanics embody a procedural rhetoric, or "the practice of persuading through processes."[44] By becoming the base units to frame user identities within digital systems, identity classifications are data that structure how processes are designed to function. Terms and data collection classify users. Menu-driven choices,[45] such as radio buttons rather than checkboxes (by asking for one type of data when categorizations have overlapped), serve as singular rather than inclusive identity classifications, where designers persuade users to define themselves through the classificatory options given. Designers may assume they are reaching out to a "universal" audience through their linguistic and architectural design choices; instead, without extensive, underrepresented group targeted user testing they are merely arranging a context or procedure for themselves and people who share in their identity and perspective.

Through digital protocol, people are reduced to aggregates of specific data to be transcoded within a given system for an intended purpose. For example, although the term "feminism" has changed drastically over time, space, community, and culture,[46] and has been decontextualized from its roots, people use the term monolithically in digital spaces. For example, in July 2016 Buzzfeed[47] provided a quiz entitled "How much of a feminist are you?" where users check boxes to illustrate the *quality* of their feminism. Yet the terms and checkboxes Buzzfeed's digital designers provided measured the *quantity* of feminist terms recognized by users. The designer asked if a user knows what "intersectional feminism" was to define feminist classification based on term identification, rather than a user's understanding of structural oppression itself. In the case of intersectionality, designers did not ask users to illustrate their contextual understanding of how oppression is differently, nonsummatively experienced through systematic and institutional treatment.[48] Buzzfeed's test offered no realistic engagement of what feminism is; its designers did not engage various layers of systemic oppression, which would have allowed for a common "vernacular" through the classification of "feminism" without accountability for classification itself. Through Buzzfeed's classification, people would be able to feel good about "intersectional feminist" self-definitions by recentering themselves as "good feminists" within a conversation, without listening, bonding, and recentering through an oppression of differences, which is at the heart of intersectionality.

Decoding an Epistemology of Whiteness

A classification like feminism functions not only as a rhetorical term but also as a data bit, to be transcoded into a digital system based on how users perceive their role in the site (both architecture and usability). Designers structure architecture to engage users based on what user information organizations desire and then use data to structure websites and filter users based on a set of rules or protocols built into a site's architecture. Architecture is part of a "vernacular rhetoric" or communication that "resonates within local communities," regardless of whether or not that rhetoric embodies or critically undermines dominant institutions.[49] While physically dispersed, digital "local" communities can connect through a vernacular of digital architecture. A website's architecture includes splash pages, home pages, and content pages, as well as how users interact with a website. Although whiteness is culturally institutionalized in the United States, for white nationalism whiteness becomes a rhetorical vernacular to create "locality." The ways in which designers expect users to immediately engage and continue to participate in, as well as expected performance (e.g., outreach) from, the site structure a rhetorical vernacular for potential audiences.

As white nationalists "cloak" their core beliefs in white supremacy,[50] their classifications become more difficult to track. For example, rather than identifying a whiteness epistemology that guides the webspace's development, Stormfront, the largest online white nationalist forum, designed the www.martinlutherking.org website, presenting it as unbiased information and burying their identity within a small link at the bottom of the page. The placement in a Google search (within the top ten links when "Martin Luther King" was searched from 2007–2017 based on metadata, like classification tags) lends credibility to the website and value to the associated classifications,[51] normalizing classifications, which cloaks the whiteness the authors present. Current iterations of a similar cloaking can be seen by looking at the National Policy Institute's website. Visually, the site appears credible—it includes a white background, Javascript-based images, sections on "About," "Issues," "Blog," "Events," "Donate," and "A call for papers," similar to an academic conference website. Yet, upon more in-depth analysis of the author and purpose of the site, users may find that Richard Spencer was its creator and primary producer.

Further design elements (like hashtags) influence how organizational and individual data is classified and systematically processed. As Bonilla et. al note, "Similar to the coding systems employed by anthropologists, hashtags allow users to not simply 'file' their comments but to performatively frame what these comments are 'really about,' thereby enabling users to indicate a meaning that might not be otherwise apparent."[52] In addition to functioning as a fast means of retrieving similarly "classified" materials, hashtags provide a window into how someone understands or associates content. Yet, term choices between users can be inconsistent. Berger found that, unlike ISIS Twitter members, white nationalists' classification hashtags are less rhetorically consistent, which make identifying and policing white nationalist authors more difficult.[53] An ideology of whiteness appears more seamless, invisible, and "normal" due to its rhetorical ubiquity. Researching how white nationalist women used classifications to design their websites offers insight into how white people use white identity politics to reify whiteness and promote inferential racism.

Intersectional Approach for Decoding Classifications

Using Adobe Acrobat, I analyzed website content in PDF form based on how white nationalist women rhetorically classified themselves, and I critically assessed their web design architecture, looking for qualities of white nationalist site design. In this study, I analyzed ten individual and ten organizational public and "semi-public" spaces (no registration or passwords required): websites, five organizational discussion pages, and five individual blogs[54] from 2007 by women (female Western name or image) who identified themselves as "Pro-White," highlight the "white" race, or called for a focus on "nationalism." I chose websites based on links from individual white nationalist women and their organizations and authority as determined by Technorati.com (credibility based on incoming links). Through my analysis[55] I detailed not only rhetorical classification, but also the architecture of white nationalist women's websites to illustrate a vernacular of whiteness.

Classification of a White Warrior/Activist and Motherhood Body

First, white nationalist women classified their white identity through empowered physical referents and motherhood. One author identified herself as "Angry White Female," creating a simulacrum of white women to attract members.[56] Women for Aryan Unity (WAU) provided the text "Evoking the Spirit of Warrior Sisters Past,"[57] further solidifying their target audience of empowered white women who will click through their websites. These words appropriated classical Greek and Native American descriptors as a representation of their own warrior identity.

In addition to warrior representations, white nationalists asserted "motherhood" classifications. For example, the WAU stated under an image of a white woman, "We walk the same path as our foremothers,"[58] calling attention to biological, maternal classifications. Similarly, when an outside commenter challenged April Gaede about her identity on her blog space, Gaede, the mother of twins who comprise the white nationalist music group Prussian Blue, identifies herself as, "a 40 year old mother of three who has spent a great deal of my life outdoors training horses on a ranch. I am still pretty sure though that many of my fellow WN men would still rather have a child with me than a mud woman."[59] Motherhood as a classification shifts the frame from men to women, along with power and agency. Motherhood normalizes white womanhood through biological racial classifications defined by "blood purity." Further, by naming other interests beyond white nationalism, white nationalist women signaled whiteness through interests such as homemaking or homeschooling, singing patriotic songs, gardening, gun ownership and usage, paganism, breast cancer awareness, Celtic music, and technology,[60] which stood as "everyday woman" identity markers. Other scholars have noted how white power music even functions as a recruitment tool[61] and an international and transnational web to share conspiracy-based ideologies,[62] but further research is needed to establish how music might normalize white supremacy. By providing multiple activity classifications to describe its membership, white nationalist women described themselves as warriors and mothers to normalize their white identity classification and reify their "archetypal (e.g., victim, nurse, mother) female role model."[63]

Co-opting Classifications of Multiculturalism and Feminism

Although white nationalist women classified themselves as "diverse,"[64] they place boundaries on a multicultural identity inclusion with BIPOC. Assertions of European heritage functioned as "strategic whiteness,"[65] where white people use historical origins as nostalgia for dominant, hegemonic white culture and reasoning for continuing power over others. White nationalist women appropriated classifications of sex marginalization to their white identity, but vacillated between locally disdaining and globally embracing feminism. When referring to the Southern Poverty Law Center's (SPLC) latest "Intelligence Report," Angry White Female accused, "In truth, it is the enemy that seeks to chain us to the kitchen sink and confine our movement role to cooking, cleaning and having babies."[66] However, in her article entitled "Feminism: A Reality Check," she stated:

As a result of the propaganda pouring in on today's girls from every sphere, women are encouraged to believe their natural limitations are society-imposed, products of the "patriarchy," just as blacks are encouraged to blame "racism" when they encounter obstacles. . . . If society did not reinforce feminist dogma and female self-delusion at every turn, women would have to honestly face the fact that they have limits, and we'd all be better off.[67]

Although Angry White Female identified the oppression experienced through expectations of being a default homemaker, she derided a feminist classification. By decontextualizing historical gains made by feminists and feminist communities, individual white nationalist women appropriated the victimhood of oppression, but not the accountability of feminism. However, by using the term they evoked a frame of oppression because "the word is defined relative to that frame. When we negate a frame, we evoke the frame."[68] By choosing the word "feminist," white nationalist women reinforced a feminist framing of their oppression.

In contrast, global white nationalist organizations use feminism as a classification to target women. For example, global diasporic organizations like the WAU have described their task as "reinventing the concept of 'feminism' within the parameters of Race and Revolution."[69] WAU classifies their target audience of feminist women who value "equality" and will fight through education. Similarly, on Stormfront's forum under the title "Germany's New Anti-feminism Movement," one author identified Germany as anti-feminist because a former career woman's letter got published about her enjoyment in being a parent.[70] Although inconsistent, feminist ideographs are powerful because they unconsciously and enthymematically transform social structures by classifying their individual "marginalization" to make seemingly "political" arguments in general about how white women perceived their equality as threatened without having to attend to the scope of oppression.

Standardizing White Filtered and Gated Community Design

White nationalist women's verbal classifications echoed through their filtered and gated architecture. For example, organizations provided images of white-skinned, female warriors[71] or silhouettes of women riding horses with large headdresses and spears in hand going to battle.[72] Homefront Publications contained images of white babies,[73] inviting independent white women or mothers and parents into their website. Images became part of an architectural vernacular and, as a composite of "data,"[74] they imply or signal white, female, warrior, or mother classifications in addition to or rather than overtly stating organizational commitments. The design filtered out users who do not fit those classifications because the images do not resonate.

Other white nationalist women designed "gateway" architecture, requiring a hyperlink-styled ideological agreement before entering their site. For example, white nationalist Elena Haskins hand-coded her website to include a six-page gateway structure. On her first page, Haskins provided a detailed narrative about the barriers to education that her family experienced due to BIPOC, hyperlinking the following statement, "Click here or on the graphic below to enter."[75] On the next two successive pages, Haskins presented similar framing about cultural and historical war on white "Gentile" people with another hyperlinked gateway: "Click on the above button or on this text link to enter Wake Up or Die through the gateway pages."[76] On the fourth gateway page, Haskins offered the audience a "choice" to "Wake Up" or to "Join the White 'Gentile' American Zombie Suicide March."[77] The "Wake Up" link took users to her main page, while the other option takes users to a fifth gateway page that included uncited statistics and biting interpretations of people of immigrant status, stereotypes about BIPOC being economic threats, and conspiracy rhetoric about the master-slave relationship between BIPOC and white people.[78] Haskins offered no interactive discussion pages or user comment sections—only her narratives, uncited statistics, and examples that users could follow by agreeing with her argument (hyperlinks). Her linear, hyperlink design ensured the white classification of her target audience.

In addition to filtering website design, white nationalist women standardized expectations of the user to strengthen white networks. White nationalist women focused on "[c]reating a web of support" with other white families.[79] Individuals and organizations like Angry White Female,[80] Sigrdrifa,[81] and Stormfront[82] shared homeschooling materials to perpetuate a culturally isolated white history and network. White nationalist women also hyperlinked their website "contributors" and/or "friends." For example, Haskins section entitled "The Love Watch Section: Links That Celebrate Our Whiteness" included David Duke and Stormfront.[83] Similarly, Prussian Blue hyperlinked "contributors," "Friends of Prussian Blue," and "Prussian Blue & Family," which illustrated a white network and community around the family and white-power music.[84] To extend white nationalist networks, white nationalists requested that users provide support for their local as well as global endeavors. For instance, the WAU encouraged mothers to strengthen the movement through friend of a friend (FOAF) networks, stating, "If you know of a mother, father or family, soon expecting a baby or with a newborn please email WAU to find out about receiving your Welcome to the World Little One package. All information is entirely confidential."[85] Additionally, the WAU provided hyperlinks to global chapters including Portugal, Argentina, Chile, and Spain. Through external hyperlinks, audience members found "sister" groups around the world.[86] By soliciting support of established white nationalist organizations, white nationalists continued to build a "shared" construction of whiteness.

Implications of Decoding White Nationalist Classifications

Due to how public policy is forwarded and funded,[87] privileged opportunities for maternity leave and homeschooling make affluent, white women prey for white nationalism in online communities where alt-right women flourish.[88] White nationalist women's rhetoric is "palatable"[89] due to the contextualized classifications (motherhood, feminism) and US value systems.[90] As a biological classification, motherhood may appeal to users seeking meaning, resources, and community during a stressful and lonely transition. The hypervulnerability of this particular intersection leaves considerable room for further coded and codified racist ideologies to have persuasive appeal.

First, intersectional analysis invites scholars to critically engage how white people appropriate classifications from critical theory to contain "feminist" identities. White nationalists pieced together a local pastiche to assemble "a unique discursive form out of cultural fragments" in which they appropriate from counter-hegemonic discourses "oppositional to dominant ideologies."[91] White nationalist women identified their "oppressed" states, but were unwilling to bond with other oppressed groups out of fear of losing individual status with white people. Further, this study called attention to the appropriation of vernacular rhetorics by "alternate" or "subaltern agents"[92] within the digital sphere through a recontextualization of meaning. However, preliminary investigation illustrated how victim rhetoric, once salient through contained agency, changes over time. When looking at Elena Haskins's website in 2017, her splash page narrative now highlighted how she has been helping BIPOC, the misogyny within the white nationalist movement, and "Anonymous" "Misogynist" harassment of her.[93] By challenging students to engage changes in arguments, we problematize white classifications of feminism. Further, pushing students toward critical histories of feminism including reading how suffrage leaders excluded Black women[94] problematizes and disrupts implied whiteness within classifications of feminism.

Second, although universities may ban white nationalist speakers like Milo Yiannopoulos from speaking on campus, white nationalist women retain their seats at the table. Lauren Southern, following her presentation at the University of Minnesota, tweeted an image of her audience with the text " 😊 they all survived the shrieking commies outside" as well as "200 people showed up to protest a 22 year old Canadian girl that makes memes."[95] Southern classified herself as credible by showing her audience "survived" the counterprotesters, while using the identity classification of "girl" to undermine her accountability for the counterprotest. Interestingly, she contained her own agency by attempting to reduce the accountability or "consequences"[96] of her actions.

People must consider the boundaries of the freedom of speech or our legal rights to the freedom of speech. However, university administrators cannot censor speakers based on political message. As the SPLC notes, "No matter how repugnant one may find a speaker's views, as long as the college has a policy of allowing student groups to invite people from outside their campus to speak, university administrators at public institutions cannot pick and choose based on the views the speaker holds. Neither other students nor administrators can stop someone from speaking merely because they dislike the speaker's ideas."[97] Publicly funded institutions must uphold the freedom of speech established under US law unless the expression disrupts learning, incites violence, or is an expression of fighting words. Yet, in addition to the disproportionate number of white, male, cisgender, able-bodied faculty members, allowing speakers who sustain white supremacy privileges a clear preference for certain types of people. Further the enforcement of "free speech" on campus may impact scholars who are BIPOC (or who align with BIPOC) more than white speakers who further white supremacy. Resources like the SPLC's "The Alt-right on Campus" handbook, Dana Cloud's article "Responding to Right-Wing Attacks," and Daniels and Stein's article "Protect Scholars against Attacks from the Right" offer suggestions like getting to know the ideologies of white nationalists to form counterarguments, finding allies on campus and holding inclusive community events away from white nationalist speakers on campus, meeting with groups "targeted by alt-right," meeting with hosting groups, and sharing concerns in classrooms.[98] Further, by amplifying conversion narratives given by prominent members, like Stormfront leader Don Black's son, Derek Black, and white women who came from "liberal" households like Corinna Burt,[99] scholars can help students learn to question and challenge appropriated classifications of victimhood and "marginalization" as forms of contained agency to press dialogue about intersectional approaches to systemic oppression. Through recognizing other white people coming to terms with their intellectual, epistemological humility, we can begin to question our own. However, the question remains if these statements function as responsive or apologetic actions. Media attention of Prussian Blue amplified the mainstreaming of white nationalism in the US. Even after the statements made by Prussian Blue singers, Lamb and Lynx Gaede, that they no longer support white nationalism, it is not clear that they have rectified the extensive fuel they offered the white nationalist movement, especially as they shift their focus to medical marijuana legalization,[100] but their efforts are a start.

Finally, pervasive digital institutions should be held accountable for the "openness" of their environments. Hyperlinked architecture makes classifications seem ubiquitous, as users are filtered enthymematically into gated communities. Preexisting networks can become diasporic means to strengthen a white community. Although authors like Levmore and Nussbaum called for organizations to create "safe work environments,"[101] institutions like AOL and Google have been slow to regulate white nationalist content, only taking action when it financially benefits themselves to do so.[102] Accepting rationalizations of "free speech" (where participants assume whiteness as an "objective" stance[103]) gates whiteness. Although we see some white nationalist websites coming down, such as Stormfront and the Daily Stormer,[104] periods of censorship are short-lived, and different classifications of whiteness are developed and "rhetorically refined" within the white nationalist movement.[105] We can pressure online agencies who assert "liberal" or "progressive" viewpoints yet gate whiteness, to develop more accountable policies and procedures, similar to steps being taken by Twitter concerning their abuse and harassment policies and banning users from creating new accounts and developing "search safe" features.[106] More recently, companies like GoDaddy,

Google, Apple, CloudFlare, Airbnb, PayPal, Discovery Financial Services, Visa, Spotify, Discord, and GoFundMe are taking steps to shut down white nationalist, Nazi, and alt-right content on their sites.[107]

By extending procedures to assess how certain architectures lend themselves to filtering whiteness (like Facebook's "like" structure), organizations can take a stronger role in how they perpetuate ethical design. Classifications associated with racial discrimination (policing, the war on drugs, the prison system, criminal justice, education, employment, wealth, the workplace, voting, media, housing) are built into the architectures of our communities. Privilege offers access through architecture; white nationalist online presence prompts concern as to how far online racism will extend and be networked globally.[108] As users and potential designers of digital environments, even Facebook groups and community or course blogs, we need to consider how we design, classify, and administer our materials (through user testing, feedback forms, and changes in our designs)[109] to ensure access to discourse through the architecture of anti-racist design.

Conclusion

Web designers use classification tags as the meta-level organization to structure how text and people are categorized. Through classification, digital design structures the way we see similar and different and, even though the classification tags may change, what ends up in "like" categories may be rhetorically coded to do so and supported by generations of people. White nationalist classifications mask white privilege to constrain agency of users. By recognizing the permanence of racism,[110] we begin to see white people's antiracist role in combating it by questioning how architecture is grounded in classifications by and for whom those systems are built and serve.

Although our parents separated us when we opened gifts and, after years of feeling less than our brother, our parents finally spoke with our grandmother, who compensated by buying us girls expensive clothes and perfume. Yet, my parents struggled to engage her more directly earlier in the process reinforced her "natural born," white hierarchy, but I also empathized with how difficult it can be to challenge a parent's assumptions. In the last twenty years of her life, my grandmother lived with one of my cousins, with whom she formed a close bond. She and I even connected as we visited her regularly on frequent trips between Indiana and Minnesota near the end of her life. People change by choice, need, and proximity. As an academic, I remind myself that, by choosing intersectional engagement, we understand the need to reframe how we understand whiteness to ensure classifications of victimhood do not become contained agency for white women. We can redesign equitable systems, rather than capture users within a design's default, by changing the proximity of classifications based on who and how we value.

INDIVIDUAL WOMEN'S VOICES AS INSTITUTIONAL CODING OF WHITE SUPREMACY

4

White Outsiderism as White Identity Politics

Situating Tea Party Rhetoric as Uncivil Testing Grounds

During the spring of my oldest son's first grade year, he was invited over to a classmate's home after school. It was one of the first solo play dates he attended and we had only met the parents a couple of times. When I went to pick him up, the mother invited me in to chat about the upcoming school referendum. When reviewing the superintendent's presentation, she agitatedly mentioned that young [white] boys were being overlooked in resource allocation. I found myself taken aback by the comment considering the "liberal" PTO and community we lived in. I mentioned to her the continued statistics on disparities between resources for and faculty representing children (BIPOC), which translated into students (BIPOC) left behind academically. I also encouraged her to speak with other parents and see what they thought concerning the issue. Uncomfortable silence followed. I felt relieved when it was time to leave. I often reflect on that interaction, especially when I see her at school functions. Other white mothers at the school had described themselves as "helicopter parents," but did that translate into advocating for white boys' continued privilege? As part of cultivating my community, what would a critical conversation about whiteness look like in my community?

Racism flourishes within environments that breed competition for resources, like environments where parents (read: default parent, the mother) feel compelled to advocate for a child. We test out our rhetorical heuristics or argumentative codes with others, especially as we figure out new roles, like being a new parent at a school or being a political outsider. However, as seen with political outsiders like Sarah Palin, motherhood can also be used to reclassify and situate one as an insider when it comes to advocating concerns. Due to their decentralized, online roots[1] and use of social media for diffusion,[2] the Tea Party became a viable network within which white nationalism could expand through a "rebranding."[3] Following the outcry by white nationalist women for empowerment, Sarah Palin embodies a white, "maternal feminist" identity, which offers and eagerly invites white women to a seat at the political table. White nationalist values and ideologies poignantly align with white libertarian, evangelical Protestant women who could test out their rhetoric within the political sphere. Through their appropriation of "outsiderism" and the "alternative," conservative white women become a tool to move white identity politics where underrepresented groups like BIPOC, especially women, fighting for rights, are brandished as "bad."

The Tea Party Movement

The Tea Party is an ideological movement with a unique political identity. Founded in libertarian roots[4] with a strong portion of converts from Republican (45 percent), independent (28), and Democratic (17) leanings, the focal points of their rhetoric construct a message that in turn attract religious right-leaning, more specifically "evangelical Protestant," members.[5] Tea Party members organized themselves within the digital public sphere, specifically within Twitter,[6] allowing a disparate Tea Party to align their views into cohesive talking points.[7] Their main goals were "fiscal responsibility," "limited government," and "free markets."[8] They argued that fiscal responsibility meant "freedom of the individual to spend the money that is the fruit of their own labor."[9] They felt that government taxation was problematic. Through their goal of "limited government," they stated, they were "inspired by our founding documents and regard the Constitution of the United States to be the supreme law of the land. We believe that it is possible to know the original intent of the government our founders set forth, and stand in support of that intent."[10] However, their support for the laws remained within their interpretation of "original intent" of these founding documents (the Declaration of Independence, the Constitution, the Bill of Rights as explained by the Federalist Papers), which disregards how context and culture has changed since that time. Last, they defined a "free market" as

> the economic consequence of personal liberty. The founders believed that personal and economic freedom were indivisible, as do we. Our current government's interference distorts the free market and inhibits the pursuit of individual and economic liberty. Therefore, we support a return to the free market principles on which this nation was founded and oppose government intervention into the operations of private business.[11]

Through their definition, Tea Party members placed themselves as outside of and hurt by the current government or administration. They argued economic earning as a "freedom" or an individual right, which they classified as separate from their community.

Not surprisingly, most "Tea Party sympathizers are also predominantly white, male and affluent, but less likely to have advanced degrees—and finally, tend to be older than the typical Republican."[12] Although a highly educated group,[13] Tea Party members assumed that education was solely earned through individual effort rather due to a privileged entrance into the university and access to course materials based on identity similarities to tenured professors who paved the way before them. Further, high educational and economic discrepancies existed between members. The Tea Party was a "grassroots populist movement" with economically elite, corporate benefactors during a time of economic recession.[14] As part of a populist movement, "American populist rhetoric . . . fires up emotions by appealing to individual opinion, individual autonomy, and individual choice, all in the service of neutralizing, not using, political power. It gives voice to those who feel they are being bullied, but this voice has only one, Garbo-like thing to say: I want to be left alone."[15] Tea Party members articulated that their autonomy and independence was threatened and they needed the means to reclaim their power.

With the election of a Democrat during a severe recession, Tea Party members were experiencing a declining power (economic, political) and perceived government-based threats to fiscal interests.[16] Similar to most social movement actors,[17] Tea Party members felt that they were victims and debated over "distributive justice," or the access of resources.[18] Through their "injustice" argumentative frame,[19] Tea Party members argued against immigration,[20] taxation and government expansion,[21] government programs that ensure "social inequality,"[22] and Obama's healthcare reform[23] as threats to their prosperity. Focused hostility toward Obama[24] as well as "racial animosity"[25] became hallmarks of the movement over time. By arguing their "American exceptionalism,"[26] a quarter of all Tea Party members may have felt a violent action against the government would be justified;[27] however, some members recognized that they needed to take other actions.

Similarly, although according to a Gallup Poll conducted on April 8, 2011, 47 percent of people oppose Tea Party efforts,[28] the Tea Party's libertarian roots are shared grounds for white nationalists to move their ideology. The Tea Party functions as a fringe movement that has gained political seats in the United States Congress and in state legislatures. Interestingly, before serving as the chief campaign and White House strategist for Donald Trump, Steven Bannon produced a documentary film entitled *Fire from the Heartland* about powerful, conservative white women such as Sarah Palin, Michelle Bachmann, and Ann Coulter. Bannon also has served as executive chair of Breitbart, which functions as the "media platform" for the alt-right. Bannon not only understands the power of women in political roles, but he poises himself to forward the next iteration of white supremacy, the alt-right (see chapter 5).

Following her vice-presidential run, Sarah Palin quickly became a major figurehead of the Tea Party movement. During her speech hosted by the Susan B. Anthony List, Palin proclaimed women were the foundation of the movement due to their strong organizational roles.[29] After her keynote address at the 2010 Tea Party convention, Sarah Palin was called the "de facto head of the Tea Party."[30] Although the Tea Party began as an outlying, online, indistinct group, they rapidly made their presence known within mainstream politics. According to the New York Times/CBS News Poll in 2010, 138 Tea Party candidates ran in House and Senate races.[31] The Tea Party found generative space in Texas, winning multiple legislative seats in 2010 and 2012[32] as well as seats in Nevada (Sharron Angle) and Delaware (Christine O'Donnell).[33] In many cases, Tea Party members beat out Republican incumbents. Tea Party members also included Glenn Beck[34] and Michelle Bachmann,[35] as well as those endorsed by Sarah Palin: South Carolina Governor Nikki Haley and Senators Joni Ernst of Iowa and Ted Cruz of Texas.

White Woman as Acceptable Outsiderism for White Victimology

The articulation of the white "race" as outside of the system was right within the wheelhouse of white nationalists. However, white women like Sarah Palin, similar to eccentric politicians before them like former governor of Minnesota Jesse Ventura, embodied what Bakhtin noted as "the fool" who transforms the political sphere into a carnivalesque atmosphere. According to Bakhtin, the fool was one figure who holds the privilege "to be 'other' in this world, the right not to make common cause with any single one of the existing categories that life makes available."[36] Due to her commitments to traditional gender roles and economic and social conservatism, Palin was able to be gendered "other" without losing her white privileged status.[37] The choice of contained agency may have been due to a "desire to be accepted [that] cuts across lines of ethnicity, race, and sexual preference."[38] As Ridgeway noted, consistent interaction between men and women with status distance can reinforce traditional gender roles.[39] Women who come from a working class who forward traditional gender roles become an ideal audience for the outsider rhetoric of the Tea Party to keep corporate men in positions of power. Further, new women voters typically "embrace conservatism,"[40] making populations who were the first in their family compelled to vote conservatively, while also seeing themselves as an "outsider" to the political system. Despite her intention to be a female "outsider," Palin may have wanted to "normalize their [re: women's] history and escape the stigma of being thought of as outsiders."[41] Her rhetoric of maternal feminism reinforced gender roles to contain the feminist agency through movements such as the Tea Party. Yet, outsiderism in Palin's rhetoric was not the same experience of being "othered" noted by those experiencing racial disparity. Short-term political access (individual empowerment) due to an administrative change is not demonstrative of social change for long-term, historical access and continuing institutional and cultural discrimination underrepresented groups experience in our government.

Sarah Palin's role as an outsider and descriptions of "other" status contributed to the Tea Party's rhetorical embodiment of "white victimology,"[42] or white identity politics, in order to secure an "outsider" status.[43] Although the Tea Party described themselves as victims, white men were having difficulty selling themselves as oppressed. By occupying a more dominant expected position than white women, "white males, have been accorded essentially a label-free existence."[44] Although originally women were less likely to be Tea Party members, the movement forwarded women as figureheads,[45] which may have appealed to conservative women while also allowing for individual empowerment of white women like Palin. By 2010, 55 percent of Tea Party members were women.[46] The decentered nature of the Tea Party provided an accessible organization for women to move to center stage.[47] Tea Party bloggers like S. E. Cupp, Dana Loesch (once identified as the spokesperson for the NRA following the Marjory Stoneman Douglas High School mass shooting in Florida), Kathleen McKinley, and Michelle Moore constructed a rhetorical reality for Tea Party members, which solidified their victimhood or "other" status.[48] Interestingly, victimhood claims by white women today mirrored those made by conservative white women during women's liberation in the 1960s and 1970s,[49] and fell prey to the same containment.

Claims of white victimhood, or white identity politics, are problematic considering the continuity and discontinuity of historic social constructions of race and races—identifiers of BIPOC change over time as they seek legitimacy, while "white" as a racial identifier changed insignificantly over time.[50] The roots of identifying "race" in the United States began as a way to retain economic social status and government stability by keeping multiple groups (poor, BIPOC, etc.) classified separately.[51] Our founding documents ensured only "free white men" would receive civil liberties protected under the law. Whether it be through enforcing rules made by bourgeois white male landowners or now through making claims to debase affirmative action programs, poor white men were offered a proverbial carrot on a stick to sell out other oppressed groups.[52] Historic conversations and extensions of whiteness illustrated not only its social location,[53] but also the economic and power advantage of extending the construction to other groups. Cultural changes in the definitions of whiteness over time included national acceptance of particular ethnic groups as white, such as people of Jewish, Celt, Slav, Mexican, and Irish descent, who were accepted as legally white due to their increased "Americanness"[54] to ensure dominance and power by affluent white men. Today in mainstream US culture, "whiteness" functions ethnocentrically by "depicting people of color as having the characteristic of race, while simultaneously assuming that white people are somehow not 'raced,'"[55] creating clear dividing lines between groups of people who may share a class or sex or other identifier. When people discuss issues of "diversity," "culture," or "race," typically BIPOC are at the forefront of people's minds. As a result, groups just outside of the fringe, in particular, poor white men, enforce an "other" status of BIPOC. White people benefit from race as a social construction because it allows clear dividing lines between populations, which is why over time the construction of whiteness has included more and more groups of people. However, as white identity politics extends, continuously underrepresented groups may continue to feel paranoid about their cultural place.

Outsiderism and "Alternative" Identity as Fueling White Identity Politics

Due to past, repeated experiences of systemic, historical, and institutional oppression, people learn defensive coping behaviors. Someone who expects judgments that may threaten their identity may modify that identity, what Einwohner refers to as "identity management."[56] Racial stereotypes not only become the expected behavior for BIPOC, but also limit racial agency by reinforcing the expectation of cultural (racial, gendered, economic, etc.) discrimination or bias due to awareness of mainstream, negative stereotypes of historically disempowered individuals.[57] Separation of the abnormal, or Other, becomes a way "of exercising power over men [and women], of controlling their relations, or separating out their dangerous mixtures," facilitating the construction of a "pure," "exceptional," or "great" community.[58] Further, historic assimilationist assertions of "blaming Black behavior for racial disparities"[59] becomes a means to preserve a white privilege filter (see chapter 2).

Due to the boundaries on a person's perspective, a privilege filter that uses rhetoric of oppression functions as a type of power. Power is an ability to use disciplinary structures, or technologies, that facilitate and reinforce social control (status quo). However, since power is based on material gains or control over objects, "gratification" is only temporary. Those lower on a hierarchical rung must continually exhibit or demonstrate their worth to those on a more privileged rung. When a privileged group appropriates "outsider" rhetoric, oppressed groups may question their oppressed state through an internalization of their oppression, where the oppressed accepts and even enforces their own oppression—which functions as a form of power for a privileged group. For example, when the Tea Party co-opted oppressed rhetoric, they framed their arguments to forefront how "others" compromise their "hard work," redistributing the money they were entitled to other parts of their community to perpetuate a color- and sex-blind politics. Their argument implied the failings (due to a lack of hard work) of others. By claiming an "outsider" or "alternative" identity when part of an insider group, actual outsiders to a system appeared as fringe or extremist. Similar to how the alt-right asserts their extreme identity as outside the norm yet part of a "silent majority,"[60] they were able to classify groups like Black Lives Matter as radical by comparison to the "trendiness"[61] of their identity. The alt-right articulated itself as slightly to the right of center rather than the extreme group they were (see chapter 5).

Because of women's continued gender oppression, white women in the Tea Party successfully articulated themselves as victims, outsiders to a political system. Through Palin's use of "outsiderism," her maternal feminist white identity manifested as [white] "mama grizzly." Motherhood functioned as a primary identity classification to cushion the professional, outsider identity, which allowed the Tea Party to use [white] women to validate their outsider status.

White <American> Outsiderism

Palin's focus on motherhood and "outsiderism" offered her credibility to challenge the existing political executive branch. In particular, Palin had the "innate ability to wrap herself in the anger that those voters felt."[62] As a woman who was thrust onto the political stage at a presidential level, she was automatically an "outsider." As a woman, her physical appearance functioned as a "material referent" or "gender performance" of her outsider status.[63] Palin capitalized on her additional "outsider" status being from Alaska, a state physically disconnected from the US and known for its rough, frontiersperson attitudes (due to the harsh winter climates) and being a traditional woman in the political sphere (due to the centrality of her white motherhood identity). Coming from a part of the United States already shrouded in ambiguity and generally not accessible in the working memory of the general US populace provided new and ideal rhetorical grounds for Palin to embody an "othered" status. As noted in the opening quotation, Palin's use of elemental, sensory description (of the bear) allowed her to potentially connect with traditionally minded audience members.

During her campaigning, Palin continued her "outsider" rhetoric and gained ground with Tea Party members. Early in her vice-presidential candidate acceptance speech in 2008 she stated, "Before I became governor of Alaska, I was mayor of my hometown. And since our opponents in this presidential election seem to look down on that experience, let me explain to them what the job involves (crowd applause). I guess, I guess a small town mayor is sort of like a community organizer except that you have actual responsibilities."[64] Palin capitalized not only on framing her outsider status based on her opponents' arguments, but then solidified her outsider identity by providing other sources, such as longstanding political and media outlets. Later in the speech Palin described herself, stating, "I'm not a member of the permanent political establishment and I've learned quickly these last few days that if you are not a member in good standing of the Washington elite that some of the media consider a candidate not qualified for that reason alone."[65] She not only described herself as a political outsider to Washington, D.C., but further used her outsider status when engaging in apologia concerning controversies over her statements. Following the shooting of Senator Gabrielle Giffords in Arizona, media outlets focused on an image released by her PAC that had a gunsight crosshairs on Gifford's district. When given the chance to defend herself, Palin noted that other people, including Democrats, used similar symbolism in maps previously. However, she took it a step further as she articulated her party as outsiders to media outlets, stating, "I know that it isn't about me personally."[66] Further, she argued that "the criticism of even the timing of this statement is being used as a diversion . . . again, it was a part of that double standard thing."[67] Although she attempted to not define this attack on her statement as personal, she described the criticism of her as a "double standard," a term people commonly use when asserting a sex-based bias. She described herself as a victim as she was wrongly "accused of murder,"[68] but attributed that victimhood to a larger political bias against her because of her party affiliation. Her own and party victim status set the tone for how she will mold herself, the Tea Party, and then Republican candidate Donald Trump's, outsider persona in the following years.

Palin's political outsider rhetoric continued in her most recent backing of US Republican presidential nominee Donald Trump, whom Kellyanne Conway touted as a "true outsider who's coming to shake up the system."[69] In Cedar Rapids, Iowa while campaigning for Donald Trump in 2016, Palin argued, "When both parties, the machines involved, when both of them hate cha,' then you know America loves you."[70] Palin created a clear distance and power differential by placing the "machines" (referring to longtime political figures like Hillary Clinton) as an unfavorable population. She described their disagreement as a victory, arguing that when the opposition to Donald Trump disagreed with you, it always meant you were right. Upon a ubiquitous belief Donald Trump was "truth," the "outsider" she focused on was not BIPOC or other underrepresented populations who experienced systemic or historic oppression. Instead, she set her eyes on the heart of the Midwest, where many families (77.5 percent) are white[71] clarifying that, "The American people are taking our country back."[72] When considering her Midwest, rural location and mainly white audience, Palin used <American> to imply white North American people, yet she did not clarify from whom <Americans> were taking their country back. However, she articulated how the movement "is telling those in D.C., those good ol' boys"[73] their demands. Palin harkened ideas of "the boys' club" feminists used to illustrate oppressive, backroom environments that excluded women, yet cast Donald Trump as the savior of patriarchal norms.

Rise of the Grizzly Mama Matriarch: Sarah Palin

Although powerful political outsider arguments were not new, most candidates described themselves in contrast to their opponents and a "change" for the political arena. However, what gave Palin rhetorical influence was her ability to capitalize on an updated version of "maternal feminism"[74] to forward the ideologies of the movement. "Maternal feminism" is when a conservative woman uses her political presence "to exercise her maternal skills upon the race at large."[75] As the assumed keepers or "default" authority on parenting,[76] white women "civilize" their communities. Devereux described the ideal maternal feminist as an "image of the imperial mother producing and raising healthy children as she also works valiantly to make the nation and the Empire as socially and morally hygienic as her own home [which] quickly became the hallmark of Anglo-Saxon feminism and the basis of white feminists' claims to social and political power."[77] Through maternal feminism, Palin identified oppressive agents of historically oppressive institutions to women, while sidestepping the implications of feminist histories and goals to ensure the empowerment and choices of underrepresented people. Sarah Palin used terms like "mother" and "woman" interchangeably,[78] which provided her short-term gains to move the Tea Party's conservative agenda forward.

Early in her campaign for vice president in 2008, Palin highlighted her family. For example, she stated, "From the inside no family seems typical. And that's how it is with us. Our family has the same ups and downs as any other."[79] Not only did she recognize her family as unique, but she also argued they were similar to other American families. Palin also focused on her "hockey mom" experience to connect with potential voters who were women and mothers. Palin reflected, "I love those hockey moms. They say the difference between a hockey mom and a pitbull—lipstick."[80] By noting lipstick, Palin reified a traditional, aesthetic-based definition of women, yet that image included an acceptable ferocity. A woman can be aggressive if she aesthetically adheres to patriarchal requirements of beauty. Yet, motherhood also functioned as a means to protect women from critique. Palin capitalized on the acceptable privilege of aggression of [white] moms through her articulation of mama grizzlies:

You don't want to mess with moms that are rising up . . . and here in Alaska I always think of the mama grizzly bears that rise up on their hind legs when somebody's comin' to attack their cubs, to do something adverse toward their cubs, you know the mama grizzlies they rear up and, you know, you thought pit bulls were tough, well you don't want to mess with the mama grizzlies and I think there are a whole lot of those here in this room.[81]

The power of motherhood was that it evokes an acceptable gender-insider end, the baby, for the gender-outsider means, aggression. When Palin appeared with her infant, Rebecca Traister explained, "I knew the baby was there to advertise Palin's maternal allure, to protect her from criticism."[82] Palin used motherhood as a shield to protect white women—it also could be a means to constrain our full engagement in dialogue. Further, by highlighting her motherhood, Palin reinscribed a "gender border" to reify a traditional gender "integrity," ensuring that her "outsider" status, achieved by being a woman politician, remained well within gender expectations.[83]

In addition to individual empowerment, motherhood became a classification for Miller's notion of agency, or a shared relationship.[84] Two years after her vice-presidential campaign in a speech to the Susan B. Anthony List, Palin argued for bonding based on motherhood. In the speech, she rallied:

The policies coming out of D.C. are allowing us to feel empowered, really, allowing us to rise up together because moms kind of just know when something is
wrong, it's that mother's intuition thing, I think. We can tell when things are off
base, off course, they're not right and we're not afraid to roll up our sleeves and
get to work and get the job done, set things straight. Moms can be counted on to
fight for their children's future.[85]

By calling on mothers to be empowered and to trust their biologically based
intuition, Palin set the groundwork for maternal feminist action. Maternal
feminism as a means to mobilize mothers, or as Deckman calls it, "kitchen
table" conservatism, asks mothers who have home budgeting experience to
economically consider the federal budget and "debt burden for future generations" as well as reduce taxes to ensure control over the family.[86] However,
these calls appear in line with a postfeminist attitude where the feminism
label or ideology does not require roots and cores of feminism such as equal
rights, choice about body, etc. with a focus on structural and institutional
inequality.[87] Maternal expectations became another form of contained agency
in that they were constructed through relationship to another person: a child.

Sarah Palin's Brand of White <Feminism> as Contained Agency

Although Palin always called to mothers, her advocacy as a feminist or use
of the feminist term was inconsistent until more recent years, yet her focus
on individual empowerment was clear. During her career, Palin illustrated
that she was torn in her relationship with feminism. On the 2008 campaign
trail, Palin did not want to identify herself as a feminist. However, following
the election, Palin began to recognize the power in invoking the term and it
became an ideograph (see chapter 2) for her.

Palin asserted that she struggled with the feminist term. In her vice-presidential campaign speech, Palin stated, "[e]very woman can walk through
every door of opportunity."[88] In a later interview with Katie Couric on
September 30, 2008, when asked the question "Do you consider yourself a
feminist?" Palin responded, "I do. I am a feminist who believes in equal rights
and I believe that women certainly today have every opportunity that a man
has to succeed and to try to do it all anyway."[89] "Feminist" was always jux-
taposed with the idea that women *already* have every opportunity, in direct

opposition to the feminist movement attempting to give as many opportunities to women as men have. Further, the focus on individual agency, rather than a recognition of systemic oppression and revolutionizing institutions, illustrated Palin's disposition toward a contained white agency. Her exclusion of recognizing intersectional oppression showed her contained disposition when acknowledging oppression. Palin demonstrated a preference toward individual empowerment, which placed responsibility of dealing with misogyny back on the shoulders of women.

Even though she called attention to women's equal agency and used the term "feminist" to describe herself, she waffled in later interviews with Senator John McCain. In a joint interview with Senator McCain while on the campaign trail, Brian Williams asked her the same question as Couric and she responded, "I am not going to label myself anything, Brian, and I think that is what annoys a lot of Americans especially in a political campaign is to start trying to label different parts of America, different backgrounds, different . . . I am not going to put a label on myself, but I do believe in women's rights," and noted "a couple of extra hurdles" that women could somehow power through by "being stronger."[90] Palin shared a post-feminist perspective that women had the agency to do what they wanted, as long as they "dig deep" to find the strength to accomplish their goals.

After losing the election and leaving her governor role in Alaska, Palin again changed her attitude. During an interview with Fox News reporter Greta Van Susteren, Palin conceded, "with a female on a ticket, Hillary went through the same thing, of course. It shows that we have a bit further to go before everyone is treated equally."[91] Although she did not use the feminist term, Palin noted the unequal treatment between men and women. However, a fundamental shift in the way she approached feminism became clear in 2010 when Palin started using a rhetoric of maternal feminism. In her speech to the Susan B. Anthony List, Palin argued, "We're getting the job done, sisters, one life, one activist, one election, one vote, one American dream at a time,"[92] and even willingly used the term "feminist" to describe herself. Media outlets recognized the constraint or containment on Palin's definition of feminism. Some media outlets were suspect of her use of the term, arguing she used it as a "catch phrase" rather than embodying the ideology.[93] As Salon author Rebecca Traister articulates, "preventing other women from exerting full control over their bodies and health, assessing their value as lesser than the value of the fetuses they carried, was, it seemed to me and many others, fundamentally anti-feminist and anti-female." Palin's image even "co-opted" feminist imagery like Rosie the Riveter,[94] yet the empowerment always centered on motherhood,[95] allowing her feminist transcendence to depend on her ability to appear as the perfect mother.

"Othering" of Not Working Hard Enough

Although possibly not as stringent as within a physical panoptic structure (every minute of every day is not contained, recorded, or observed as in prisons), sex-based coding becomes a strong method of discipline and control. Functioning as an informal panopticon, internalized oppression guides interactions between people, prompting people to reinforce particular stereotypes. For example, if people deride women for not privileging their motherhood over other things (such as their career, friends, etc.), they may highlight only positive experiences of motherhood in fear of judgment from others. Palin never critiqued her experience of motherhood; instead, she used it to illustrate what the expectation of womanhood was to her. People who did not fit that identity did not fit her version of motherhood. As Szymanski et. al discuss, internalized sexism correlates with psychological distress for women.[96] Women who are not mothers, or are mothers who do not function as the mother archetype but internalize pressure to do so, may experience more psychological distress and seek ways to alleviate that stress.

Further, by articulating the gender divide as either nonexistent or minimal, Palin reinforced women's internalized oppression to contain agency. Instead of attending to systemic, oppressive barriers that enforce gendered oppression, women held themselves accountable for not working hard enough to achieve their goals because of the frameset around working hard to achieve everything within the system, to "do it all." As the Combahee River Collective articulates, "The fact that racial politics and indeed racism are pervasive factors in our lives did not allow us, and still does not allow most Black women, to look more deeply into our own experiences and, from that sharing and growing consciousness, to build a politics that will change our lives and inevitably end our oppression."[97] Without recognition of oppression by the oppressor through specific institutions, the oppressed remain disparate from one another, unable to recognize a collective impact due to their fear of being a true outsider. bell hooks calls this internalized coding the "legacy of negative socialization."[98] Breaking the disciplinary coding for ourselves and toward others was at the root of antiracist and antisexist politics. Instead, based on the appropriation of the rhetoric of white identity politics, conservative white women articulated themselves as "outsiders" from a political identity system without recognizing it as an institution of systemic oppression.

Conclusion

The presence and embodiment of contained agency of women like Palin allowed the Tea Party to thrive. Although motherhood served as a strong frame to drive social movements,[99] the Tea Party leaders were economic patriarchal puppet masters, which begged the question of the sincerity of Palin's message. Sarah Palin opened the door for the recognition of women like Michelle Bachmann and others[100] within larger political arenas, yet I find myself wondering how her white identity politics influenced women in the political sphere. Evoking motherhood as a founding rhetorical ideology to women's identity contained the longevity of women's political involvement. Due to a lack of intersectional engagement of motherhood, Palin's arguments fueled Tea Party and white nationalist ideals as well as cultural identity paranoia in those who did not achieve similar expectations. American values of meeting a person's potential, determining his or her future, striving to do his or her best, facing adversity as an "outsider" and not giving up, and being an independent person all contributed to Tea Party justification of why they worked so hard to enact their belief in the "American Dream." As Donald Trump's campaign manager, Kellyanne Conway highlighted by stating that Donald Trump is a "true outsider who's coming to shake up the system,"[101] outsider claims translated to underdog status. Tea Party members like Palin, similar to those white nationalist women I noted in chapter 3, wanted feminist or individual empowerment, but did not desire the responsibility of a legacy of feminism (empowering rather than having power over marginalized people). Tea Party members wanted to feel justified in their anger against other people rather than against systemic oppression itself. We continue to see the expression of anger by women of the movement increase (Palin, Loesch, etc.), which can become another interesting rhetorical strategy white women use in US politics, especially when people pair it with ad hominem attacks.

I hate to admit that I still feel inadequate to the task when it comes to the parent noted at the front of this chapter. After a challenging interaction with her son, I tried to engage her in a conversation to help her understand how she expected more for her son than what she was willing to preserve for other children. The overarching fear of never doing enough for a child can result in focusing on equal rather than equitable distribution. Without having to mention her concerns loudly, her reservations concerning resource distribution resound through her silence or questions, which preserve white privilege. When equality of resources is the focus, "outsiderism" and "alternatives" do not account for inequitable distribution. Instead coded arguments justify a hierarchy of resources to allow the privilege of advocacy to influence access of resources for those already privileged, perpetuating inequitable institutions.

5

Reckoning with White Fragility by Alt-Right Shield Maidens

Disassembling "Contained Agency" of the Alt-Right

Although I started teaching to help students develop their voice, my resolve was tested in a public speaking class during the fall of 2018. After using the alt-right as an example in class, a student, a young white woman, asserted that she wanted to give a speech on the <freedom of speech> to which I encouraged her to be more specific. She turned in her annotated bibliography which included ungrounded claims, like many ([alt]right) people are being censored and, when referring to the 1967 *National Socialist Party of America v. Village of Skokie* case, stated that no one is harmed by seeing swastikas. In my feedback I mentioned concerns with her ungrounded claims and linked to five studies that illustrated how swastikas do psychological harm to people. I also contacted the public speaking coordinator and my department chair, who sent me to the Community Standards liaison, who pointed me toward the student code of conduct Subdivision 6, Harm to Person: "Harm to person means engaging in conduct that endangers or threatens to endanger the physical and/or mental health, safety, or welfare of another person, including, but not limited to, threatening, harassing, intimidating, or assaulting behavior." Since the student's speech outline did not contain "harmful" information, the Community Standards liaison recommended that I "hold to my rubric." When I arrived early to class the next day, I heard my student sharing with a peer that she had not even looked at her annotated bibliography feedback. I used that opportunity to invite her into the hall and reassert my feedback on her assignment about symbols and harm. She then verified that she was not planning to present on those symbols in class and clarified what she planned to present. Our conversation was amicable and focused on the course criteria and, because I did not escalate the situation (ban her speech, admonish her, etc.), I felt able to potentially deescalate a potential victim-magnifying situation. I wondered how my decisions to ask more questions might have influenced her as a person. The default victim status used by a vocally powerful, privileged student offered a parallel example of how "contained agency" not only functioned for white nationalists, but also could be mobilized by alt-right women to secure a platform via social media for their agenda.

A Pew Internet study in December 2016 found that 54 percent of US adults had not heard of the alt-right movement.[1] In August 2017 41 percent of US adults had no opinion of the alt-right while 10 percent of people supported it.[2] A poll by Reuters/Ipsos/University of Virginia Center for Politics Race clarified alt-right support closer to 6 percent with 52 percent of people polled opposing it and 23 percent who did not know if they support or oppose it.[3] The rise of the "alternative right" is, in part, due to their selection of digital spaces as well as maintenance of their message, even by introducing new terms.[4] According to the Southern Poverty Law Center, "[u]nder the banner of the Alternative Right—or 'alt-right'—extremist speakers [have begun] touring colleges and universities across the country to recruit students to their brand of bigotry, often igniting protests and making national head-lines."[5] Whether it be through asserting dehumanizing beliefs in class using the <freedom of speech> as a justification (see chapter 2), giving speeches on college campuses,[6] or attacking professors[7] via social media, the alt-right has made its assault on academic freedom and expression clear. However, as long as their rhetoric does not disrupt the academic environment, incite violence, or include fighting words, it is well within their legal right to exercise their freedom of speech. In their "The Alt-Right on campus" guide, the SPLC notes "mostly young men" as the leaders and proponents of the alt-right who push for the infiltration of academic spaces and wield <freedom of speech> as their shield (Richard Spencer, Stephen Bannon, Milo Yiannopoulos, Jared Taylor, Greg Johnson, David Horowitz, Matthew Heimbach, Mike Enoch,

Andrew Anglin, Nathan Damigo, the Proud Boys, and the Fraternal Order of the Alt-Knights); they identify no alt-right women.[8] The *Atlantic, Harper's Magazine*, and NPR bring into media discourse the women of the alt-right movement, noting women such as Lana Lokteff and Tara McCarthy, [9] while social media such as YouTube videos of conversations with Lokteff and McCarthy and Brittany Pettibone posted by Brittany Pettibone[10] and "Virtues of the West" with Lauren Southern[11] solidified value and ideological similarities in their views. Using a foundation of the biological determinism (motherhood) of women as a major vehicle to propagate their message(s), alt-right women validated their white privilege through a motherhood-based rhetoric of "contained agency" to justify their attack on independent, feminist women. Within social media, alt-right women's classification functioned rhetorically to retain a hierarchy of whiteness by amplifying conflict between people who were similarly oppressed.

Classifying the Alt-Right?

Coined in the mid-summer of 2008 by Richard Spencer, the term "alt-right" was first used to argue for "identity politics" for [white][12] "European Americans" in the United States. By December of that year, Paul Gottfried gave an address at the H. L. Mencken Club's annual meeting, where he argued his intent to organize "an independent intellectual Right."[13] Both Spencer and Gottfried speak to the current alt-right iteration of racism in the United States as "identitarian[ism]," or a focus on racialized identity politics for white people.[14] Spencer argues his interest in "get[ting] away from mainstream conservatives" to form "a new beginning" for the conservative moment.[15] Gottfried argues that "paleoconservatism,"[16] a perspective the neoconservative Republican Party rejects, was well within the constitutional rights for "self-actualizing" people to reject "a failed leftist utopia" of the "welfare state" he claims the United States to be.[17] The alt-right rejects the "moral traditionalism, economic liberty, and strong national defense" the conservative movement espouses,[18] instead focusing on white identity politics.

White identity politics provides three coalescing factors to alt-right members: a sense of self, community, and purpose.[19] The SPLC clarifies the alt-right as groups or individuals who argue their "'white identity' is under attack by multicultural forces using 'political correctness' and 'social justice' to undermine white people and 'their' civilization."[20] Groups that comprise the alt-right include white supremacists (e.g., neo-Nazis), religious racialists (e.g., Kinists), neo-pagans (e.g., Germanic Neopaganism), and internet trolls (e.g., 4chan/pol/).[21] Framing themselves as different from past white nationalist organizations, the alt-right attempts to create rhetorical distance from mainstream discourse concerning racism. By placing themselves in a counter-hegemonic light, they hope to classify their identity as just to the "right" of the conservative right. As Cheney-Lippold notes, "The process of classification itself is a demarcation of power, an organization of knowledge and life that frames the condition of possibilities of those who are classified."[22] Although they are not formally organized,[23] by naming themselves "alt-right" they take hold of how people define them to contextualize their movement. Illustration of that power is found within the considerable debate that has arisen concerning whether or not media organizations and academics classify this movement as "alt-right" rather than white supremacist or white nationalist.[24] My goal within this analysis was not to assess the accuracy of their choice of name but instead to illustrate how white nationalist values, ideologies, and classifications refine and code white identity politics through their color-blind rhetorical choices, like "alt-right."

Using apocalyptic and revolutionary terms, the alt-right spread their values through Twitter and Reddit to gain political pull in the United States.[25] Trump's campaign strategist and former White House chief strategist Stephen Bannon identified Breitbart (a media outlet where he served as executive chair) as the "media platform" for the alt-right,[26] yet other outlets such as Takimag and VDare support their views[27] and white nationalist ideologies (see chapter 2). In addition to larger outlets, alt-right members like Spencer post videos on privately owned Russian sites like Geopolitica.ru. On these spaces where they control the flow of information, Spencer articulates "alt-right" as a "political theory,"[28] using philosophical or "intellectual racism"[29] to illustrate their value systems. Values of alt-right members include "libertarianism, men's rights, cultural conservatism, isolationism, and populism."[30] As seen through Spencer's video and the SPLC's interpretation of their interests, alt-right members "both inspire and define by a discourse of anxiety about traditional white masculinity. Alt-right members argue that white masculinity is being artificially, but powerfully 'degenerated,' with catastrophic consequences for the nation."[31] Yet media analysis and academic scrutiny primarily has focused on the masculinity and men who associate with the movement, thus giving those who identify as male a privileged position in the movement and critique. However, a male-centric analysis subverts the actual power of the movement and begs the question: how do alt-right women articulate themselves?

Rhetorics of "Alt-Right" Women

Similar to the white nationalist movement, the "alt-right"[32] requires women, even the specters or simulacra of supportive white women, in order to survive. Although scholars complete research on alt-right men and how they are moving from Facebook and Twitter to VKontakte and Gab,[33] alt-right women's rhetoric and digital mediation have received less mainstream media and scholarly attention. Alt-right women also noted they were overlooked, as Lana Lokteff asserted:

> Anytime they [media outlets] mention the alt-right, they make it sound like it's just about a bunch of guys in basements. They don't talk about how these guys have wives—supportive wives, who go to these meetups and these conferences—and they are there—so I think it's important for right-wing women to show themselves. We are here. You are wrong.[34]

Yes, "women have always played a determining role in white-supremacist movements"[35] and, regardless if they are not overtly violent in their actions,[36] they need to be held accountable for the violence they justify and spread through communities. Similar to white nationalist and Tea Party politics, white women have been at the organizational center of the alt-right movement. Although alt-right men garner media attention, white women serve as shield maidens, shouldering the implications of white supremacy for the movement. As interviews with alt-right men like Richard Spencer illustrate, a clear tie exists between racism and sexism for alt-right members.[37]

However, for white supremacy to continue, white women must accept their oppression as white men use them as shield maidens. I used the term "shield maidens" because, not only do some of these women use the term (see Lana's Llamas organic clothing line by Lana Lokteff), but the term embodies an explicit willingness to fight for a "white" cause. For the alt-right movement, white women are a protective barrier between white men and white fragility. Robin DiAngelo defines white fragility as the lack of "psychosocial stamina that racial insulation inculcates"[38] when white people struggle to come to terms with slavery and mass genocide of the Indigenous peoples in the United States by white people. Yet, as seen with the Trump administration's resolve to place people of immigrant status in overcrowded internment camps, without society coming to terms with racism, oppression continues in new forms. Instead, white people develop "racially coded language"[39] to insulate themselves from dealing with the quantitatively and qualitatively verifiable distribution of benefits, sustaining white privilege. Due to white people's inability to engage their racial privilege, white fragility is "a state in which even a minimum amount of racial stress becomes intolerable, triggering a range of defensive moves."[40] Those defensive moves can be seen as an apologia, or defense, of white privilege. Similar to white nationalist women's rhetorical refinement of values (found in chapter 1), alt-right women used ideological classifications to shield white men from race-related stress or to "protect their ego."[41] When people are less accountable for their conduct, they are more likely to engage in unsavory acts.[42]

DiAngelo notes multiple factors "inculcate" white fragility to preserve white privilege: segregation, universalism, individualism, racial arrogance, entitlement to racial comfort, racial belonging, psychic freedom, and hierarchical value. Segregation is the isolation from BIPOC that white people experience and come to expect without thinking critically about it.[43] Universalism and individualism allow white people to center our experience as though our experiences are representative of all people's experience. As a "universal reference" for racism, white people assert color-blindness to race, or declare that "all people are the same."[44] Further, although white people's frame of reference is centralized, we are taught to value ourselves as individuals in a way that is not reflective or respectful of others' perspectives.[45] Racial arrogance is an internal locus of control as explanation for the success of white people, or that our success is a result of our effort rather than our white privilege.[46] Racial belonging relates to the ubiquity of white privilege built into US culture through mediated role models, textbooks, and even institutions. White people rarely feel isolated by racial identity, but may also become uncomfortable when boundaries are set by BIPOC for collective, communal racial reflection.[47] Whiteness can create a sense of racial access, where white people and their desire for racial knowledge validates an entitlement for the acceptance and privilege of white people within any community. Psychic freedom relates to the freedom from having to consider race and racism in our everyday lives.[48] Instead, white privilege allows white people to relegate race and racism to a problem for BIPOC rather than a systemic community or institutional problem. The privileging of white role models and content creates a sense of hierarchical value to whiteness.[49] Through the continued images within magazines, television shows, religious iconography, etc., the "centrality" of whiteness codes into culture to delineate [white] ideals. When experiencing feelings of white fragility, each of these factors provides means to intellectually rationalize and reassert white privilege rather than humbly listening to and engaging unequal and inequitable distribution of resources.

Using the lens of contained agency I noted earlier in chapter 3, I offer a brief overview of four alt-right women central to the movement as illustrative of white women's identities and ideologies. Women like Lana Lokteff, Tara McCarthy, Brittany Pettibone, and Lauren Southern materialized within social media spaces such as YouTube, Twitter, online radio shows of their own creation, and identitarian conferences to articulate their views. I studied the rhetoric of these women because of their identity classifications and value assertions, which place them squarely within an alt-right perspective as they forward white identity politics. The digital articulations by these women served as case studies to understand the values, ideologies, and classifications of alt-right women and how their reactions to experiencing white fragility rationalized their white privilege.

Lana Lokteff

Lana Lokteff is an American citizen. Historically, Lokteff has labeled herself a libertarian and an anarchist,[50] but over the last few years she has identified with "identitarian" and "alt-right" classifications. On her Twitter feed, where she had 35,000 followers, Lokteff used the classifications of "Ethnically #Russian. Wife of a Swedish Viking. Mother. Producer of #Identitarian#Nationalist Media for @redicetv Founder of @reallanasllama organic clothing."[51] Although she later noted a "nationalist" classification tag, Lokteff privileged a European lineage, specifically a Russian "ethnicity" and not American. In an interview with Brittany Pettibone and Tara McCarthy, Lokteff said, "you are talking to a Russian. . . . both sides. I am almost entirely Eastern European."[52] Then she defined herself in relation to her spouse as a "wife" and to her children as a mother. Considering her perspective on European identity as family (see below), all three identities (wife, mother, Russian on both sides) were familial classifications. Further, Lokteff provided classificatory "data" through terms like "identitarian" and "nationalist" to place her identity clearly within the alt-right movement with interests of forwarding white identity politics. Last, Lokteff's classification of "organic clothing" crossed right/left political party lines, from conservative to seemingly liberal interests. However, historic concerns for "purity" by white nationalist or alt-right members made associations with organic products more understandable and potential for a connection with women into organic production including gardening more concrete, similar to arguments made by white nationalist women (see chapter 3). By defining herself as a wife, mother, teacher, homemaker, artist, "maker," or gardener, an alt-right advocate could connect with audience members who define themselves similarly.

In addition to her identity classifications, Lana Lokteff hosted a talk radio program named Radio 3Fourteen for Red Ice, an organization that forwards "diverse topics from Pro-European perspective."[53] Although she claimed that the name stems from the day she was born, March 14,[54] I would be remiss to not identify 3 and 14 numerology associated with white nationalism. In an interview about women and nationalism, Lokteff claimed, "There are three important things for a woman and they are ingrained into our psyche and no matter how hard you try, they will never be removed: beauty, family, home. . . . exactly what nationalism gives to women."[55] Additionally, as I noted in chapter 4, the "fourteen words" associated with white nationalists were "We must secure the existence of our people and a future for white children."

Tara McCarthy

Tara McCarthy is a British and Irish citizen. Although in 2015 she defined herself as a socialist, anti-natalist feminist,[56] currently she identifies herself as a "mixed race ethno-nationalist" who is "more libertarian and authoritarian."[57] Other alt-right movement members critiqued McCarthy about her great-grandparents' half Jewish and Indian backgrounds, and she "finds it frustrating that people cannot understand why I consider myself to be white . . . because I am mostly white."[58] Her great-grandfather died in Auschwitz. She also noted that she is engaged to marry a "white guy"[59] to legitimate her "whiteness." Rather than a biological background, McCarthy claimed that a difference in "ideological" roots was tied to race and ethnicity.[60]

McCarthy was a co-host of the "Virtue of the West—The Golden One" program with Brittany Pettibone (see below). Although removed from iTunes, McCarthy also authored the podcast *Reality Calls* and claimed to be finalizing a book she titles *Irreplaceable: How and Why We Must Save the West*.[61] When speaking about her upbringing, McCarthy stated that she was "born right-wing in a left-wing area" and that her conservative views were her "exercising my common sense."[62] When asked during a video interview to sum up her ethno-nationalist views, McCarthy stated, "white people are consistently blamed for the poor performance of nonwhite people in their countries. . . . from what all the science is showing today, from what all the cutting edge genome research is showing is that they [nonwhite] actually have a limited intelligence genetically as a group."[63] Although she historically produced extensive social media content, in December 2017 McCarthy removed most of her content from online sites like YouTube and even left Twitter. Many screenshots of her tweets were taken and videos were captured and posted on other sites.

Brittany Pettibone

Brittany Pettibone is an American citizen. Pettibone classifies herself as "Political Activist. Author. Independent Journalist. Catholic"[64] and as a "white identitarian."[65] Although I initially did not plan to write about Pettibone, her emergence as a major alt-right media figurehead became clear when researching Lokteff, McCarthy, and Southern (see below). Pettibone was born born in California, and raised in a liberal household with her twin sister, Nicole, in Kansas.[66]

Although she began as an "independent . . . writer,"[67] her YouTube page has 61,000 subscribers. In an interview on the "Virtues of the West" vlog she co-hosted, she contrasted American and European identitarianism:

> we [white Americans] were made to be ashamed of ever approaching the issue of identity. . . . the different ethnic groups are all very much in touch with their identity and it's encouraged, it's very encouraged except for us. They want to separate us from it and if we show any kind of desire to be in touch with it or proud of it it's the worst thing you can do.[68]

Similar to Lokteff, she described a white identity under attack. Alt-right women constructed their "fringeness" by setting themselves in contrast to BIPOC withholding their ability to fully embody their white identity. They articulated a clear yearning to fully identify with others—to find their "community."

Lauren Southern

Finally, Lauren Southern is a Canadian-born woman who describes herself as a "Best Selling Author. Lover of hedgehogs & Freedom. Retweets ≠ endorsement"[69] and classifies herself as "secular."[70] Southern sought to shepherd the return of the "traditional woman."[71] Out of all women I detail within this chapter, Southern may adamantly separate herself from holding "alt-right" views, yet her values, ideologies, classifications, and conversations with other alt-right women, *signaled* "alt-right." As a "traditionalist," Southern focused on issues such as sexuality before marriage, image and fertility, happiness, and femininity versus feminism, which placed her among other alt-right women.[72] Southern framed her perspective as "someone who is super against identity politics" because she saw it as an "intellectually corrupt political practice."[73] Although she articulated her interest in seeing people come together and grow, Southern argued, "identities based on levels of oppression are not identities worth spending tons of resources preserving or basing political action around. They're not ones that have created civilizations—quite the contrary, these identities seek to destroy them."[74]

Southern's Twitter feed connected with 329,000 followers while her YouTube channel had 437,000 subscribers. Further, various university and college conservative or Republican groups have invited Southern to speak. In November 2017, Southern spoke at the University of Minnesota, which resulted in a small counterprotest.[75] At a speech given in May 2017 at Cal Poly in San Luis Obispo, Southern argued that "women are happier" being married and as a homemaker with children.[76] Southern used "data" to prove her assertions, yet did not provide any sources for her statistics. Although she made a trip to Africa for her documentary, which she was documenting online, in 2019 she announced that she had "retired" because she has "found a husband and started a family."[77]

The Power of Alt-Right Women

Alt-right women described their agency in ways that focused on European historical and biological disposition and in relationship to other white women. In response to stereotypes they articulated as "neo-nazi, white trash trailer park girl" and the religious doting mother and wife, "weak and naïve,"[78] alt-right women described white women as emotionally vulnerable and alone and seeking support. Through a "fear of criticism," they argued that white women were crippled without the "support" of a man and even avoid alt-right conferences because "they [protesters] harass people coming in even if you are a woman."[79] Similar to claims of the "silent majority" made by alt-right men and Tea Party members, alt-right women claimed that other alt-right women "prefer to watch our livestream in their homes in the comfort of their families."[80] Instead of being leaders within the alt-right movement, alt-right women argued that other alt-right women served in central organizational, supportive roles to the alt-right movement and that they should be vocal in their communities. As a contained agency within interest in home, beauty, and motherhood, alt-right women classified their purpose in four main ways: #Diversity as biologically separate, #Motherhood as immediacy and primacy, #Alt-Right as #Alt-Feminist, and #[White]Sisterhood as individual white woman empowerment. As viable white sex partners, mothers, and ethereal muses,[81] alt-right women argued that white women should be in service roles to white men and children to argue for biological separation as diversity against feminist and feminism.

Diversity as Biologically Separate

Alt-right women solidified their white identity politics by using <diversity> as a rationale for keeping people separate. For example, McCarthy asserted potential conflict as a reason to avoid "diversity." Specifically, she noted that in schools, "that is how they want it . . . [schools] try to promote diversity as though it is a good thing, as though it is our strength. When in reality it creates a whole load of unnecessary friction and identity politics and . . . nonsense really, that we have to put up with."[82] McCarthy described diversity as something that causes "crazy friction" between people[83] rather than recognizing the inevitability of conflict, and identifies race interactions as a "victim perpetrator cycle" between people of one racial identity and those of multiple racial identities.[84] Alt-right women focused on the "hassle" they experience by engaging in dialogue with someone different from them.

Further, similar to white nationalist women, alt-right women conflated <diversity> with BIPOC, typically focusing on Black people. For example, on her Twitter feed, using an image of Chadwick Boseman in his role of king of Wakanda in the movie *Black Panther* (2018) with the quote that "The cast of Black Panther is hella diverse. 90% of the black Panther cast is black," Southern responds, "Diversity literally just means less white people lmao."[85] Similar to white nationalists (chapter 2), Southern tried to create a contradiction in usage of the term *diversity*, leaving room for other alt-right women, like Lokteff, to redefine the term. At an Identitarian Ideas conference in Stockholm, Sweden, Lokteff argued that diversity means having "different" racial identities. Lokteff appropriated <diversity> to shift its definition to illustrate how separation meant protecting diversity. Yet when faced with the prospect of living near others who come from different backgrounds, in a video on Red Ice Lokteff stated, "By racist white people she [Oprah] means people who don't want their neighborhoods to be enriched by so-called diversity . . . people who want to be left alone to live with whom they choose."[86] Lokteff argued that multicultural neighborhoods should be a white person's choice (read: privilege). Similar to past efforts by white supremacists, alt-right men expected white women to "police the relationships and racial identities of their neighbors."[87] Lokteff argued for a form of white tribalism to preserve a white privilege filter. Similar to insights made by Harris, assumed "privilege" of whiteness included "a right to exclude,"[88] a right to separate oneself and one's neighborhood. Similar to white nationalist women, alt-right women used <diversity> in contradictory ways. Lokteff conflated definitions of privacy with racial separation. Yet her arguments cannot stand together: one either values diversity or privacy from that "diversity." The latent hypocrisy of alt-right women's discourse surrounding diversity served to further prove the employment of white ignorance.[89]

Alt-right women prompted white protection by racial separation of people, yet they viewed their "race" as better than others. As she clarified why she became a nationalist, Lokteff claimed, "it is the way to protect white people. To protect black people. To protect Mexicans. To protect Indians[,] that is diversity. We all have to have our own separate territory . . . to thrive. And people need to be free to have their culture."[90] Similar to white nationalists, "protection" was used as a shibboleth to signal values of safety and security because they felt their "white race" was superior or less violent than other races. The subtle rhetorical (re)introduction of segregation and "separate but equal" platitudes created a discursive landscape where white identity politics supposedly benefits BIPOC.

Sisterhood as Individual White Woman Empowerment

Although alt-right women believed that alt-right men should bring about the traditionalist and anti-multicultural changes alt-right women would like to see, arguments about white female empowerment pervaded their discourse. According to alt-right women, finding the voice of white alt-right women required developing white women's voices. For example, at her presentation at the Identitarian conference noted above, Lokteff argued that white women need to show themselves because "we are here."[91] No arguments are made about listening to white women to recognize systemic or institutional sexism; instead, alt-right women noted that they want to "redefine . . . [the] strong woman"[92] as the "lovers, mothers, friends, teachers, and now shield maidens ready to go to battle."[93]

Alt-right women pushed the expectation of alt-right women's action further by highlighting a need to become vocal about the movement. Lokteff asserted, "this is the time for female nationalists to be loud" as "shield maidens" to "fight in emergency situations."[94] In her joint interview with Pettibone and McCarthy, Lokteff clarified that women's voices were especially useful because "women can get away with saying more than guys can because we can't hurt anyone . . . we can get away with saying a lot more than guys can."[95] Lokteff recognized that, due to their identities as white women, they existed within a unique position to say challenging statements without being challenged. However, using their voices did not mean embodying leadership roles. Lokteff reasoned, "women are too emotional for leading roles in politics. . . . women by themselves cannot emotionally put up with the hits that come along with coming out as a nationalist and in America as a white nationalist and defending white people.[96] Lokteff argued that women were not equipped to be the primary advocates of change. Instead, alt-right women reduced white women's primary roles to being a beautiful muse for sex and vessel for children with white men, as they ironically spoke at conferences and interviewed one another on YouTube channels.[97] Alt-right women's arguments served as a form of contained agency in that women's voices are reduced to inspiring men. However, the alt-right recognized that women's involvement in the movement changes the magnitude of its influence. Placing the onus on her "adversaries," Lokteff reasoned, "they know when women get involved, a movement becomes a serious threat."[98]

Similar to the white nationalist women noted by Blee,[99] alt-right women recognized that they have means to become activists to move the alt-right's movement interests. For example, alt-right women noted the impact white women voters had on getting Trump elected and used that information to push their movement's victim status to the media. In their joint interview, McCarthy asserted, "[m]ost white women in America voted for Trump, yet the media is spinning as though we are against Trump even though it is not true."[100] By focusing on their civil engagement through voting, alt-right women argued that widespread support exists by white women for alt-right values. Yet, I envisioned that Southern and Spencer differed significantly in how they saw women's participation in civic life, government, and/or democracy. In a *Newsweek* interview, Richard Spencer, when asked (twice) about women voting in US elections, stated, "I don't necessarily think that that's a great thing."[101]

Since they felt former white feminists might become future alt-right allies, alt-right women sought to further the discord in the feminist movement by building a white sisterhood. Lokteff argued, "white women are starving for a true sisterhood. Blacks have it. Mexicans have it. Jews have it. White women need to have it again."[102] Alt-right women targeted white women who wanted to be empowered, but felt alone. They even attacked women further by preying on a large fear of being a "nuisance"[103] or useless rather than a supportive, contributing member of the feminist movement. Dyer articulated this apologetic reaction as "a feeling that, amid all this (*all* this?) attention being given to non-white subjects, white people are being left out. One version of this is simply the desire to have attention paid to one, which for whites is really only the wish to have all the attention once again."[104] When the focus was taken off of white people to a place where white people felt excluded, a color-blind corrective kicked in. Yet, in their search for "equality," alt-right women sought for a recentering back on whiteness.

#Motherhood as Immediacy and Primacy

Although they exhibited agency through individual empowerment of white women's voices to build a white sisterhood, alt-right women described motherhood and having a family as the central role for white women. During a YouTube video on the "Virtues of the West," hosted by Tara McCarthy and Brittany Pettibone, an interviewee named "Rebecca" described:

After college I worked on Wall Street and I was seeing a lot of working moms and was like there is no way that I am going to be able to do both of these things. And when you realize that it kind of primes you for more conservative thinking. . . . you just move into traditionalism because you know that at some point you are gonna have to choose.[105]

Alt-right women recognized the problematic negotiation of work and home life for mothers and reasons that home life would always take priority. Further, according to alt-right women, home life should start in the early twenties for women. In a YouTube video with Lokteff and Pettibone, Tara McCarthy reasoned:

In Western Europe throughout all of our advanced stages of history, the average age of marriage for women was 23. . . . so you should really start looking when you are 21 and then by the time you are like 23 or 24 then you'll find someone . . . you haven't had a chance to be away from your parents and think about things for yourself enough until you are about 21 or so.[106]

Pettibone followed up by stating, "give us time," and Lokteff added, "it is never too late. . . . as long as you have them [children] . . . great."[107] The expectation and sole responsibility of having children and developing and maintaining a household shifted a power balance for women in the political sphere. As Kitch notes, state formation of patriarchal households influences the breakup of female-based groups and further expands men's power within political arenas. The household has functioned as a form of social control over women.[108] For alt-right women, arguing for domesticity as a primary function acted as a containment of their rhetorical power and influence under patriarchal control.

The only stipulation to getting married that McCarthy, Pettibone, and Lokteff provided was that the "right" person needed to be found,[109] yet timing seems to also be an issue for younger alt-right women. The constraint of the lack of support for working moms provided exigency for these women who illustrated their dedication to forwarding whiteness through a service of motherhood. These constructions of "finding the right person" and having kids in the mid-twenties not only required someone to be not found but *chosen*, but also implied the "whiteness" of that hypothetical person and assumed a possibility of and ease in biologically conceived children. Even

Lokteff acknowledged that her own relationship did not progress as such (she had children in her thirties), yet they all reinforced an alt-right simulacrum of how they should continue their lives as shield maidens in order to biologically solidify their place as mothers of the movement.[110]

Since they expected white women to have children in their twenties, alt-right women articulated agency in ensuring that white women did not make their largest regret *not* having kids. As Lokteff noted, she feared that white women might "[wake] up to those things a little late."[111] Lokteff even described herself as a proud "matchmaker" at alt-right conferences because, for alt-right women, one's family was connected to one's nation. As Lokteff articulated, "a nation is your extended family, your tribe, your support system. The comfort of your home and way of life remains uncertain without your people as your neighbors."[112] A white biological motherhood classification was vital to alt-right women's rhetoric because it offered opportunities for a white family to extend into a white neighborhood, community, and nationhood.

Although these young, unmarried, childless alt-right women argued that white women should develop families in their early twenties, exceptions were made for themselves. In early December 2017, McCarthy and Southern faced a barrage of comments about their single and childless status. Through Twitter and YouTube comments, people identifying as alt-right supporters questioned why McCarthy and Southern did not have children or were not married yet. McCarthy noted in an article published by Salon that they "are constantly harassed by low level anonymous trolls trying to put us in our place."[113] In a series of Twitter posts, McCarthy wrote, "Women of all ages, who do or don't have children, are harassed for various 'reasons.' The ultimate goal seems to be to bully us off the internet"; "Men in the Alt Right are going to have to decide whether they will continue to passively/actively endorse this behavior, or speak out against it"; and "If you want more women speaking publicly about ethno nationalism, I suggest you choose the latter."[114] Using a mothering tone, McCarthy directed alt-right men who were bullying her to stop if they hoped for the movement to continue. When it came to standing up for themselves, women in the alt-right gave "suggestions" in the form of if–then dichotomies before they removed themselves altogether from the situation (e.g., "if they hoped to keep white women in the movement, then they should be nicer to them").[115] In response to similar forms of harassment, Southern restated her data, yet described herself as an "exception" to, rather than example of, the rule.[116] In a YouTube video she stated, "I am not trying to sell the idea that myself, as a twenty-two-year-old, needs to be married right now for the sake of traditionalism and not being a degenerate."[117] Even though a year earlier, at Cal Poly San Luis Obispo, Southern had argued that women are happier when they have children, she rearticulated her "data" stating "on average women are happy being married and having kids."[118] Southern reasoned, "we are living in a very different age right now. . . . we are longing for an age that we've never lived in."[119] Yet, more recently both McCarthy and Southern have taken a break from promoting the alt-right agenda by moving their "ethno-nationalist" and "traditionalist" Twitter and YouTube materials, either by removing their content or moving on to another project.[120]

However, by arguing for a limited role in the movement, alt-right women further contained white women's agency. They recognized the challenge to engage in equality and inclusivity within the feminist movement and attempt to capitalize on that discord using young, single women to advertise for an idyllic, yet unrealistic "traditional" model of motherhood. However, as these women reached the expected age of marriage and child rearing (mid-twenties), the alt-right movement began to turn in on itself. Further, future research on alt-right women after they have children might offer insight into the longevity or change in their arguments concerning their roles in the movement.

People within the alt-right described the infighting between alt-right men and women as stemming from their "adversaries,"[121] furthering the extremist, conspiracy rhetoric that connects to their apocalyptic, victim style. Yet social media wars (on Twitter, YouTube, etc.) illustrated another story. Alt-right men disciplined alt-right women. However, in contrast to their treatment of the feminists they derided and attacked, alt-right women expected their viewers to be sympathetic and understanding of their shortcomings or misinformation. As Southern noted, "I want to bring you along on that journey of asking questions and looking at statistics and taking the piss out of the hard core feminist and making fun of the silly things they do. But the reality is that I am going to fail, people are going to mess up."[122] True to the privileged ideological claims made by white nationalist women before them, alt-right women expected no accountability for their words and actions and then received bullying, shaming, and harassment from inside their movement.

Due to the expectancy of and need for white women to solidify the movement through marriage and procreation, alt-right women have continued to be more prolific through social media earlier in their lives until they reach the "pinnacle" of their existence within the movement—bearing white children. Then, most of these women experience a silence similar to other mothers when they become the default parent and other white women will serve to perpetuate white nationalist/alt-right simulacra. However, these women's silence may be more profound as white men, who believe women's contribution is less intellectual than men, move white women further to the back of a movement. But as seen with white nationalist women, alt-right women will return as public advocates for the movement.

Alt-Right as Alt-Feminist

Although alt-right women desired individual empowerment, they accepted contained agency of their voice when they became mothers and derided what they perceive as attacks by "feminists" on the family structure. For example, in her speech for college Republicans at Cal Poly in San Luis Obispo, Southern opined:

> Women are now being told that childbearing is oppressive. If you look at Simone de Beauvoir's book *The Second Sex* she says that "motherhood leaves a woman riveted to her body, like an animal, and made it possible for men to dominate her and nature." So for these feminists it wasn't enough to just pit women and men against each other, to pit wives and husbands against each other, they had taken to setting mothers against their own children and not just that abortions were not enough for them. The womb, the incubator of life itself, is an oppressive thing.[123]

By using a primary source, Simone de Beauvoir's text, and her reductive explanation of Beauvoir's meaning, Southern attempted to tar all feminism as antithetical to motherhood. However, what Southern, as a childless young woman, did not understand was the context of motherhood. The context for Beauvoir's quotation focused on the endless, intensive, and constraining responsibility and household management duties that default to mothers,[124] which subsume a woman's identity. Without experiencing the depths of expected servitude of motherhood, it was difficult to understand Beauvoir's meaning. Further, Southern's rejection of the identity oppression women experience through motherhood (e.g., as their individual identity is subverted by their mother identity) did not take into account the implications of the institution of marriage and motherhood (mother as default parent). Further, the classification of individual empowerment without feminism mirrored white nationalist women and conservative white women. Similar to Tea Party members, alt-right members argued that beauty, home, and family are the most salient issues for [white] women.[125]

In line with all their calls for white women to become vocal (but not in a way that contradicts traditional patriarchal modes of women's activism), alt-right women derided feminism and attacked a caricature of feminists. In their attempts to discredit feminists, some alt-right affiliates attacked feminism as a problematic ideological turn. In her speech at Cal Poly, Southern rebranded herself as a "traditionalist" (not a "maternal feminist," although the distinction between the two is unclear) under attack by "Marxist feminism."[126] Alt-right women distanced themselves from "feminism," instead arguing for the "power" women gain from traditionalism, which was another form of contained agency. Southern identified "socialism, feminism, Black Lives Matter, the free love movement from the sixties, and globalism" as "branches of the tree of Marxist thought" and "politics of envy," which "deconstruct the family."[127] Similar to alt-right members like Richard Spencer, by providing philosophical terms for their arguments alt-right speech sounded intellectual, gaining them access to college campuses under the guise of free speech.

Similar to white nationalist women from the United States, alt-right women made attacks on feminists to contain the agency women had in the movement. For example, Lokteff reasoned, "If you point out the pattern which reveals the majority of rape is by non-European men a feminist will say, what does their race matter? And it would have happened by white men eventually anyway?" and "In order to be a feminist your top priority must be open borders and anti-white male politics above all else."[128] In another interview, Pettibone identified "right wing or anti-feminist" as the same thing.[129] Their reductions did not account for the differing viewpoints of feminists; instead, they created a uniform, pseudo-intellectual, straw-person enemy. However, their concerns spoke to a significant issue about how boundaries around feminism were be drawn. While clarifying groups like a book group for feminists by Emma Watson or other celebrities, Pettibone clarified, "but then as an anti[-feminist]. . . . someone who didn't subscribe to the current feminist views, which I don't believe personally is even feminism, you kind of feel left out."[130] Alt-right women identified a feeling of isolation from the feminist movement, which served as reasoning for why they virulently attacked it as well as recruited from the conflicts in it. Lokteff admitted, "I got sucked into feminist thinking. . . . a lot of my twenties without even realizing it . . . and you find that you are happier when you actually settle down and find the right guy."[131] In an attempt to be critical of racial experiences, alt-right women provided surface-level analyses of feminism as a weak and feeble ideology and a means for ready-made conversion narratives for others. Alt-right women described inter-feminist conflict as a place to recruit potential alt-right members and offered white women a central role in the "victim Olympics" they conveyed. Pettibone reasoned, "I think that anti-feminists are looking for a group,"[132] and alt-right members poised themselves to engage those white women seeking empowerment through white privilege—specifically, white women who felt silenced in feminist groups who ensured that BIPOC, transwomen, also have a voice. Through relational agency, alt-right women sought to use white identity politics to centralize white women within the alt-right.

However, since alt-right women did not understand or engage the structural and political layers of oppression (intersectionality) that came with being both a woman *and* BIPOC, their relational agency was a contained one. In response to the rejection of white women from feminism that alt-right women perceived, they sought to connect with white women seeking individual empowerment. In a video she titled "Intersectional Feminism Wages War On White Women," which received 54,916 views within the first four days it was published, Lokteff jibed:

> You can have it. Leave and take feminism with you. If white feminists are irredeemably racist, then stop including them and asking for their help. In fact, push them away. Tell them off. It's doing us a favor . . . Some white women will have to learn the hard way about their so-called female allies who are actually their worst enemies. But when they do, women like me will be waiting to welcome them with open arms.[133]

Similar to white nationalist women, alt-right women illustrated relativism when it came to racial experiences, ignoring or diminishing the compiling factor of historic and systemic racism toward BIPOC as well as systemic sexist oppression.

As Lokteff stated, "Oprah calls white southerners who want to live with other white southerners racists. And whites celebrating other whites also racists. Yet blacks celebrating other blacks is a moving and magical experience."[134] Like many white people, Lokteff did not recognize her own ability to choose where she lives, something denied to BIPOC for generations. By taking a color-blind ideological stance concerning systemic, historic, and institutional racism, Lokteff constructed her desire for and choice of racial community as relative to BIPOC's experience of community. Yet, she did not address how BIPOC have been historically and legally forced into identities (race through census) and communities together (reservations, housing discrimination, etc.) or physically separated from one another (immigration, slavery, etc.).

Classifying White Female Empowerment as Contained Agency

Similar to their white nationalist predecessors (see chapters 1, 2, and 3), alt-right women found a contained agency of voice and individual empowerment within the alt-right identity. Diversity as biologically separate, sisterhood as individual white woman empowerment, motherhood as immediacy and primacy, and alt-right as alt-feminist provided alt-right women with organizational clarity. By developing their "voice" through redefining <diversity> as racial separation while forwarding a desire only for an agency of relation or recognition, and accepting a comprehensive, all-consuming, yet theoretical motherhood identity while critiquing praxis of a balanced motherhood/womanhood experience and feminist agency (collective or communal responsibility), alt-right women articulated a contained agency of isolation for white women.

Instead of critically and humbly assessing their white privilege, alt-right women sought to redefine themselves as <diverse>. Alt-right women's ideographical interpretations were examples of white fragility, where white people coded themselves as victims instead of a dominant group in conversations about racial inequity.[135] Due to their explicitly white supremacist values, their color-blind rhetoric was much more clear. Yet, when white people used similar ideological rhetoric, although not identifying as alt-right, the racism was similarly preserved. For example, merit-based arguments for accomplishment pit racial <diversity> against merit to preserve white supremacy through a hierarchy of implied whiteness. As an apologia, white fragility preserved white supremacist institutional structures through an ideological explanation of white supremacy. By classifying <diversity> as separate from equity or equality or merit as a form of "entitlement to racial comfort,"[136] white people justified their hierarchical separation (white privilege).

Through a similar desire for connection and community, alt-right women sought a "white sisterhood," yet refused to accept collective care and responsibility of other people. Instead, by noting how they were not included, alt-right women focused on their lack of individual empowerment as white women or their "outsider" status from BIPOC to construct a collective white identity. Alt-right women wanted to feel a sense of "racial belonging,"[137] but community required valuing group relational needs over individual power. By creating a classification of white sisterhood, alt-right women solidified white women's containment from addressing systemic oppression with other oppressed people as well as their own gendered oppression. Most interesting was alt-right women's move away from an emotional connection when engaging a racial conversation to a pseudo-intellectual stance. Similar to rhetorical moves noted in Singleton and Linton's theory of courageous conversations, instead of sustaining difficult dialogues these women used an apologia of whiteness preserve their white privilege. [138]

Instead of gaining a theoretical community, alt-right women used [white] motherhood to articulate their immediate and primary purpose and community in their lives. Single, childless alt-right women envisioned their individual lives (careers, interests, etc.) ending with motherhood, and rationalize when their theoretical stance did not align with their actual lives. Married alt-right women with children sought to marry off eligible white women and vocalized a contrary message that their voices were not important as the men's. Yet they gave speeches at identitarian conferences, interviewed on radio shows, held their own businesses, etc. Alt-right women sought individual empowerment through their voice and discussion, but not through collective action with other women, which became especially important after women have children and expectations of default parenting came into play.[139] White women could gain control over their families, neighborhoods, communities, and nations to illustrate their "value,"[140] but it came at the expense of addressing the systemic oppression they face as women. White supremacist groups could easily connect with women through the isolation of motherhood[141] to shift that isolation into an acceptance of the network isolation white supremacist groups require to facilitate their agenda.

Due to their lack of sisterhood and equitable inclusion, alt-right women classified alt-right as alt-feminist for white women. The ideology of feminism, with its focus on equity for people based on sex and gender oppression and not at the exclusion of intersectional racial equity, challenged alt-right women to clarify their empowerment of white women in terms of the individual. Alt-right women desired a "psychic freedom" not only from recognizing themselves as racialized subjects,[142] but also from recognizing themselves as gendered subjects. Alt-right women ignored or responded to systemic oppression with rhetoric of individual exceptionalism, while feminist groups were seen as a place for recruitment of disenchanted white women seeking individual empowerment. Former white nationalist Corrine Burt, who left white nationalism, noted the pain of rejection she has experienced in life that led her to white nationalist organizations in the first place, even though her parents expressed "liberal" politics.[143] The short-term gains for white women within the alt-right movement illustrated a contained agency. By rejecting the very feminism that has historically allowed them voice, alt-right women allowed men to silence them, as alt-right men vocalized a recognition that alt-right women did not live up to their own standards.

Conclusion

Similar to white nationalist women before them, alt-right women allowed alt-right men to forward values, classifications, and ideologies that hamstrung their agency. Instead of protection by a cloak of the alt-right knight, alt-right women were being told their independent time was up—the movement required their stability to gain more support. Alt-right women made the argument for "traditional values" of motherhood as a necessary sacrifice to fuel white men's interests. White nationalist, Tea Party, and alt-right women used values, ideologies, and classifications that harkened motherhood and female empowerment to forward their white supremacy. In addition to portrayals as "goddess/victim" and "wife/mother,"[144] Blee alluded to white nationalist use of an ideology of female empowerment[145] or shield maidens (young, white women fighting for a white idealized, unachievable nation-state), yet many alt-right women separated themselves from feminism. Blee noted how a woman named Elizabeth Tyler, who was trained in public relations, was used to "publicize and recruit" new members,[146] similar to Lokteff's role in identitarianism. A similarly tenuous PR role can be found for alt-right and conservative white women and white supremacy.

Since I had inklings of my student's political commitments early in that semester, I worked hard to maintain an amicable relationship in hopes that something would resonate with her while ensuring that I maintained my professional integrity and grading consistency through my speech rubrics. I would be remiss not to mention that I felt nervous for the next "protest speech" unit. I discussed the university conduct code materials in class before the protest speech, trying to illustrate the seemingly "color-blind" neutrality inherent in the "codes of conduct," but felt frustrated by that neutrality because it did not address inequity that was placed on our shoulders as instructors and professors. Although this student identified as "Republican," the rhetoric she was forwarding created boundaries between us as we both made moves to connect as women. When she came to my office to make up days she had missed and talk about her assignment grades, I started to see how not being revered by earning top scores (merit) due to not meeting the rubric criteria could influence how she felt about the objectivity of a professor. The privilege of white entitlement moves white women to voice a sense of discrimination when it comes to them not being able to have access to the merit they seek or feel they deserve. She focused her protest speech on a friend's physical assault, calling for people to speak up and say their accuser's or accusers' name(s), yet her call was markedly different from those of her peers, who identified their own victimhood as a means to call for structural and political change. I saw her "story" as a way to shield herself from responsibility, similar to responses from the current Republican-inhabited White House as it uses white women to shield white men from engaging their experience of white fragility when faced with white privilege, rather than voice their stories as illustrations of how we can improve the systems in which we live.

6

Responsibility of a White "Privilege Filter"

Dismantling Conservative White Women as Color-Blind Maiden Shields

"Question for you: what is your take on the book and concept of White Fragility presented there? How has the field accepted or rejected it?" I received this message in my Facebook feed one afternoon from a white scholar with a PhD in Communication Studies and found myself not sure of how to respond. To afford myself some time and space to deliberate, I indicated that I had used the concept in my scholarship and had seen others use it. I inquired why she was interested. Her response surprised me: "I saw it used this week as a totalizing concept for stonewalling, and it bothered me. I like the concept, but the term feels like it digs into white shame concepts, which feels less useful." As we continued our conversation she noted, "From someone who studies trauma, it feels like especially right now when so much trauma is activated from the Kavanaugh stuff, that blocking of agency feels like it would not help anything for those traumatized on either side of the racial divide . . . To shut down all dialogue." (By "Kavanaugh stuff" this scholar refers to the testimony given by Christine Blasey Ford concerning Brett Kavanaugh's sexual assault, during Senate confirmation hearings for his nomination to the US Supreme Court, which was ultimately confirmed.) During our conversation I found myself considering the adage about "crabs in a barrel" crawling on one another to get out of a constraining situation or what Crenshaw describes as a basement with levels based on disadvantages.[1] Academic work sometimes feels similar as people promote new theories and approaches and vie for prominence only to attempt to tear down other theories as a means to illustrate the strength of one's own theoretical commitments. Although I did not see my peer's assertion as competitive or nefarious, I found myself wondering about how the theories we are taught influence the lens in which we understand future scholarship. In this setting the epistemological concern that only one master theory could elucidate them all made me cringe as the possibility of the whitening (recoding) of critical race theory through trauma studies, yet we had been dialoguing critically about whiteness. Watching Republican white women use challenging and traumatic events, such as negotiating motherhood and a career and the #metoo movement and feminism, seemed to illustrate a similar line of thinking.

In the economic crisis of a shrinking middle class that the United States is currently experiencing[2]—tax cuts, program cuts, etc.—an increase in economic stress is prompting competition where, in order not to get lost or underfunded, groups are vying for identity and significance. As voices continue to vie for economic stability and survival, it is imperative that we pay attention to how decision makers frame issues, not only by what issues they support but also in how they communicate their decisions. In political institutions such as the White House, significant staffing changes occurred. Specifically, Trump has appointed 62 percent of his communication roles to women,[3] including Kellyanne Conway, Ivanka Trump, and Sarah Huckabee Sanders. Although many may call their token presence a mark of "progress,"[4] their inexperience has manifested in extreme loyalty, making them ideal women to sacrifice their voice and power to function as maiden shields for Donald Trump. Unlike the last chapter where alt-right women acted as "shield maidens" who explicitly took to arms to fight for a "white" cause, Conway, I. Trump, and Huckabee Sanders functioned as "maiden shields": white women placed in strategic positions within the campaign and cabinet to insulate Donald Trump from the accountability of his oppressive rhetoric seem to embody a specific, more defensive role as maiden shield. The primacy of white-collar motherhood and inexperience with needing to engage in advocacy for themselves as affluent, well-positioned white women creates slippage in professional identity accountability: the idea that "people necessarily have a stake in each other's quality of life."[5] The ways in which they articulate that support are unique to each of them, yet all echo white nationalist and alt-right individual empowerment values, motherhood classifications, and color-blind ideologies. I am not indicating that these women are undeserving of their families or positions. Instead, I elucidate the similarities in their values, ideologies, and classifications with white nationalist and alt-right women's color- and sex-blind ideologies. Specifically, through their classification of motherhood, internalized -isms, and color-blind ideology that they couch in "hard work" and "merit-based" claims, these women used a white privilege filter to frame their "individual feminism" as a form of contained agency to shield Donald Trump from the impact of his oppressive rhetoric. As illustrations of their privilege filters, these women extend color-blind ideology through the guise of [white] female empowerment to simulate, but not actually engage in, feminism that dismantles power structures.

Boundaries of White Feminism

Feminism continues to be a debated topic within the public sphere. Many definitions compete for viability, but the history of the movement provides a touchstone to understand the context in which it began, continues, and may exist in the future. Many scholars have defined the first wave of feminism as a struggle for women's basic rights.[6] Women such as Elizabeth Cady Stanton, Alice Paul, and Susan B. Anthony fought for the recognition of women's "human" status by advocating for issues such as suffrage and the elimination of men's political control over women through institutions such as marriage, family, and property laws. In the first wave of feminism, middle- to upper-class white feminists fought for their rights at the expense of other groups, such as economically deprived classes and BIPOC.[7] Many women fought for women's equal right to vote, but did not seek a universal right to vote. Many first-wave feminists did not see voting rights as a race or economic issue. In part, the exclusion may have been due to the perception that limited rights were available to *either* BIPOC *or* women and that BIPOC did not deserve equal rights.

However, women activists, such as Emma Goldman and Sojourner Truth recognized limitations in the first wave of feminism. Goldman did not claim the "feminist" label out of fear of what limitations the label might place on her actions, in particular economic-based action and limitations that the label might not address.[8] Further, Sojourner Truth, in her speech "Ain't I a Woman," challenged assumptions of womanhood by historically recognized, white, affluent first-wave feminists. By challenging ideas about universal experiences of motherhood, Truth advocated the inclusion of women of color into the definitions of woman. bell hooks continued Goldman's and Truth's concerns by noting how liberationist organizers of the 1960s and '70s focused on sexism rather than class or privilege issues as they painted [white] women as victims. Yet first-wave feminists ignored ties between classism, sexism, and racism built into the capitalist system.[9]

Although womanhood may be seen as similar for some feminists, feminism does not always simply equate all forms of oppression. As Paul Smith clarifies, "Feminism speaks not only for women as a heterogeneous grouping, but also against the homogenizing logic of masculinist domination."[10] Feminism is not just for women or about identity politics; instead, gender and sex as well as systemic oppression define difference. Masculine instrumental, efficiency-based, and totalizing logics of oppression are at the root of feminist work. Every social movement organization has a variety of activists; some feminists only focus on particular issues facing specific classes, races, or cultural backgrounds of women for which they do not identify. As the Combahee River Collective notes:

> As Black feminists we are made constantly and painfully aware of how little effort white women have made to understand and combat their racism, which requires among other things that they have a more than superficial comprehension of race, color, and Black history and culture. Eliminating racism in the white women's movement is by definition work for white women to do, but we will continue to speak to and demand accountability on this issue.[11]

More recently, people have used the term "white feminism" to illustrate a similar feminist disconnect from intersectional realities of many women's identities. Through Adrienne Rich's term "white solipsism," or the "passive collusion" of "snow-blindness," she defines white feminism as when white women have "ignored or discounted the experience" of BIPOC within the feminist movement.[12] Through "a tunnel vision blind to nonwhite experience," white women assume their experience of feminism as a common experience with women (BIPOC).[13] By forwarding [white] feminism, white women allow racism to continue through a color-blind ideology. Although we may associate limited perspectives with less educated people, Bonilla-Silva's preliminary data analysis illustrates that

> younger, educated, middle class people are more likely than older, less educated, working class people to make full use of the resources of color blind racism. This does not mean they are less "racist." It just means that they are more adept at navigating the dangerous waters of America's contemporary racial landscape and to know all the stylistic tools available to save face.[14]

Affluent white women and men have become more adept at using color-blind racism to preserve and protect their white privilege. Using a particular framing of feminism, white women forward white identity politics to protect their privilege filter and positions to white men.

White Women in the Political Sphere

White women have gained a small mainstay in the global political arena. Since 2000 the number of world leaders who are women "has more than doubled"; however, "these women still represent fewer than 10% of 193 UN member states."[15] In the United States, although we have had no woman as chief executive, we did experience our first leading candidate for a presidential election (Hillary Clinton). Since 1916 the trailblazing efforts of Jeannette Rankin (Republican), who became the first woman appointed to US Congress, many women have been elected to office. Elected in 2016, Senator Mia Love was the first Republican woman of color to serve in Congress.[16] Of the 327 women elected or appointed as of 2018, approximately 20 percent of congressional seats (House, 22 percent and Senate, 19.3 percent) were filled by women[17] and 7.1 percent were held by women of color.[18] In 2018 nearly one third (32.2 percent) of all legislative offices were held by Democratic women and 9 percent of all legislative offices held by Republican women.[19] In 2019 approximately 23.7 percent of the congressional seats (House, 23.4 percent; Senate 25 percent) were held by women[20] and 8.8 percent of total congressional members were women of color.[21] Clear gains have been made, yet women did experience a significant drop from 289 in 2012 to 272 slots in 2016.[22] Despite a

Republican being the first woman to serve in the US Congress, Republican women are currently less likely than Democratic women to be elected, with women of color experiencing an even more profound gap.[23] In 2018, of the 89 Democrats and 13 Republican women elected, 46 Democrats and one Republican were women of color.[24]

Similar to many other underrepresented groups (color, ethnicity, sexuality, gender, class, different ability, etc.), women, and specifically women of color, are not seeing equal or equitable representation within the US political sphere when compared to affluent white men. Researchers of a Pew internet study found that 47 percent of women felt their lack of access to public office was due to women candidates being held to a higher standard than their male counterparts.[25] Public audiences hold women to different expectations of gender performance from their male counterparts. In the political arena, "men are normalised as politicians, and women are treated as 'other,' reinforcing binary gendered positions"[26] to reestablish gender expectations and roles. Professional endeavors, structural barriers, electoral gatekeepers' choices, and political ambition contain women's access to the political arena. Women were "significantly less likely than men ever to have considered running for office," making them an outsider presence even when elected.[27]

Although their presence is less statistically representative than men, women politicians are represented in photographs more than men, reifying their identification with their body rather than their words or ideas.[28] Media outlets feminize female leaders and describe women's strength as "emasculating" male politicians. Unlike their male counterparts, women who are politically successful have "learned to balance these dual roles and reconcile being the primary caretaker of the home and children with their ambition to become lawyers, executives, school principals, professors, and heads of political organizations."[29] Professional success for women means that women must embody traditional roles in their relationships and families while gaining and maintaining professional career positions. "[W]omen and men who are similarly-situated professionally are not similarly situated at home,"[30] meaning women continue to take on more of the household management and child-rearing duties than their male partners. Women are found in political spheres through marriage or by appointment, yet continue to be a novelty in the political arena.

Trump's presidential appointments have brought a range of women in proximity to political office through a dramatic increase of appointments of women to positions in the Republican-held White House. This may be surprising considering the Republican Party has been known as a traditionalist party focused on "restoring the American Dream,"[31] "American exceptionalism," and individualism over government involvement.[32] According to their 2016 platform, Republicans highlighted values like American "strength," "an America that is the most powerful and respected country on the face of the earth," and "control" of institutions such as education, agriculture, and religion within their preamble as they seek to "take back our country."[33] In her book *Trendy Fascism*, Love argues that the Republican Party has embraced "radical right issues, such as gun control, anti-immigration, Islamophobia, and states' rights, and may now provide a more respectable outlet for potential hate group members"[34] making it important that their rhetorical similarities to hate groups like white nationalism was analyzed.

As a traditionalist party that statistically demonstrates unequal access and advancement (political representation for elected offices) in leadership roles for women, the White House appointments of Kellyanne Conway as presidential campaign manager, Ivanka Trump as a White House advisor, Sarah Huckabee Sanders as White House press secretary, Omarosa Manigault as director of communications for the Office of Public Liaison, and Hope Hicks as communications director[35] illustrated a significant departure that some heralded as proof of women gaining ground in the political sphere. Some media outlets even called it a "feminist double standard" for not heralding their accomplishments as feminist.[36] By their very physical presence, women were a "material referent"[37] of "outsider" status (see chapter 4),[38] and, therefore, an asset when political parties indicated an interest in change.

Three Maiden Shields: Kellyanne Conway, Ivanka Trump, Sarah Huckabee Sanders

Although many women have been appointed, three women have represented Donald Trump's campaign and presidency due to their proximity to, longevity with, and vocality for the campaign: Kellyanne Conway, Ivanka Trump, and Sarah Huckabee Sanders.

Kellyanne Elizabeth [Fitzpatrick] Conway grew up as an only child in Atco, New Jersey, within a female-dominated household: her mother, grandmother, and two aunts.[39] At the time of publication, she is a fifty-two-year-old entrepreneur who graduated magna cum laude from Trinity College. She studied at Oxford University as well as George Washington University Law School, where she earned her law degree.[40] In 2001 she married George T. Conway III, a New York lawyer, who also played a role on the *Jones v. [William] Clinton* case as well as aided Linda Tripp with her legal counsel.[41]

In addition to her education, Conway has extensive business and some political experience. She was the president and CEO of a political polling company (The Polling Company), which she started in 1995 due to her interest in earning a profit by highlighting how women vote.[42] In 2012 she worked with Newt Gingrich during his presidential run as well as with Ben Carson and Ted Cruz in 2015.[43] While serving on the Manhattan-based condo board of the Trump World Tower,[44] Conway met Donald Trump.[45] During Trump's presidential run, she became the first successful woman to fulfill the role as presidential campaign manager.

Another prominent woman within Trump's campaign and presidency has been his daughter, Ivanka Trump. Born Ivana Marie Trump in Manhattan into the wealthy Trump family, she graduated from the University of Pennsylvania's Wharton Business School with a degree in economics in 2004.[46] She modeled in 1997[47] and went on to found her own namesake brand and act on television shows such as *The Apprentice* and *Celebrity Apprentice* with her father. In 2010 she published her first book, *The Trump Card: Playing to Win in Work and Life*, and in 2017 her second book, *Women Who Work: Rewriting the Rules for Success*.

Ivanka Trump also served as an advisor to Trump during his campaign and became a top White House advisor when Trump became president. Due to her distinct lack of knowledge about politics or policy, the White House press secretary, Sean Spicer, was asked about her role. Spicer stated, "I think that Ivanka. . . . has built a very successful business. She's been working with women to talk about empowerment and education for quite some time— it's a passion of hers. I think for her to bring both her business acumen and success—her passion for women, empowerment, education."[48] In some ways, Ivanka has seemed to replace Melania Trump as First Lady of the United States (FLOTUS) on the international political scene, making her an ideal person to study. Further, considering the scandal concerning allegations of

Melania Trump's plagiarism of Michelle Obama's speech[49] and her less fluent spoken style, her oral rhetoric did not carry as much weight as Ivanka's
might with audiences. In comparison to Conway, Ivanka took a more "soft-
spoken" approach.[50]

Sarah Huckabee Sanders is the daughter of former Arkansas Republican
governor and former presidential candidate Mike Huckabee. She was born
in Hope, Arkansas, and served on her father's campaigns as she grew up.[51]
She attended Ouachita Baptist University in Arkansas. Sanders had extensive
experience organizing and soliciting campaign funds for PACs (political
action committees). Under President George W. Bush, she worked for the
Department of Education as well as on his 2004 reelection campaign. In addition to working on John Boozman's 2010 Senate campaign, Tim Pawlenty's
2012 presidential campaign, and Tom Cotton's 2014 Senate campaign, she
also worked on her father's presidential campaign in 2008.[52] At the time of
publication, she is thirty-eight years old and became the third woman to
serve as White House press secretary on May 5, 2017, yet she also resigned
from the position in 2020.

Although we cannot ignore the clear individual accomplishments these
women have earned, it would also be shortsighted not to mention their families' monetary trusts and political coexistence with powerful men (fathers
and spouses), which provide these women access to or additional presence
in the political sphere. These three white women have been present and vocal
about their continuing support of Donald Trump. However, through their
white privilege filters of color-blind merit arguments, these women have
used motherhood, individual "feminism," and internalized -isms (contained
agency) as means to disarm attacks on Donald Trump concerning his political, historical, and structural ethical responsibility.

Three Means of Using White Privilege Filters as Disarming Shields

By their existence as women in roles of power where women have been
underrepresented, these women illustrated strides for feminism; however,
their physically implied feminism or material referent did not supersede the
values, ideologies, and classifications they presented with contained agency
for the feminist and anti-racist ideology. Their responses of contained agency
illustrate a color-blind ideology in ways that hinder feminism. Conway,

Ivanka Trump, and Huckabee Sanders strategically used their white privilege filters of motherhood, "individual feminism," and internalized misogyny, similar to classifications, values, and ideologies white nationalist and alt-right women used, as disarming argumentative shields to keep political, historical, and structural responsibility away from Donald Trump.

White privilege filter of motherhood as disarming authority

These conservative white women use motherhood as their white, affluent privilege filter to stabilize traditionalism during Donald Trump's campaign and early days in office. They use motherhood as a disarming shield to illustrate themselves as "traditional" women to disarm claims on Donald Trump's ethics. In order to court women voters, Donald Trump approved of an advertisement campaign featuring his daughter, Ivanka Trump, in which she stated, "The most important job any woman can have is being a mother. And it shouldn't mean taking a pay cut."[53] This advertisement came out right after the Access Hollywood scandal in which a tape was released of Trump saying he could "grab them [women] by the pussy."[54] As a response to sexism, Ivanka's response about motherhood became a way to illustrate "family values" that he would share as her father, yet they also signal an internalized sexism. Further, by focusing on economic issues that invoke white feminist concerns of the "glass ceiling," Ivanka Trump ignored issues like the "concrete ceiling," Ilene Lang notes as not even being able to see barriers for advancement women of color face.[55] Similarly, following Trump's defense of Roy Moore's sexual abuse accusations, Conway stated, when considering her role in the White House, that she struggles with the decision due to the ages of her children since she "obviously loved being a mom most of all—that's the greatest privilege of my life."[56] As a mother, I empathize with Conway's consideration when taking on an involved and personally exposing public identity due to how it might influence her children. These White House staff members' insistence that motherhood was their first and foremost identity reifies feminine archetypes,[57] making womanhood seem synonymous with motherhood.

However, negotiating their identities as mothers and career women became an arena where their expert decision-making skills functioned as an economically situated privilege filter. As Conway noted, "The work-life balance that we all talk about is not elusive to me and I don't have any

Responsibility of a White "Privilege Filter"   131

specific advice to America's women, but except to know who you are and put your priorities in order . . . nobody understands your life but you."[58] Although her message appeared individually empowering, Conway highlighted her ability to successfully navigate both without highlighting her economic status. Further, Conway argued at a CPAC (Conservative Political Action Conference), "It is also just in conversation with the president, vice president, and their two wives, all of whom are very, very respectful toward and accommodating toward working women, in particular working moms. I've never asked for a special privilege at all. I just try to blend in there."[59] By focusing on a mother's ability to "prioritize," Conway individualized motherhood rather than recognizing it as a cultural struggle, something that has become very apparent during the COVID-19 outbreak. Clarifying "working moms" rhetorically privileged the ability to take care of children as a key task/carrier of value for women.

Similarly, Ivanka Trump argues in her book *Women Who Work* that mothers need to plan well:

> When my father was running for president, my schedule was even crazier than usual, but the way I made it work was through meticulous planning. I was incredibly disciplined about looking at my schedule and ensuring that I prioritized plenty of great quality time with my kids. . . . In the max peak craziness of October, I was so grateful for the Jewish holidays, which forced me to take a break and allowed me to spend several days focused entirely on my family.[60]

Without addressing the inequality of religious holidays in the United States, let alone afforded by particular institutions or organizations based on class, Ivanka localizes her ability to plan her household schedule as the backbone of her success. She not only illustrates the centrality of her family and her matriarchal role as mother within that family, but also touts her individual empowerment to control her schedule and life. Similarly, during a press briefing at the White House, Sanders called attention to her family multiple times to skillfully evade potential criticism of the current administration. She took this evasion a step further when she facilitates an "I am thankful" ritual in the pressroom, turning the press room journalists' focus onto family.[61] Through this ritual, Sanders embodied the archetype of a "matriarch"[62] within the room. These three women used their motherhood identity to disarm the controversy they faced due to the inflammatory comments made by Donald Trump.

Further, they used their position to illustrate how mothers, in particular, should appreciate and be loyal to Donald Trump. In the abovementioned July 26 press briefing, Sanders stated:

> To the best of my knowledge, I am the first mom to hold the job of the White House Press Secretary. That says less about me than it does about this president. . . . Empowering working moms is at the heart of the president's agenda, particularly when it comes to things like tax reform. I have three children and the oldest, Scarlett, starts kindergarten in a few weeks. Scarlett and every little girl in America should grow up in a country, that if we deliver on the president's agenda of better jobs, better health care, and a better tax system that incentivizes women to work and raise children. As a working mom it is not lost on me what a great honor, what a privilege it is to stand here at the podium, and I thank the president for the opportunity.[63]

Calling to the "honor" and "privilege" of her situation as a "working mom," Sanders expressed gratitude for being able to "work and raise children," as though women should be grateful for the opportunity to do both at the same time. Working during motherhood became a means for blind gratitude for and loyalty to an employer, yet "special privileges" people (e.g., women, BIPOC, differently abled, trans people, etc.) should not ask for to complete one's job. As an ideologically oppressive blindness similar to color-blind racism (see chapter 2), acceptance of a motherhood blindness ignored the gender inequity of parenting, where the default parent (responsible party) is most often the mother.[64] Although Conway argued that she "work[s] for a man in the White House where that work-life balance is welcomed," she also noted, "it is a different set of considerations for women [mothers]."[65] To stay in line with a color-blind ideology, women should not have to ask for special privileges; yet, clearly there was a "different set of considerations" for women (read: mothers) when they worked. It was this bind that became particularly sticky for these women who recognized their own experiences of discrimination as women, yet forwarded the color-blind policies (see below) of the Trump administration.

Specifically, these women highlighted how they were able to manage their schedules as mothers and career women. In her book *Women Who Work* in the quotation above, Ivanka Trump does not note issues of class (e.g., cost of daycare), race, gender, or sexuality (e.g., access to inclusive daycare) that are a major part of access to close, quality child care that allows for "meticulous" planning of one's schedule and self-sacrifice rather than self-care and compassion.[66] Instead, she highlights her own ability rather than her privilege. Similarly, Conway noted her ability to work hard that she learned from her mother:

> My mother didn't feel sorry for herself. My mother was left with no child support, no alimony at a very young age, with a child to raise and a high school education and she just figured it out. She didn't complain, she didn't rely upon government. She relied upon her own skill set, her own self confidence, her own drive and moxie, and her own duty to me and her and she relied upon her family and her faith and I believe those are timeless lessons and timeless opportunities for all women in similar circumstances and situations.[67]

Although Conway called attention to her hardworking mother, she seemed to forget that her mother lived with Conway's grandmother and two aunts in the house to support her and her only child, Conway herself. When she spoke at CPAC in 2017 about her success, Conway clarified that she not only "worked hard, but I also got my opportunity, which puts me in a different category of blessings."[68] However, she did not expound upon those "blessings." In a later speech at the #WomenRule Summit, Conway stated, "we are privileged people who work really hard in our lives and got lucky along the way as well."[69] Conway emphasized how "really hard" she worked, though also that she was privileged and got lucky. Conway did not clarify the privileged connections, white skin, or other attributes that aid her ability to work hard, which illustrated what Carroll called a dynamic liability: a discourse that feigns critical engagement through a paraliptic form.[70] Conway simultaneously named the issue of privilege, while negating any structural advantage. By focusing on how she worked hard, Conway sought to transcend the "other" or outsider (see chapter 4) status she gained by being a woman in the political arena.[71]

White "privilege filter" of individual white "feminism" to disarm political, historical, and structural responsibility

Conservative white women validated their individual feminist experiences as victims of sexism to shield criticism of Donald Trump's misogyny. First, conservative white women defined themselves as "individual" feminists.

Conway did this early in her career as she articulated her upbringing. Conway described her childhood as being raised in a home where

> nobody ever had a single political conversation—my mom, her mom, two of my mother's unmarried sisters. My father left when I was very young, we have a great relationship now and he certainly does with my four children. But I was raised to be a very strong and independent woman without anybody saying the word feminist or having a political conversation. We were taught to be free thinking, independent, to look at your goals, and that old saying you can never go home is never true.[72]

Conway framed her childhood without the term feminism because it offered her individual empowerment without the need to recognize the oppression of others, in particular intersectional concerns. Although she tried to identify with "millennial voters," who she noted did not like labels, she defined her brand of feminism as "individual" or "conservative feminism" where "you make your own choices." Conway argued that she "look[ed] at myself as a product of my choices not a victim of my circumstances. And that really to me is what conservative feminism, if you will, is really about."[73]

By definition and use, "individual" or "conservative feminism" appeared similar to white nationalists' and alt-right members' implications of maternal "feminism" in that they localized power for individuals within specific contexts (business or motherhood) that contain the empowerment of certain people and when they can be empowered. Instead of focusing on the institutional, historical, or systematic oppression, conservative white women portrayed feminism as individual, non-intersectional, economic empowerment of women where other women in power are held to sexist standards.

Conservative white women used individual feminism to disarm sexist claims lodged against Donald Trump. In an interview with Anna Palmer at the #WomenRule Summit, Conway noted that she had a "Me Too" moment as well:

> Yes, I did, but mine was very public and nobody cared about it, respectfully. So when you want to make that exchange with whomever . . . You should think about me going on national TV on October 9th, 2016 and the spin room, my first interview after that second debate, Access Hollywood weekend, when I said to Chris Matthews and Rachel Maddow and Brian Williams on live TV I talked about how I had, how there were a couple of members of Congress on the list

that Chris was holding up or referencing that I said, "oh I recognize a couple of those names," maybe when I was younger and prettier they had tried to shove their tongue down my throat or rub or do worse oh, yes, of course I've had a Me Too moment, but nobody cared about that and nobody cared that I was saying it because of whose campaign I was managing.[74]

Conway raised an interesting concern about victimization and context. Considering when she brought up her "Me Too moment" and her role in the presidential campaign, it seemed strategic rather than empowering for the MeToo movement. Conway recentered the conversation on the response to her initial telling of her assault, rather than focusing on how to stop other assaults. Her attempt to refocus the issue on herself through a "narrative justification" (similar to other white feminists, Zajicek notes)[75] and away from the other victims coming forward illustrated an individually focused outcome. Conway displayed her individual power to be a distraction to the issue rather than one ideologically aligning with developing feminist agency against a systemic issue of sexual assault. Further, through her own experiences of disrespect Conway articulated a color-blind ideology. After a different interview, in which Anderson Cooper of CNN rolled his eyes after Conway repeatedly evaded a question, Conway described the eye roll as "possibly sexist, definitely what I call Trumpist. People who go on TV are treated like a houseguest and then when we go on we're not."[76] Conway switched the sexist interpretation to decontextualize her oppression to make any "discrimination" against Trump seem relative to widespread oppression, similar to white nationalist women (see chapter 3). Similarly, at the G20 summit in 2019, Ivanka Trump inserted herself into a conversation about social justice and economics with world leaders such as Prime Ministers Emmanuel Macron (France), Theresa May (Britain), and Justin Trudeau (Canada) and Christine Lagarde, head of the IMF (International Monetary Fund), attempting to centralize herself in the conversation by mentioning the economics in a male-dominated workplace.[77] Instead of listening to insight on macro-level, transnational policy issues, she shared a contained example of job discrimination. In order to engage in the delicate dance of contained agency that retained white privilege, these White House staff members separated themselves from feminism and social justice *for all*. We should expect that their "success" may be behind closed doors, not transparent. After she was appointed to the White House Staff, Ivanka said that the public should not to conflate lack of public denouncement with silence . . . there are multiple ways to have your voice heard. In some cases it's through protest and going on the nightly news and talking about or denouncing every issue which you disagree with. Other times it is quietly and directly and candidly. So where I disagree with my father he knows it and I express myself with my father with total candor. Where I agree, I full lean in and support the agenda and hope that I can be an asset to him and make a positive impact. But I respect the fact that he always listens . . . most of the impact I will have over time most people will not actually know about.[78]

Her assertion illustrated a form of contained agency or internalized misogyny. Although not all forms of regulation were internalized, her statement about not saying anything publicly, especially on issues of sexism, illustrated her ability to stay silent instead of vocal when facing sexist materials. Part of her concern stems from supporting her father by presenting a united front, like most White House offices hope to perpetuate.

The containment of Trump administration women's individual feminism included using traditional feminine traits to persuade their audience and to sustain a white privilege filter. Sanders used smiling to disarm her audience. After her first briefing, a reporter used her first name "Sarah" and welcomed her to the podium, to which she responded, "Thank you . . . does that mean you are gonna be super nice today, right?" while smiling at the reporter, who was asking multiple pointed questions about healthcare.[79] Sanders used smiling to head off potential "attacks" she perceived from the reporters present. Also significant was the gender dynamic that people harass women more than men, yet media and other politicians politically engage women less virulently than men. Conway reinforced this expectation as she attacked senators, who happened to be women, for not being "congenial" or accessible. Following the 2017 State of the Union address Conway asserted, "I think Nancy Pelosi looks like that all the time. I think that she should smile a lot more often and I think the country would be better for it. She seems to embody the bitterness that belongs to the Democratic Party right now."[80] By focusing on Pelosi not "smiling," Conway reified the unequal gender expectations women leaders face[81] and enforced the idea that women not performing feminine gender traits are seen as aggressive and therefore transgressing gender roles. Although she argued that women attacking women are a concern (quotation at the beginning of the chapter), she had no problem attacking other women who do not perform gender[82] in submissive ways.

Further, Conway did not shy away from mentioning how Hillary Clinton did not receive the vote and support of women, stating, "She should have gotten 60 or 62 percent of the female vote" and that people should have been marching or protesting to get her elected,[83] citing her inability to be "likable" by her audience. "Smiling" or "liking" can assert dominance, but people also identify them in gendered attacks. Attacking other women for being serious or "unlikable" does not engage their policies or their positions but rather reduces women to their looks and gender. Conway ironically made victim claims (e.g., how people have made fun of how she looks) to illustrate how other women treat her unfairly. Although she asserts an interest in empowering women while working for Trump, Conway reduced women to being "young" or "mean" when facing conflict with them in public settings. When a student asked Conway about her rationalization of her personal success as a woman with the sexual assault allegations directed at Donald Trump, Conway replied,

> anti-woman . . . women tired of the same argument and same thing you are pre-senting to me now even though you are trying to be personally mean about it. . . . I am glad that people looked at that and saw that and said that is an argument that will not create a single job in my community, will not bring a single of the 75,000 factories that have been closed, will not deter one member of ISIS doing their bloodletting here or in Europe or anywhere else in the world.[84]

By embodying smiling and articulating critical questions as "mean" behav-ior, conservative women reify standards of beauty and a need for likeability that feminists continue to fight in order to establish equitable treatment. Further, through her attack on a young woman who posed the question about the equity of women (independence value), Conway shifted the conversa-tion from independence to safety values. Conversations about safety values allowed for her dominating behavior, where she embodied gatekeeping to ensure archetypal femininity (not questioning authority) to perpetuate fear against an unknown other to preserve her white privilege and authority.

White privilege filter as color-blind politics to disarm intersectional and structural oppression

By attributing their ability to "work hard" for their success and relativizing their victim status, conservative white women opened space to argue color-blind politics. In addition to people revering these women for their household organization mentioned above, each white conservative woman promoted specific policies or means in order to forward color-blind merit. Spicer noted (above) Ivanka Trump's business (economic) acumen. Interestingly, during an interview Conway even told people to buy I. Trump's merchandise (a likely violation of ethics rules for which she received rebuke from the White House),[85] which furthered merit-based claims of I. Trump's business success. Yet, their privilege to have media access or her financial base, both ties to I. Trump's network and historic white privilege, to promote her products was not addressed. Similarly, when debating about running for office, Conway argued that she was not sure she wanted to give up the comfortable economic life she had made for herself;[86] however, she did not tie her financial success to her education or family background. Instead, she provided advice to other women. In her CPAC speech, Conway told a story about a speaking engagement with a peer in 1996 where she did not know how to answer the question about her speaking fee. She clarified that "often in my career I literally did not know how to express my value and ask for what I deserved and what I had earned," summing up her story with a paraphrase of the well-known quote from the film *When Harry Met Sally*: "I'll have what he's having."[87] Through pithy pieces of advice found in I. Trump's book or anecdotal examples of Conway's success, these women appeared to be offering means for success: plan well, work hard, and ask for what men have rather than question the systematic and institutionalized misogyny. Yet similar to alt-right women in chapter 5, instead of engaging with oppression-based discrepancies, conservative white women framed their success from a universal stance and individualized effort perspective. Conservative white women coded an outside "other" as the enemy, illustrating a method of masking misogyny by facilitating racism through an assertion of color-blind merit.

Additionally, individual empowerment of women came in the form of "advocating for the economic empowerment of women,"[88] yet intersectional concerns illustrated the contained definition of women. For example, when facing questions about Trump's proposed cancellation of DACA and his immigration policy preferring white people, Sanders explained:

By definition a merit-based system is color-blind. It's not basing it on any of that criteria. It's not based on race. It's not based on religion. It's not based on country of origin. It is actually based on the merits of whether or not this person's going to contribute into society. So actually it erases all of those things and makes it a much more fair system instead of picking and choosing . . . trying to meet different quotas of different things.[89]

By using color-blind as an ideograph, Sanders ignored historic discrimination against underrepresented populations in the United States, while values like "American exceptionalism" (lionized in the RNC platform) legitimated entitlement and privilege of some, but not all, members of the community. By her definition, a merit-based system was color-blind, which illustrated Sanders's privilege within that system because she did not experience the bias that occurred in multiple "color-blind" institutions.[90] Sanders did not critically contemplate how designers' and historic users' perspectives influence systems; instead she rationalized and forwarded policies to institutionalize racism. As Noble noted, "you cannot have social justice and a politics of recognition without an acknowledgement of how power—often exercised simultaneously through White supremacy and sexism—can skew the delivery of credible and representative information."[91] By creating and codifying some classification of "informational" criteria of "merit," the policy's impact will benefit white men. Through their white privilege filter, merit became a means to pit equitable otherness or "diversity" versus "merit" to preserve a particular merit, which sustained white privilege.

Without critical introspection, blind loyalty and apologia continue in political arenas and further illustrate boundaries of color-blind privilege filters. For example, following the Charlottesville protests and death, when asked a question about the president's rhetoric inflaming people against the immigrant community with snap judgments, Sanders responded, "Not at all. The president has been incredibly outspoken against crime in any form, fashion . . . to call into question his rhetoric to be anything other than somebody who has condemned hate and violence in all of its forms is simply just a complete misrepresentation of not only who the president is but also of what he has said."[92] Sanders relativized Trump's outspokenness to all forms of violence; yet, it took him three public statements to get around to condemning white nationalist violence in Charlottesville.[93] The relativization of oppression continued as Conway reached out to conservative students. At her CPAC speech, Conway praised a student by saying, "The courage that so many of you show in your communities, in your places of work, places of worship, certainly on your college campuses where you definitely feel that you're in an ideological minority, that kind of courage, that kind of outsider status, is what Donald Trump is."[94] Similar to the Tea Party rhetoric of out-siderism (chapter 4), Conway relativized racial oppression ("minority," see chapter 2) with an experience of the conservative college student. Sanders further embodied a color-blind ideology when facing questions about the president engaging in racist statements. For example, after a ceremony to honor Native American World War II "code talkers" in which Trump made a comment about "Pocahontas" (sarcastically referring to Senator Warren), a reporter asked Sanders if he was making the claim that "Pocahontas being in the Senate" was a racial slur. Sanders replied, "I believe that is a ridiculous response."[95] Similarly, when asked a question by a reporter about Trump's response to Jemele Hill's tweets ("Donald Trump is a white supremacist who has largely surrounded himself w/ other white supremacists"[96] and "His rise is a direct result of white supremacy. Period"),[97] Sanders responded, "I think that is one of the more outrageous comments anyone could make and certainly something that is a fireable offense by ESPN."[98] Rather than respond to the critique, Sanders implicated the reporter ethically, blaming the reporter to "dismiss the initial criticism."[99] When facing further ques-tioning about a reported comment that Trump called Haiti, El Salvador, and some African nations "shithole countries," Sanders called senatorial attention to this issue an "outrageous and ludicrous excuse"[100] and later rationalized, "Look, no one is going to pretend here like the president is always politi-cally correct. He isn't" and that "Sometimes he does use tough language."[101] Similar to white nationalist women using <freedom of speech> (chapter 2), Sanders shielded Donald Trump from responsibility or accountability for his words within a color-blind defense of "political correctness" and preserved his white privilege filter.

In addition to justifying a lack of accountability of Donald Trump for his words, these conservative women and representatives of his administra-tion illustrated no awareness of intersectional feminism. In particular, they engaged in statements that illustrated their ability to separate oppression of women from oppression of BIPOC. During an interview on the CNN show *Larry King Live* (March 7, 2008) while defending John McCain, Conway stated, "While Hillary and Obama argue whether or not she should let him sit on the back of the bus on her presidential ticket."[102] It is difficult to miss the use of Hillary's first name (familiarity and no acknowledgment of her title, Senator) and the racial signaling of Obama's Blackness through using the example of the "back of the bus." Examples like these articulate Clinton and Obama through subjugated identity reductions, reifying sexist familiarity and racial histories. Further, Sanders reified racial reductions by connecting topics such as Cinco de Mayo and immigration. During her first press briefing on May 5, 2017, Sanders stated,

> It is also Cinco de Mayo, an opportunity for us all to celebrate the extraordinary contributions that Mexican Americans have made and continue to make in this country. Yesterday at the president's personal request the vice president joined Labor Secretary Acosta, the Mexican ambassador to the United States, and many others for a celebration, reception. The vice president closed his remarks by echoing the president's promise to show great heart as we move forward with real and positive immigration reform and sharing the story of his own grandparents who themselves took a chance by leaving Ireland for the land of opportunity and freedom.[103]

By tying a Cinco de Mayo celebration to Mexican Americans and immigration, Sanders reified racial reductions of Mexican Americans as immigrants and outsiders. In both cases, Conway and Sanders detailed historical events from a perspective of white privilege—one asserting authority and vantage over location within a bus and the other by conflating people with an immigrant status with Mexican American people.

Assertions from a white privilege filter by conservative women were based on skin color; yet, verbal platitudes limited responses of concern based on racism. One of these women made a clear assertion concerning racism and Nazism: Ivanka Trump tweeted on August 13, 2017, after the Charlottesville protest and violence, that "There should be no place in society for racism, white supremacy and neo-nazis,"[104] breaking her rule about being silent, but also not saying much in specific content. However, her silence was apparent when it came to institutional and systemic forms of intersectional oppression. I. Trump did not engage in critique of sexual oppression or misogyny in local settings nor did she critically engage racism for BIPOC. Instead, she contained her outrage to a surface-level, vague claim about how racism, white supremacy, and neo-Nazis should not have a place in the United States, with little to no introspection as to how her father's policies perpetuate these concerns in US culture.

Implications of Conservative White Women Using White Privilege Filters

While I applaud the efforts to have more women in the White House, I recognize that constraints came with their appointments. Continuing claims by Conway and others of "liberal women" not highlighting these women in positions of power offered surface-level critique (e.g., women should support all women). Nepotism, whether it be through family or community ties, is what offered these women access to positions of power and what will continue to contain their agency within the roles they play as they responses were tied by their appointment, which preserve white privilege filters. Being grateful for an opportunity forced an allegiance or loyalty to someone in a high-ranking position of power, at the sacrifice of engaging larger forms of oppression.

These women became token simulations of "empowerment." Considering the rhetorical implications, the Republican Party's easiest method of appearing as agents of "change" with a traditionalist agenda became appointing women, specifically white women, as political actors. Similar to the appointment of Sarah Palin as vice presidential candidate in 2008 (see chapter 4), women in the traditionalist Republican Party become the material referent of outsiderism without having the complications of actually addressing systemic, historical, and institutional oppression in an intersectional manner. As the women who were politicians surveyed by Fox and Lawless note, conservative women argued "the feminist ideal that women can try to 'have it all'"[105]—spouse, children, and profession. However, having it all required no intersectional identities or attention to intersectional oppression. Similar to past white women within the rhetorical sphere being valued for their silence, purity, or domestic place,[106] some people preferred women as silent bodies unless defending a domestic sphere (whether motherhood or borders) to ensure the "purity" of the United States and its institutions. Yet, rhetorics of "purity" are fraught with "attempts to meet and control a complex situation that is fundamentally outside our control" which "shuts down precisely the field of possibility that might allow us to take better collective action,"[107] making it necessary to be wary of them as a posed solution.

Further, scholars noted the constraint associated with reifying traditional women's roles within political arenas. In his study of adult Brazilian women's identity, Neuhouser argues that when "woman" is "virtually synonymous with mother,"[108] feminist transformative identity politics are connected to or even limited by access to child care and class considerations. Dana Cloud notes the constraint of such definitions of women when she analyzes the mythic political vision of family values, which "depends upon the construction of women's identity as the keeper of the family utopia and guarantor of national unity and prosperity."[109] By placing pressure on women to uphold the vision of a nuclear family unit, the expectations of default parenthood constrain women.[110] People expect women to be mothers, household managers, etc., as well as professional women with men as their gatekeepers to the professional realm. However, women must consider the "knight in shining armor" to whom they are beholden. Similar to disaster relief victims receiving aid or a nation responding to a crisis situation, "[t]he 'compassion' of chivalry, protectiveness over the feminine, and the power of gatekeeping through parental-like decision making produce this illustration of invulnerability. . . . Valorized 'compassion' depends on and perpetuates the invisibility or racial and gender subordination."[111] White conservative men appoint white conservative women who continue to be loyal to those men, especially when the carrots conservative men provide maintain traditional family dynamics. Loyalty comes in the form of being maiden shields of white privilege based on traditional motherhood, individual feminism, and color-blind racism.

Conservative white women produce classification of motherhood (as primary to all women) similar to white nationalist and alt-right classifications of women and, therefore, fall to the same critique that women's ability and choice to reproduce grounds our oppression. More troublesome is how conservative white women articulate motherhood as an arena where not only should children be the center of a mother's life as a woman but her children should also see her as the center of theirs. In an interview with *People* magazine next to a picture of herself, Ivanka Trump said, "I want my children to see me first every morning, so I wake up at 5 and make sure to shower and exercise before they get up."[112] Her image (low-cut, tight-fitting white dress, fully coiffed) resembles those white nationalist women used to illustrate values of health through sexual vivacity and power I note in chapter 1. Further, her assertion as the central feature in their lives appeared similar to alt-right women (see chapter 6) who refocused their communities within the family. These images and claims are in contrast with former first lady Michelle Obama, who, in a campaign speech for Hillary Clinton, articulated motherhood as a means to educate critically through historical recognition in order to challenge institutional and systemic oppression. During her Democratic National Convention speech on July 26, 2016, Michelle Obama contextualized:

That is the story of this country, the story that has brought me to this stage tonight, the story of generations of people who felt the lash of bondage, the shame of servitude, the sting of segregation, but who kept on striving and hoping and doing what needed to be done so that today I wake up every morning in a house that was built by slaves. . . . And I watch my daughters, two beautiful, intelligent, black young women playing with their dogs on the White House lawn.[113]

Rather than focusing on her home as contextless, Obama placed her daughters' identities within the context of historical oppression to illustrate her concern about how they, as women (not girls), encounter and engage racism in the future rather than recentering their focus on her.

In turn, through their maintenance of white privilege filters, conservative women become the gatekeepers of whiteness where they use "individual feminism as a color-blind ideology. Conservative white women refocus issues of feminism on their individual person rather than on larger societal issues. White women supported white supremacy more openly in the past by influencing local and federal policy through lobbying for the Racial Integrity Act, genetic family tree mapping, letter-writing campaigns to solidify racial classifications and Jim Crow laws, challenging textbook selection, and even petitioning for educational desegregation;[114] yet these white women carried a similar segregationist agenda by supporting barriers to educational, economic, and housing access for BIPOC.

When compared with Michelle Obama, my analyses revealed a massive difference in the way these conservative women approached feminism. While these women recognized their ability to work hard to break through glass ceilings, M. Obama questions how to ensure her daughters and other people flourish as independent individuals pursuing their lives within contexts of systemic misogyny. Rather than focusing on individual actions, M. Obama recognizes the structural inequity facing her daughters. Following the release of the Access Hollywood tapes with Trump's comments about "grab[bing women] by the pussy," Michelle Obama responded by stating at a Clinton-Kaine rally on October 13, 2016:

What message are our little girls hearing about who they should look like, how they should act? What lessons are they learning about their value as professionals, as human beings, about their dreams and aspirations? And how is this affecting men and boys in this country? Because I can tell you that the men in my life do not talk about women like this. And I know that my family is not unusual. And to dismiss this as everyday locker-room talk is an insult to decent men everywhere.[115]

Notably, Michelle Obama recognized cultural and institutional problems rather than refocusing the issue on one individual's ability to challenge a system, like Kellyanne Conway. By recognizing a larger oppressive system, M. Obama acknowledged a larger, intersectional scope of racism and sexism.

In addition to a limited concept of racism and sexism, conservative white women reduced class to an individual problem of work ethic or focus. One of the most consistent critiques of Ivanka Trump's second book is that her assertions about giving up "massages," "meditation," "time with friends," as well as perfect, dirt-free photographs[116] illustrate how class shrouds her white feminism. Similar to Sandberg's claims about women "holding themselves back" (introduction), I. Trump did not acknowledge how economic class, race, appearance, or sex allowed her competitive advantages in her field. Instead, she said people hold themselves back, articulating her advantage as only "psychological."[117] Her denial of privileged access and status is especially surprising considering her unorthodox fulfillment of first lady roles for her father. Yet denial of privilege facilitates "a rhetoric of dysfunctional silence" inherent to whiteness.[118]

Asserting individual feminism only reified problematic boundaries of feminism, allowing for continued silencing of intersectional experiences of feminism for women (BIPOC). Conservative white women's contained understanding of systemic, historical, and institutional oppression reinforces their white privilege through color-blind politics. Rather than address the critiques about Donald Trump's racist statements, conservative white women used an apologia based in white privilege to sidestep addressing his racism. Conservative white women attacked critics' assertions as "ridiculous" and dismissed institutional oppression. Based in their contained agency, these women excluded other oppressed group members who might need services that they did not require, like access to immigration, Planned Parenthood, or maternity leave policies. Their claims served to discredit or distract attention from large-scale cultural oppression to preserve white privilege filters. Instead, conservative white women attempted to stand as models of "American exceptionalism," which fueled a sense of entitlement that sometimes manifested as violence against others.[119] Conway further rationalized that individual empowerment supersedes sisterhood:

Turns out there are a lot of women who have a problem with women in power. This whole sisterhood, this whole let's go march for women's rights and you know constantly talking about what women look like or what they wear or making fun of their choices or presuming that they are not as powerful as the men around—this presumptive negativity about women and power I think is very unfortunate because let's just try to access that and have a conversation about it rather than a confrontation about it.[120]

However, individual empowerment requires multiple layers of privilege (race, economic, sexuality, etc.) and no intersectional recognition. Conservative white women's rhetoric only includes cisgender, heteronormative constructions of mothers, encouraging "others" to be silent or calm, which invokes arguments for civility.[121] Due to contentious assumptions about people's universal agency, these calls for "civility" and "communicative spaces" require further study.[122] As Audre Lorde notes:

Anger is an appropriate reaction to racist attitudes, as is fury when the actions arising from those attitudes do not change. To those women here who fear the anger of women of Color more than their own unscrutinized racist attitudes, I ask: Is the anger of women of Color more threatening than the woman-hatred that tinges all aspects of our lives?

It is not the anger of other women that will destroy us but our refusals to stand still, to listen to its rhythms, to learn within it, to move beyond the manner of presentation to the substance, to tap that anger as an important source of empowerment.[123]

Change requires conflict; continuous and denied recognition of oppression warrants anger, which can fuel productive dialectic about how we need to change the institutions that contain agency. Further, by coming to the defense of Jewish [white] people and not other BIPOC, Ivanka Trump reifies Jewish [i.e., white] people as worthy of a verbal defense. By reifying racial worthiness of concern, conservative white women reify a problematic, racialized hierarchy of people and subsequent care for individuals rather than a systemic recognition of white racist acts that continue to occur. As Ibram Kendi, a leading scholar of anti-racism at American University, notes, "If the fundamental problem is ignorance and hate, then your solutions are going to be focused on education, and love and persuasion. But of course [*Stamped from the Beginning*] shows that the actual foundation of racism is not ignorance and hate, but self-interest, particularly economic and political and cultural."[124]

Conclusion

By using a white privilege filter to reinstate racial hierarchies, conservative white women shielded conservative white men, like Donald Trump, from the implications of their racist speech. Conservative white women like Conway, Ivanka Trump, and Sanders functioned as maiden shields for Donald Trump because they simulated empowered women while, in praxis, their political rhetoric was similar to that of white nationalist and alt-right women where women were contained by values, ideologies, and classifications which preserve white supremacy (see chapters 1, 2, 3, and 5). Conservative white women did not take into account intersectional concerns of women; instead, they tried to block powerful critiques about Trump's supposed dedication to the empowerment of all women. They offered "outsider" appearance, while sticking to "individual" or "maternal feminist" agendas. Dismantling their rhetoric as contained by a lack of intersectional considerations revealed why their agenda was such a significant threat not only to feminism but also to all people's right to combat oppression for equal access to their civil liberties.

Individual feminism provides *a* solution to oppression—work harder against each other—rather than an institutional corrective. When people bring up oppression, a lack of receptivity to that oppression can limit possibilities to engage it through a victim's own terms. As noted in the Facebook message example that begins this chapter, decontextualizing terms can offer meaning, but it can also usurp perspective and agency. Instead, claims for "civility" or reinterpretation only serve to pacify and "whitesplain" interpretation, and change in ownership of the narrative recodes the meaning through a white privilege filter. Although trauma is definitely at play within the US, without recognizing the racialized rhetorical correctives we miss the cycle of racism at work within our institutions. White fragility offers a means to critically confront white insecurity standing in the way of our epistemological humility, or our ability to be humbled enough to listen and be responsive to change the impact of our racism.

Epilogue

Amplifying Intersectionality
as an Ethical Response

I started this research in 2005 and fifteen years later it was ready for print. I recall the first time I submitted my book manuscript to an editor in 2010. I was elated to receive feedback that the book should be fast-tracked for a full review. As a young assistant professor, I was buoyed that a major international publisher was interested in my work. However, when the reviews returned, they indicated that the book fell short of my intention. One reviewer even indicated that the way that I was conveying information seemed problematic due to my use of objective language. I was devastated to hear that my work seemed to amplify rather than unmask whiteness. At that time, I stepped away from the project, unsure of what to do with it, unsure of how I might make a necessary epistemological shift. However, if I had stopped my research at that point, the value of understanding how people—regardless of race, class, gender, different ability—code whiteness to support white supremacy would have been lost.

After leaving my position as an assistant professor, I recall chatting with more scholars at conferences about my work. Some indicated that racism was addressed by other scholarly work, yet more young scholars, particularly BIPOC, recognized a need to engage racism in renewed ways. These conversations motivated me to return to the manuscript. I recalled notes from my dissertation co-chair about critical race theory and kept pushing myself to return to and find materials new to me. When reviewers for this book offered me additional critical race theory scholars to engage, I felt that I had finally found how to ethically engage my work. I knew limitations existed on what I would understand and how I might perpetuate whiteness. Reaching out to other scholars working in critical race theory is what has allowed my work to flourish, yet those steps required a necessary epistemological humility.

A similar humility is necessary for people to become responsive in critiquing whiteness. As Radcliffe notes, a rhetoric of listening requires "recognition, critique, and accountability;"[1] yet will that ensure an anti-racist stance? In addressing the three questions I pose in the introduction that frame my research, I conceptualize a need to embody epistemological agency as an anti-racist accomplice, which requires an ethical methodological approach and responsiveness. As an accomplice, white people should not be intent on saving ("white savior") BIPOC; instead, agency is found standing and working with BIPOC to dismantle the processes within institutions and organizations that facilitate white privilege.[2] Working with critical scholars, especially those who are BIPOC, not only ensures that we are listening to and learning from and with people who experience the very oppression we hope to combat, but also allows space for dialectical engagement of white culpability, where white fragility may mask whiteness from our immediate perception. Building on George Yancy's call for "epistemological humility"[3] and "vigilance,"[4] white scholars have to *choose* to actively seek out and listen and be responsive to critical scholars (BIPOC) when engaging racism to ensure we recognize when we are caught within "a sticky web of privilege that permits only acts which reinforce ('reinscribe') racism."[5] Through our continued choice to cultivate anti-racism within the academy we ensure they are "hospitable," even habitable, for BIPOC.

By critically assessing contained agency and white privilege filters, I distinguished between identity politics and systemic oppression to understand the impact of how white supremacy politically and structurally codes the institutions in which we participate. By continuing to engage in epistemological humility, we start to resist the complacency of white supremacy[6] and find ethical agency for social change.

Further, when analyzing white nationalist and alt-right women's rhetoric within a digital context, positional ethics and reflexive conversations with critical scholars (BIPOC) provided a means to unmask color-blind politics rather than perpetuate it through an analytic approach. To clarify how

I respond to each of research question, I briefly address how the state of white supremacy at this moment in the United States situates this research, a digital context's conduciveness to empowering white women, and an analytic approach to studying white women who spread white supremacy. By engaging the power and control of institutional white supremacy through an anti-racist stance and engaging how critical race theory dismantles a white privilege filter, we can breach possibilities for challenging white supremacy in meaningful ways.

What is the state of white supremacy in the present moment in the United States? How has the digital medium enabled the spread of white supremacy? By electing Trump, his voters in the United States weaponized multiple institutions of white supremacy. Following the neo-Nazi rally in Charlottesville, Reuters and the University of Virginia polled people in the United States about their attitudes concerning the endorsement of racism. One of the questions asked is whether or not white people were under attack—39 percent agreed or strongly agreed, while disagreeing with the statement that nonwhite people were under attack. Almost a third (31 percent) strongly or somewhat agreed that the United States needed to "protect and preserve its White European Heritage," while another third disagreed and 29 percent neither agreed nor disagreed. However, about 70 percent of respondents strongly agreed that "all races are equal."[7] Norton et al. clarify that many white people saw racism as a zero-sum game for them, as though they are under attack culturally by BIPOC.[8] Based on these statistics concerning racial injustice, it is clear that people believe in equality as a value, but a disjuncture exists between US cultural vision and reality, or how we embody the value of equality. Contrary to the value of equity which may directly acknowledge historic, systemic, and institutional disadvantages and privileging, equality perpetuates a contained agency for white people. Yet, due to an epistemological "threat" of learning that people have been taken advantage of and abused throughout US history to retain white supremacy, a strong contingency of white people from the United States are choosing to fuel white identity politics to avoid feelings of insecurity.

Values of equality perpetuate a color-blind ideology and create a foundation for white people to use ideographs like <diversity> and <free speech> to bully BIPOC into a contained agency of white identity politics. White men use white women, as an embodiment of "difference," to convey strategic, color-blind communication. Ivanka Trump, Kellyanne Conway, and Sarah

Huckabee Sanders function as Trump's new "guards"[9] of white supremacy; however, they are not the only white women to attempt to appease the US populace's concern for ethical engagement. Even the FLOTUS, Melania Trump, "campaigns" against bullying, which functions as a means to downplay issues of harassment, reception of unwanted attention, or intimidation by her partner.[10] When facing intersectional critiques concerning oppression, through an apologetic defensiveness white women can place themselves/ourselves in a perpetual victim stance to recenter conversations away from experiences of racial oppression.

As a scholar who envisions a more equitable democracy, I critically contemplate and "curate" the ways in which we rebirth and cultivate our communities. Confronting academic institutions marred by puritanical politics may challenge how our processes have historically been done. Charles Mills notes the dire need for ethics and political philosophy to mainstream discussions of "conquest, imperialism, colonialism, white settlement, land rights, race and racism, slavery, Jim Crow, reparations, apartheid, cultural authenticity, national identity, *indigenismo*, Afrocentrism, etc."[11] By critically contemplating historical exclusion of BIPOC from the democratic process, we can further our discussion on equity within political spheres. For example, during the spring of 2019 in the field of Communication Studies, we witnessed an abrupt apologetic defense of white privilege as a group of primarily white "distinguished scholars" defended their right to solely appoint their members rather than share the responsibility with the National Communication Association's executive board. In one response signed by multiple "distinguished" scholars, merit was pitted against diversity, without recognizing how their epistemological assumptions about assessing "merit" were built into facilitating processes and structures that cultivate white supremacy.

Further, due to continued threats to regulate and control academic work challenging white supremacy, professors' academic freedom continues to be under attack. As Daniels and Stein note based on a 2013 survey of faculty,

> 70 percent of faculty use social media for personal reasons at least monthly, while 55 percent use it specifically for professional use at least monthly. People who take stands on controversial issues, particularly if they're members of marginalized groups, are more likely to be subjected to scrutiny and even, at times, intimidation. By and large, college and university administrators are not prepared for these new challenges.[12]

University professors who undermine or unmask white supremacy through critical scholarship continue to be targets of both alt-right and conservative political efforts in their personal digital spaces. As targets of the alt-right, academic institutions need to do more to preserve learning environments and human rights of underrepresented BIPOC, transgender, differently abled, and women scholars from the scapegoat-like harassment they may receive from outside sources.

Critically contemplating the tree-branch nominating and mentoring model may help further ethical scholarship at the university level. Similar to white fragility, mentoring is about being humbled but not humiliated. In academia the ways in which we are "disciplined" may have taught us to scar in unhealthy ways (fear being humbled through learning in lieu of feeling powerful, controlled, territory preserving). As we attempt to alter how we have been disciplined, either we must deliberately make a break in the "forms" (processes) we have been taught or we perpetuate unhealthy power and control dynamics. Much like parenting, we make a deliberate and repeated choice to parent differently in some respects from the ways our parents did. Rhetorically jarring or unsettling choices offer opportunities for us to see different alternatives to furthering our knowledge within our fields. In the apprenticeship model we discipline based on sameness rather than on centering difference in order to have a vibrant discussion to further scholarship. Instead of protecting tenured scholars who may constrain ethical communities from forming within institutions, institutions may need not only to recruit but to actually support critical faculty (BIPOC), transgender identity, and other underrepresented groups to sustain ethical, critical scholarship within our institutions.

Further policies concerning tenure need to be modified, by administrative bodies of faculty and staff, to include addendum concerning harassment, assault, and abuse of incoming faculty from oppressed groups to ensure that tenured faculty (who may perceive that they are defending their intellectual legacy) do not ethically compromise departments and universities for the sake of their personal egos. Administrations that act on an anti-racist stance, rather than waiting for individuals to "die out," reduce possibilities that their mentees will continue a legacy of whiteness. Instead, we need to revolutionize our academic tenure policies with anti-racist and anti-sexist addendums. Further development and investment into how institutions become more resilient in practically addressing attacks on scholars who engage in challenging and "risky," yet meaningful and ethical, work can help our administration support faculty as they face attacks. University administrations can develop clear policies and procedures to respond to and combat harassment by endorsing the statement made by the American Association of University Professors, American Federation of Teachers, and the Association of American Colleges and Universities[13] (including mentoring) and build those statements into tenure contracts, even retroactively. Additionally, by developing "a response plan and protocol for when faculty members are attacked,"[14] administration can offer faculty, staff, and students clear ways to document and process attacks.

It is important to know how to deal with harassment, not only in the classroom and departments, but also in digital space. Daniels and Stein suggest having "a clear policy in place about social media and public scholarship" within faculty senate.[15] Last, offering, publicizing, and incentivizing equity workshops (sponsored by a diversity office on campus) for instructional faculty and graduate employees can help more faculty become aware of and practice how to bravely address ethical attacks within the classroom and beyond. Through prioritization of anti-racism, administrations can begin to revolutionize how they ethically sustain themselves without relying on the privilege of whiteness.

What I propose is an academic revolution. As such I find myself revisiting what Abigail Adams once wrote to her husband, former president John Adams:

> I long to hear that you have declared an independency—and by the way in the new Code of Laws which I suppose it will be necessary for you to make I desire you would Remember the Ladies, and be more generous and favourable to them than your ancestors. Do not put such unlimited power into the hands of the Husbands. Remember all Men would be tyrants if they could. If particular care and attention is not paid to the Ladies we are determined to foment a Rebellion, and will not hold ourselves bound by any Laws in which we have no voice, or Representation.[16]

This revolution cannot be contained by a narrow, token focus on white women's empowerment. A revolution is here to change the way we have historically, legally, culturally, economically, and socially functioned; however, if we focus so much on our identities—in lieu of a democracy that requires us to equitably address anti-racist, anti-sexist, anti-heterosexist, anti-ablist, and to work against systemic and specifically intersectional oppression—we fall prey to whiteness. As the Combahee River Collective notes:

> Material resources must be equally distributed among those who create these resources. We are not convinced, however, that a socialist revolution that is not also a feminist and anti-racist revolution will guarantee our liberation. We have arrived at the necessity for developing an understanding of class relationships that takes into account the specific class position of Black women who are generally marginal in the labor force, while at this particular time some of us are temporarily viewed as doubly desirable tokens at white-collar and professional levels. We need to articulate the real class situation of persons who are not merely raceless, sexless workers, but for whom racial and sexual oppression are significant determinants in their working/economic lives.[17]

A socialist revolution must be feminist and anti-racist,[18] meaning we cannot trade on one for the other, or on any other oppressed group. By unmasking white identity politics, we begin to reveal the contained agency carrot privileged people offer to token, individual members from underrepresented groups by white men in powerful positions, and can instead fight for access to designing the garden.

Why is a digital context conducive to forms of empowerment for white women?
Digital spheres have become new "gardens" in which to cultivate community. With extensive techno-optimism, which continues to herald a digital era, many white people may find the prevalence of racism within digital spheres surprising. Yet, social movements have historically found growth through using budding media forms. Similar to research of past media, critical analysis of the constraints and affordances within the media themselves help scholars analyze how social movement actors may be able to recruit new members or share their values, ideologies, and classifications.

In my initial analytic process, I systematically analyzed a large breadth of written and coded content by white nationalist women and broadened my methodological approach to include self-promotion and political advertisements such as speeches, interviews, and commercials. Since I did not agree politically with white nationalism, I started this work with a fear of not being "objective" and, as a result, I systematically analyzed documents consisting of a thousand pages of text and links four times, one for each tier of my dissertation analysis. Yet, by attempting to "objectively," unemotionally operationalize my analysis, my early work suffered from the same decontextualization of evidence that white nationalists forward. To resist the ideological reduction into analytic sound bites, I started to analyze the medium mechanics and architecture [how pages flow from link to link, who is uploading materials, how content is structured (interview form), how alt-right media are linked or separated from business identities, and within historical contexts (when speeches or commercials were given after a story broke or Donald Trump's tweets, etc.)]. Further, by learning HTML and CSS, I have been able to contextually understand the multilayered classifications that takes place within online communities to solidify those communities, as well as how digital media facilitated cultural and procedural coding.

Programmatic knowledge, or knowledge of the code, can shift our understanding of ideologies built into programming languages. In the book *From A to A: Keywords of Markup*, Dilger and Rice note the ideological influences of markup languages such as HTML, recognizing that when one is fluent in the automation of a language, one can understand the procedures set in place by a particular code set.[19] Similar to arguments made by Michael McGee concerning the ideograph, ideologies built into coded systems carry multilayered, typically uncontemplated meaning. Translation: markup moves meaning. Markup languages such as HTML and CSS provide designers and developers tools to "hack" the languages. Open source code develops as an "uttered language"[20] (HTML, CSS, or other programing languages) from multiple globally located coders/hackers as well as through standards the W3 Consortium cultivates.[21] Coders hack or modify a code to suit their needs or to develop their own classification or <class> systems to help them develop the form of their webspace/argument. By understanding the underlying cultural and programmatic protocols for codes, WYSIWIG (What You See Is What You Get) editors will no longer reduce our digital agency. When able to understand how specific CSS can influence the language of code, scholars can recognize and engage digital utterances or new systems of classification. Bakhtin argues that language evolves in polyglossic ways through "utterances," where speech patterns blend and adapt to meet needs of a given context. Hacking code is a form of utterance. Specifically, feminist engagement of these classificatory design protocols aid in developing more inclusive, accessible, and flexible linguistic systems,[22] or embody the "generative power of the spoken word" generations of African people identify.[23] The feminist dictionary captures a similar reclassification process, by contextualized examples rather than vague signifiers, to the development of programming language.[24] Critical choices include choosing to analyze technological systems and choosing alternatives or redesigns (open system) to ensure more democratic forms of technological engagement. To influence how people embody their difference, users must learn how to understand and reshape the rules and codes that shape digital contexts and critically choose technologies that resonate with feminist value systems.

Digital processes, like gateway pages and games, function like digital syllogisms, where users participate in the argument to gain the information from and play on sites. For example, Flash-based games like Border Patrol, found on a popular gaming platform like Steam, require users to shoot non-player characters (NPCs) who embody a stereotypical Mexican identity (including a pregnant mother with a child) crossing a border. As users miss hitting the NPC, the game process slows down and NPCs get closer to the screen to "help" users succeed. When playing Border Patrol, users accept and complete the racist argument to play the game. The rhetoric of racist code, or how designers privileged content through classifications content within HTML and CSS (even more so now within C++), influences not only how a site is read and "played," but more so how other systems filter and process it. The way people design their process-based arguments, or their "rhetorics of form," offers insight into the visual and processing ideographs or what I call "ideoforms" that signal meaning for users as they play through a mechanic or process. Further research on how whiteness is imbued within digital media will help unmask how seemingly color-blind digital code functions to privilege whiteness. Analysis of how participation in a process facilitates information may help us better understand how media, especially those people identify as for "entertainment," forward meaning.

Scholars like Noble challenge how digital media companies, especially social media like Google, use crowd-sourced data to build infrastructures that perpetuate racism, but more research needs to be done on racialized infrastructures, both in corporate and public forum spaces. Research on social media community cultivation may help us further understand what accomplice-based equity looks like within a digital democratic sphere. For example, by restricting how people communicate, webmasters and moderators set the procedures and privilege content. Languages like HTML and CSS offer means to reclassify content to design how people understand and experience the information they see online. Rules, or terms of service, guide online communities, while web administrators enforce the boundaries and mechanized processes of those rules.

Most recently, steps taken by Ravelry, an online yarn-crafting site, illustrate how social communities can cultivate communities by taking an anti-racist stance. In June 2019, Ravelry stated that they "are banning support of Donald Trump and his administration on Ravelry . . . We cannot provide a space that is inclusive of all and also allow support for open white supremacy. Support of the Trump administration is undeniably support for white supremacy. . . . This includes support in the form of forum posts, projects, patterns, profiles, and all other content."[25] Although they are not deleting project data users purchase, they are removing content that marginalizes groups of people. They challenge their community to "help by flagging any of the following items if they constitute support for Trump or his administration:

- Projects: Unacceptable projects will be provided to the member or made invisible to others.
- Patterns: Unacceptable patterns will be returned to drafts.
- Forum posts: Unacceptable posts will be removed
- Profiles: Unacceptable avatars or profile text will be hidden or removed."[26]

By taking an active responsibility and steps to ensure that they do not perpetuate white supremacy within their spaces, Ravelry is developing an accomplice-based, anti-racist community. Ravelry acknowledges that they took guidance from gaming sites like RPG.net.[27] Further research on social media sites, like digital gaming communities, offers insight as to how webmasters can feasibly cultivate anti-racist democratic communities.

Additional interrogation on how social media affords and constrains democratic exchange may help further legal precedent and also illustrate how we can ethically and equitably engage one another. As determined in *Knight First Amendment Institute v. Trump, Hicks, Sanders, and Scavino*, public figures are not allowed to block critics on social media, due to designations of Twitter as a "public forum" with tweets, retweets, and such falling under First Amendment rights.[28] Yet, our academic institutions need to critically contemplate how they may be coding white supremacy messages by requiring digital programs to address community problems such as harassment and racism. For example, at the University of Minnesota, after a series of internal sexual harassment cases and hearings between administrative staff, tenured professors, assistant professors, athletic students, and graduate students, the university updated its sexual harassment policy and developed a procedure for reporting concerns.[29] However, the process was shared via a game-based program, where users chose an appropriate response. Although the university may have been attempting to address individual issues, without dialogue and sustained, anti-sexist choices, power and control dynamics within department and university communities may continue problematic contexts. Similar to institutionalized racism, the institutional process of dealing with harassment may favor the institution—and potentially the harassers, if they have been with the institution longer. As institutions continue to struggle to adequately address institutionalized sexism and racism, emerging media will continue to be an outlet for people seeking voice for their oppression.

Audre Lorde, bell hooks, Marilyn Frye, Kathleen Blee, Ruth Frankenberg, Stephanie Jones-Rogers, Elizabeth G. McRae,[30] and many other scholars recognize that we do not adequately study white women's voice in connection to white nationalism and supremacy. Yet few studies have engaged with how white nationalist and alt-right women spread white supremacy by refining a rhetoric of whiteness for conservative white men and women. White women are powerful rhetors whose rhetoric resonates with audiences without having responsibility attached to their ethos because women are "outsiders" due to their sex difference from men. As seen by Ivanka Trump's example at the G20 summit I note in chapter 6, due to her lack of experience she is not seen as credible, yet her presence speaks. With identity politics, white women's gendered positionality allows them to be heard within organizations, especially those laden with overt white supremacy, as token voices of <diversity> to silence more critical, intersectional voices who focus on institutional implications of oppression. A racial hierarchy serves white women by allowing white men to protect us (and our positions) and allowing us to defend them and shirk our accountability to a rhetoric of whiteness for their vision. By identifying and analyzing the rhetoric of white nationalist, alt-right, and conservative women in particular, I validate the power of women's rhetoric while unmasking the contained agency and white privilege filters people use to sustain white women's individual empowerment. However, due to their positionality, white women's rhetoric is qualitatively different from men's rhetoric and can accomplish "great" things as it serves as an apologia of whiteness. Considering a US history of constrained democratic access, digital contexts are conducive to forms of empowerment for white women. White women, who have not been heard within traditional political arenas, find other means to communicate. The World Wide Web is a space where white women can develop their voices, yet those voices may be more individually focused. Due to the medium (YouTube video, tweeting, etc.) and a desire to empower themselves, predominantly in those spaces, through the white privilege they experience rather than address the oppressive systems and institutions that constrain them and others based on their "difference" from white men, individual white women may flourish in digital spheres.

Because white women may not feel centered within an organization or in response to how our labor has been taken advantage of in past organizations, white women may struggle to invest within off and online communities. Social media programs allow privileged (white, cisgendered, economically affluent) women to cultivate digital spaces, especially during times of solitude: in college, as we transition into our careers, or motherhood,[31] or when we may be without adult companionship for long stretches of time. During these times of seeking support, white women become an audience with specific needs for information and even mentorship, making it ethically necessary for scholars to study rhetoric directed at and by them. By challenging ourselves to study rhetorics of white supremacy by women within digital spaces, we strengthen our ability to understand how rhetoric functions contextually and procedurally to unmask how white women may utilize new media to reinforce a status quo of white supremacy.

How can we respond ethically as white scholars to engage whiteness within our research practices?

In addition to pushing further analysis on medium and white women's rhetoric, scholars must critically contemplate our epistemological agency based in privilege to ensure we preserve our ethics through our research. I am grateful for the colleague and friend who candidly shared her concerns about racist implications of "objective" work and challenged me to be vulnerable again. After working with one persistent and brilliant scholar, Andrew Boge, I chose to ask critical scholars (BIPOC) to read my introduction and conclusion chapters rather than analytic sections, for it was not their job to correct my analysis. However, I want their insight on how I respond to concerns about white people who made overtly and covertly racist statements without crossing over into territory where I appropriate or "whitesplain" critical race theory or my research becomes a source of revisiting racialized trauma. While some white scholars have pushed back on my use of critical race theory, I found myself citing CRT as a form of collaborative conversation and challenged myself to resist the temptation to overstep into thinking I can embody CRT.

Only through making missteps, facing my insecurities, choosing an epistemological humility, and continuing this project have I realized the presumption and confidence that comes with a white privilege filter. Well-meaning white scholars who assert that they can be objective or profess universal theories embody some of the most egregious offenders of covert racism. If we accept that as scholars we (and other scholars) will make mistakes, yet be compassionately responsive through our insecurity, ground will be gained together. If we hold people accountable to perfection, we fall prey to the white supremacy we are seeking to dismantle.[32] This chapter does not completely encapsulate all that I have learned through the research process, but my reflection offers how my research—which started as an attempt to understand racism—influenced my perspective to spur epistemological changes in my work. I found that precarity shifted into a form of "performative agency"[33] as I read challenges of whiteness within critical race theory, which provided a praxis of confront whiteness in face-to-face settings. Although people and communities are never perfect, by taking anti-racist actions we move in a more equitable direction. As author and social activist Ijeoma Oluo notes, "The beauty of anti-racism is that you don't have to pretend to be free of racism to be an anti-racist. Anti-racism is the commitment to fight racism wherever you find it, including in yourself. And it's the only way forward."[34]

Since I am white and do not experience racism, limitations on my understanding of racism will always exist. During my life I have engaged in coded racist behavior, and have even found myself "ambushing" scholars (BIPOC) with my whiteness.[35] And I've had to learn to reflect, apologize, and choose differently the next time as a means to influence my white privilege filter. To help me learn to learn how our epistemologies afford and constrain, I found myself contacting friends who are critical scholars (BIPOC) and listening closely to other scholars (BIPOC) that I have yet to meet interpersonally and asking reflective questions that made me feel uncomfortable and vulnerable. Through my attentive and persistent, yet admittedly naïve, curiosity and their generously kind and patient brilliance, I grew to understand more about how contained agency and white privilege filters function to support white supremacy.

Similar to Tina Askanius, I fear being socialized into racist perceptions.[36] During my research the realities of the emotional labor in reading abusive content[37] left me feeling anxious, paranoid, and even resistant to trust new people, which speaks to how reading white nationalist content can influence our perspective even when we do not agree with it. I counteracted the isolation of researching extremist groups by reconnecting with friends, colleagues in the field researching a similar area, and supportive family members. When the research felt difficult, I took breaks and reminded myself that what I was experiencing is not even a fraction of the emotional labor we expect of BIPOC on a daily basis, and returned to the meaning of the work. Some emotional perceptions lingered, prompting me to wonder about the low-level trauma of doing "risky" scholarly work on extremist groups; as a white person, I had the privilege to take a break or even walk away.

Additionally, I considered the privilege of using an authorial and/or subject pseudonyms, yet I realized how using pseudonyms continues white privilege because we have the choice to accept responsibility or evade accountability. At times I have been afraid to publish this work and even more times I worried that other white folks will leave their white privilege filter unquestioned. After reading an early draft of this work, an advanced scholar argued that I was studying a "minority" (white nationalists) of a "minority" (women) group, implying the content didn't matter. Yet, I am fortunate to have other mentors who continue to remind me that I need to recognize the value of my work. Part of reckoning with my white privilege is not hiding, but letting the meaning of my work stand without self-image, because the content of this book isn't about me but rather about understanding how whiteness functions and continues to afford me privilege. As part of my antiracist activism, I choose to deliberately unmask that privilege and channel my influence to change the institutions in which we participate.

White scholars have the convenience to not experience racism, yet we have an ethical duty to engage it. In addition to studying rhetorics of BIPOC, women, trans-identifying people, and other marginalized groups, it is time white people study the darkest corner of how we gain from inequitable power dynamics. Due to this research, I can no longer epistemologically or ethically avoid the call for anti-racist scholarship our field needs. Taking an anti-racist stance can aid white scholars in becoming more critically reflexive of our work because it challenges us to see how our institutions are invested in white men's privilege and success. Anti-racist work has to go beyond citation politics where we provide an author or two of color within our courses or our literature reviews. It requires us to reflect on how our everyday communities and practices perpetuate whiteness, as is done by a scholars like Karen Teel, who interrogates the white privilege within the Catholic Church, in her decision for her kindergartener, and through her university tenure process.[38] Yet, lest we become mired in the unproductive feeling of white guilt,[39] by interrogating our privilege white people must recognize not only racist fallibility but also the potential for intellectual and community accountability and agency. Our fields' and institutions' use of ideographs of <diversity>, <freedom of speech>, and even <culture> function as color-blind rhetoric to sidestep accountability for historic discrimination and systemic oppression, while preserving white privilege.

The research I present will hopefully provide other scholars an in-depth understanding of how activist online work can influence political agendas and rhetoric. Not agreeing with the content of the work offers me a healthy reflexivity about how people engage in racism and the addition of critical race theory reinstates my ethical foundation. It would be too convenient to use a white privilege filter to argue to the "objectivity" of my study, a rhetorically constructed stance that shows in early drafts of this book. The words and digital constructions I study are written by and part of someone, reminding me that critical reflection helps us challenge how we've been coded. I am also grateful to those critical scholars (BIPOC) who continue to patiently engage my work. As white people engage racism, we need to connect with critical scholars (BIPOC) to ensure that shared values do not placate us: ideologies or classifications in the form of our privilege filters and fears of contained agency.

In addition to contained agency, without recognizing how a white privilege filter functions, we struggle to understand how racism and sexism fuel one another. In the same Reuters/Ipsos/UVA Center for Politics Race poll I note above, about 70 percent of respondents strongly agree that people of different races should be "free to live wherever they choose" and 89 percent agree that all races should be treated equally with "political correctness."[40] These responses of desiring to "live wherever they choose" mirror claims made by alt-right women (see chapter 5). A white privilege filter is clear when assessing the value of white privilege location as well as <free speech> as a color-blind lens. Yet, as I note in the introduction, due to the tie between sexism and racism, people at the intersection of race and sex are at the heart of the fight against nationalism.[41] As seen with the maiden shields of Trump's political campaign and administration, white feminism lends itself to ignoring and invalidating other groups of people who are fighting against oppression. Trump and his administration seize a movement where white women could forward a white privilege filter, allowing white nationalism to flourish. Intersectionality, as a foundational analytic lens when studying white supremacy, changes the way we approach theorizing about the impact of white nationalism in order to disrupt a white privilege filter and move us toward building a more equitable democracy.

By focusing on the value of safety and security of [white] American people, white nationalist women, white conservative women, and Trump retain a white privilege filter, which excludes some of the most vulnerable people: people of immigrant status. When considering racial categorization as well as institutional bias built into disciplinary processes in US communities, it is no surprise that white nationalists flourish through white identity politics. What is disheartening is how easily white people continue to accept and apologetically defend white privilege and supremacy. Values like "American exceptionalism"[42] perpetuate entitlement and white privilege, and, through the presidency of Donald Trump, illustrate how power naturalizes realities, identities, and ideologies. By establishing disciplinary mechanisms, such as immigration policy enforcement using concentration camps, dismantling of racial and gender equity programs, and attacks on protections for transgender rights, the Trump administration seeks to retain white supremacy and social control. In the face of such atrocities, white privilege filters become means to interpret the shadows in Plato's cave or simulations of reality[43] and calcify further white supremacy as the chief architecture that influences the processes of our institutions.

By perpetuating blanket identity fears about people of Mexican descent or people migrating who are perceived to be engaging in criminal or dangerous behavior, white nationalist women and Trump create a justification for the abuse of people of immigrant status, such as separating children from their parents and placing people in detention centers without proper medical support. Raising hypothetical fears in [white] Americans that they have something to lose when the United States admits people encourages and justifies a similar narcissism and self-centeredness in the American people when it comes to immigration. Only 17 percent of people of immigrant status had a prior violent felony conviction before coming to the United States and only

3.8 percent of those being detained in the US were due to violent action in 2010.[44] Although many Americans have never experienced any violence at the hands of people of immigrant status and longitudinal studies find that undocumented immigration does not increase violent crime[45] (accounting for less than 2 percent of crimes committed by people of undocumented status in 2018), amplifying hypothetical fears allows white Americans to retain a white privilege filter. The reduction of "immigrants" to a monolithic group creates a sense of an identifiable difference or Other. In general, violent crime continues to decrease in the United States, yet the perception is fostered that crime is on the rise,[46] allowing fear-based rhetoric about a "violent" Other (read: nonwhite) to feel justified.

In addition to how white nationalists, alt-right members, and politicians prioritize white people using US values by employing a white privilege filter, they also preserve their power through an ideographic apologia. Dr. Rita Whillock argues that, although "[w]e cannot detect the intent of a rhetor unless he or she provides that information to us,"[47] we can further shape our understanding of "racism" through its impact. Specifically, when considering <diversity> or <multicultural> programs, white nationalists argue that they are racially discriminated against. <Diversity> and <culture> continue to be problematic terminology because of their use of color-blind difference.[48] As seen with white nationalist and alt-right rhetoric, <diversity> is transformed through arguments about separatism. Further analysis of how policy actions detrimentally impact BIPOC over white people illustrates an inability to listen and equitably respond to BIPOC's experience of discrimination. A consideration of contextual power, or recognition of cultural, economic, media, social, and institutional dominance can help unmask the white privilege filter a color-blind identity politics of <diversity> or <culture> reinforces. We need to rename and revise our programs to address issues of difference and equity.

In addition to Trump's and other Republicans' apologia, scholars need to analyze the use of <freedom of speech> in the university setting through the lens of a white privilege filter. Publicly funded institutions must uphold the freedom of speech established by US law unless the expression disrupts learning, incites violence, or is an expression of fighting words. As the SPLC notes, students and administrators cannot stop a speaker because they "dislike" their ideas.[49] However, we need to investigate uses of power and control within the classroom that incite violence or use fighting words to silence others, not by making someone uncomfortable but by dehumanizing people, which disrupts the learning process and infringes on another person's free-dom of expression. Protesting against the dehumanization of a group of people seems ethically different to a community from protesting a group whose purpose is dehumanizing people. Continued legislative efforts to *not* condemn neo-Nazi and white nationalist organizations[50] and teachers in schools infusing their curriculum with white supremacist views[51] present us with a future where these organizations will continue to flourish. Only by clarifying how social identity versus institutional discrimination politics are different do we move toward an anti-racist stance.

Until we recognize the validity and power of white women's rhetorical abilities, we will hinder societal recognition of white women as having a viable voice and as citizens of democracy. More research needs to build on how women's unique rhetorical forms can lead to preserving white privilege filters or collective and collaborative opening of dialectical conversation concerning social change with difference. Scholars have an opportunity to engage in "courageous" rather than safe dialogue through our scholastic endeavors, to embody the change we hope to achieve. We need to critically contemplate what it means to label someone as "different." We have to engage how digital systems are built to uphold certain already-privileged groups of people and sustain a "different" status for other groups of people. Through their text *A Revolution in Tropes*, Sutton and Mifsud sow historic rhetorical seeds for this conversation, but more cooperative, collaborative, and coali-tional scholarship needs to be done.

The values and ideologies that constrain possibilities of engaging systemic racism also offer a system of classification to empower already privileged white women. By using classifications of motherhood and individual empow-erment, white nationalists, alt-right members, and conservative white women illustrate that a rebirth of white identity politics secures their individual power and helps them regain control over the US racial narrative. Through a defensive white reaction, white women can subsume voices of BIPOC. Although most movement activists may view power held by the established system negatively, Foucault argues that a negative impression of power must be reconceptualized to address the capabilities of power to create rather than to disable. He explains, "[w]e must cease once and for all to describe power in negative terms: it 'excludes,' it 'represses,' it 'censors,' it 'abstracts,' it 'conceals.' In fact, power produces; it produces reality; it produces domains of objects and rituals of truth. The individual and the knowledge that may be gained of him belong to this production."[52] Power is a medium that determines and allows individuals and their knowledge to exist. The ability to create and naturalize categorizations of people and systems of behavior—who is "exceptional" or "worthy" and who is not, based on a white administration's criteria for "merit"—is a potential mechanism of a color-blind ideology and manifests as an embodiment, and institutionalization, of white power.

Using classifications based in a white privilege filter, the Trump administration continues to forward policies such as those based on "merit." However, by critically interrogating and challenging whose classifications "merit" implies by addressing who is appointed and fighting for how people are appointed, we can alter problematic systems. Appointment of women or BIPOC does not change the structure oppression of our systems. Instead, appointments simulate agency through a token, contained agency and offer means to relativize oppression. In the case of racism, these policies use color-blind ideologies to return us to the Jim Crow era. By studying white people's racism, white people can begin the journey to unmask white privilege to learn to recognize how white privilege filters become contained agency of personal and institutional responses. White women can perpetuate a contained agency where we expect ourselves and other women to be the perfect caretakers and scapegoats, which will continue to undermine our validity and agency. Through that contained agency of a white privilege filter, we reinforce the oppression of others. Yet, conservative people are not the only ones who need to critically contemplate their agenda.[53] As seen from the narratives that begin each chapter as well as research on Democratic policy and campaign strategies,[54] we need to understand how white women who identify as liberal or progressive also preserve their power to retain white supremacy.

Our scholarship must move to engage intersectional analysis, where multiple identities complicate and enrich the depth of our understanding of oppression. We must subsume our critical lens so that we expect antiracist work—not *just* when chosen. Understanding racially focused social structures may provide agency to recognize experiences of hardship and discrimination and challenge dominant ideologies that perpetuate racism. According to Freire, social change within a particular culture lies on the shoulders of oppressed people, and the oppressed must continue to strive for their freedom because "[o]nly power that springs from the weakness of the oppressed will be sufficiently strong to free both."[55] However, where is the accountability for white people and the sanitized history they perpetuate to preserve their privilege? People must continue to challenge themselves to reflect on their position and societal processes to shape a larger entity than both the oppressed and the oppressor: the community.

Intersectional feminist engagement moves us not to settle for individual empowerment. Instead, we recognize the tie between oppressions and challenge ourselves, our communities, and our politicians to reach further to ensure the civil liberties of everyone in our community, lest we become complacent in our whiteness and accomplices in the oppression of others. As Audre Lorde eloquently put it, "I am not free while any woman is unfree, even when her shackles are very different from my own. And I am not free as long as one person of Color remains chained. Nor is any one of you."[56] However, inclusion also requires patience, questioning, humility,[57] and compassion from those we see as different as well as a desire to recognize and end discrimination to achieve our collective desire for a common good.

Conclusion

The National Communication Association conference sessions in Utah during the fall of 2018 felt qualitatively different form previous NCAs. I started with a panel in intercultural studies about intersectionality where scholars (BIPOC) offered insightful critiques on the reduction of intersectionality to identity offered by Rachel Griffin by white scholars.[58] I focused on listening and taking extensive notes to critically reflect on and revise my work. I felt fortunate for the intellectual and emotional labor offered by these scholars to help develop a necessary depth in scholarship, even if it meant that I was compelled to sit in my discomfort (I did not want to ask a question for fear of placing my academic labor on the shoulders of scholars (BIPOC)). Later in the day I attended a "#rhetoricsowhite" panel, which was composed of not only scholars and administrators of color but also the current and past white journal editors of the *Quarterly Journal of Speech*. For the first time at an NCA panel, I saw generative, tension-sustaining dialogue concerning how and why rhetoric excludes scholars (BIPOC). I was surprised to hear an experienced white scholar rely on stock color-blind merit rationalizations as to why such a massive discrepancy exists. Silence followed his comment and the conversation turned to scholars (BIPOC) who provided narrative accounts of the bias they experience. The history of the white editors of major journals as carrying the historic credibility in the room shifted as scholars like Dr. Bernadette Calafell spoke of the bias of textuality and performativity within public address, Dr. Fernando Delgado called for an editorial intervention when it comes to training reviewers, and Dr. Eric Watts asked editors to become deliberate "curators" of knowledge.[59] Scholars made calls to "curate" academic institutions, not only through hashtagging to reclassify interpretation and vocalizing examples of how that coding occurred, but also by offering agency when it comes to breaking the coded-racist form of review. Instead of responding directly to the white scholar's claim, Calafell, Delgato, and Watts, and other panelists and audience members sustained dialectical tension with the critical scholars (BIPOC) to help unmask the impact of racism in the field. By calling to, amplifying, and continuing critical conversations on political and structural oppression within larger NCA panels and forums, scholars curate an opportunity not to lay the burden of racism on BIPOC's shoulders. These panels offered hope of a dialectical future of sustained conflict necessary for the communication studies discipline to engage the white privilege it affords. My hope was solidified as multiple organizations and divisions spoke out and took actions in response to a similar merit-versus-diversity claim many asserted by NCA's "Distinguished Scholars" to NCA's Executive Committee during the spring of 2019. However, I would be remiss not to see the coded racism as consistent with white nationalist, alt-right, and conservative white women. Even those deemed "smart" through traditional credentials like degrees and other accolades can ignore the disproportionate impact certain procedures have on different groups of people. As Ta-Nehisi Coates notes, even "good" and "moral" white people can engage in racist behaviors because it is ingrained in our history, democratic systems, institutions, and language.[60] Rather than forgiving or ignoring those who make racist comments and commitments, questioning the process of rationalizing and mechanisms of disciplining people into gendered and racial power differentials may help us ensure a more equitable democracy.

Following the 2018 NCA panels, I found not only purpose for my scholarship, but also a need for changing the ways in which we mentor our students. Without critical race theory, our interventions will fall short. As D'Arcangelis notes that Sara Ahmed's "double turn" is necessary as a critique of whiteness studies, critical race theory can serve as a necessary historicization of racism to help radicalize reflexivity.[61] I found myself insisting on CRT within any article on racism I reviewed. People can be receptive to change, but without attention to critical race theory, racism and prejudice are just recoded through different classifications and justifications. Racism will not just "die out" with older generations; it is recoded in more savvy ways as our intellectual peers protect their privilege. Scholars (BIPOC) have been making intellectual moves to curate rather than code our academic environments—to focus on what we hope to foster rather than control and mechanize the process as to how they will work. Change is a mutual duty for members of society to take steps together to rebuild social structures on multiple levels. Through this research endeavor, I challenge myself to recognize the privilege that comes with my white skin growing up in a culture that perpetuates a color-blind ideology and how I must continually be vigilant in recognizing and challenging the privilege I experience on a daily basis to ensure I do not fall prey to assumptions of whiteness and, when I do, challenge myself to humbly recode. By breaking the code of whiteness, we afford a metamorphosis of our classification systems that reify white privilege and reclassify inclusive systems to influence an *Isegorias* that preserves equitable civic discourse. Until that transfiguration includes "chang[ing] the narrative" of race in the United States[62] where white people are not held to engage in shared labor of historical responsibility, future generations will continue to be hamstrung in our fight against oppression. As Donna Haraway notes, "[l]iberation rests on the construction of consciousness";[63] as we move into this next generation, rhetorics must embody an intersectional consciousness.

As scholars we need to curate our organizations based in a praxis of our research. We are living in a generation where we feel we have lost a sense of common ground as an American people. We are struggling culturally. We are struggling economically. We are struggling collectively. We are struggling personally. However, hope can be found in places of learning more about each other to understand the implications of our rhetorics. We must understand our values and the constraints that come with the value priorities we embody. We must understand the ideologies we forward when we choose particular terminology—not that we can legislate language, but we must understand how ideological apologia can perpetuate color-blind politics. Considering how our values and ideologies frame our commitments, classifications solidify those commitments by categorizing our identities in ways that exclude people based on what descriptors go unsaid. The classifications we use can be sources for common ground, if we ensure more inclusive and intersectional boundaries, like choosing to recognize racism and sexism as mental health crises. These analyses leave us with many questions: What values, ideologies, and classifications function as forms of apologia against anti-racist rhetorics? How do we choose and use our values, ideologies, and classifications in ways that illustrate an intersectional engagement? How can white women find their voice in politics without sacrificing or becoming wardens to people from oppressed groups? How do we recognize a vernacular of liberal white supremacy? How will we find common ground to move revolutionary political engagement in the United States when continuing opportunities for token success perpetuate a system of enforcing inequality? How will people's conversion narratives illustrate levels of contained engagement of oppression? How do we challenge our seemingly ideologically aligned "liberal" communities to share in a collective need to engage oppression? What responsibilities do we have in fighting color-blind classifications in our digital communities, which perpetuate oppression? This study provides groundwork for further research of color-blind rhetorics, intersectional rhetorics of feminism, and contained agencies of the "oppression Olympics" within the digital and political arenas. Only through continuing work can we work to dismantle the oppressive rhetorics within our cultural agoras.

To embody the democracy we so cherish, we have to rethink who counts as having a voice, whom we expect to do the labor and how that labor counts, and who "we" are when we talk about "we the people." All these women in this book deserve a voice—yet, so do all the people they, our institutions, agencies, and organizations silence through their expression and regulations and processes. Without working not to integrate but to cooperate with the "differences" people embody, we will continue to hamstring our collective development into the "more perfect union" we pride ourselves to be. We cannot stop the revolution, but we can choose to redefine, revise, reclassify, and reconfigure the "we" we envision ourselves to be by engaging in anti-racist ways not only by engaging racism but choosing to listen and amplify voices who experience the situational contingency of its implications.

As I reflect upon my opening example, I find myself frustrated by my own inability to just talk to this close family member when facing racism. I am sad that my fears of saying the wrong thing or potential tension or even silence from my relative might prevent me from always challenging the racism my spouse and I both witnessed. Yet, through a community of support, I said something and I have figured out ways to prepare to respond to racism. I have found my voice; and every time I have faced racism since, I (as well as my spouse and that relative) have more easily found our voices. We continue to prepare ourselves for the tension, to even sustain the tension, to challenge the complacency that comes with being white. Through an anti-racist responsiveness and responsibility, white people become accountable and place a boundary on what is ethically valued, ideologically envisioned, and meaningfully classified when it comes to preserving voice, community, and democracy. Only by confronting white fears do we know with what we are shadow boxing versus what is worth fighting for and for whom.

Appendix
Values

Rokeach, Steele and Redding, and Stewart and Cash acknowledged five core values with corresponding sub-values that persuaders target in US audiences.

Survival	Social	Success	Independence	Progress
preservation of health	generosity and considerateness	ambition	power and authority	education and knowledge
safety and security	patriotism	competition	freedom from authority	change and advancement
peace and tranquility	affection and popularity	happiness	freedom from restraint	efficiency and practicality
personal attractiveness	sociality and belonging	pride and prestige	equity and value of the individual	quantification
	conformity and imitation	material comfort and convenience	equality of opportunity	science and secular rationality
	cleanliness	accumulation and ownership		
		sense of accomplishment		

Notes

Introduction

1. The term "identity politics" was first used by the Combahee River Collective to describe focusing on one's own oppression. However, Tea Party and alt-right (identitarian movement) members have appropriated this term to construct their victim identity based on "outsider" or "alternative" (see chapters 4 and 5) status.

2. Brian L. Ott and Greg Dickinson, *The Twitter Presidency: Donald J. Trump and the Politics of White Rage* (New York: Routledge, 2019), 31–41.

3. Josiah Ryan, "'This Was a Whitelash': Van Jones' Take on the Election Results" (CNN Politics, November 9, 2016). http://www.cnn.com/2016/11/09/politics/van-jones-results-dis appointment-cnntv/. Accessed December 15, 2016.

4. Amanda Taub, "Behind 2016's Turmoil, a Crisis of White Identity," *New York Times*, November 1, 2016. http://www.nytimes.com/2016/11/02/world/americas/brexit-donald-trump -whites.html. Accessed December 15, 2016.

5. Gene Demby, "It's Gotten a Lot Harder to Act Like Whiteness Doesn't Shape Our Politics," *All Things Considered*, NPR, May 13, 2016. http://www.npr.org/sections/codeswitch /2016/05/13/477803909/its-gotten-a-lot-harder-to-act-like-whiteness-doesnt-shape-our -politics. Accessed December 15, 2016; Wilson Dizard, "Fear and Whiteness on the Campaign Trail," Mondoweiss, July 25, 2016. http://mondoweiss.net/2016/07/whiteness-campaign-trail/. Accessed December 15, 2016; Hua Hsu, "White Plight? In Working-class America, an Elite-resenting Identity Politics Has Emerged in Which Whiteness Spells Dispossession," *New Yorker*, July 25, 2016. http://www.newyorker.com/magazine/2016/07/25/the-new-meaning -of-whiteness; Kathryn Moeller, "Whiteness in an Era of Trump: Where Do We Go from Here?" Huffington Post, March 8, 2016. http://www.huffingtonpost.com/kathryn-moeller /whiteness-in-an-era-of-tr_b_9404240.html. Accessed December 15, 2016; Eric. D. Knowles and Linda R. Tropp, "A lot of People in the US Are Suddenly Identifying as 'White'—and a Lot of Them Support Donald Trump," Quartz, October 25, 2016. http://qz.com/816229/a-lot -of-people-in-the-us-are-suddenly-identifying-as-white/. Accessed December 15, 2016.

6. Eli Saslow, "The White Flight of Derek Black," *Washington Post*, October 15, 2016. https://www.washingtonpost.com/national/the-white-flight-of-derek-black/2016/10/15/ed5f906a-8f3b-11e6-a6a3-d50061aa9fae_story.html?utm_term=.3cd769cacfc7.

7. Similar to Burke's critique about surface analyses of Hitler's *Mein Kampf*, I use the term "genius" similar to how Burke defines it as the "essence" or personification of a quality. Kenneth Burke, "The Rhetoric of Hitler's 'Battle,'" in Kenneth Burke, ed., *The Philosophy of Literary Form* (Berkeley: University of California Press, 1941), 165.

8. Reni Eddo-Lodge, *Why I'm No Longer Talking to White People about Race* (London: Bloomsbury Circus, 201), 63–64.

9. Eddo-Lodge, 65.

10. Eduardo Bonilla-Silva, "The Linguistics of Color Blind Racism: How to Talk Nasty about Blacks without Sounding 'Racist,'" *Critical Sociology* 28 (1–2) (2002): 9.

11. Charles A. Wilkinson, "A Rhetorical Definition of Movements," *Central States Speech Journal* 27 (1976): 91.

12. Charles J. Stewart, Craig A. Smith, and Robert E. Denton Jr., *Persuasion and Social Movements*, 6th ed. (Prospect Heights, IL: Waveland Press, 2012), 63.

13. Michael Calvin McGee, "The 'Ideograph': A Link between Rhetoric and Ideology," *Quarterly Journal of Speech* 66 (1980): 6.

14. Edwin Black, "Secrecy and Disclosure as Rhetorical Forms," *Quarterly Journal of Speech* 74 (1988): 133.

15. Eduardo Bonilla-Silva, *Racism without Racists: Color-blind Racism and the Persistence of Racial Inequality in America* (New York: Rowman & Littlefield, 2014), 5.

16. According to the ACLU, "14 Words" is a reference to the most popular white suprema-cist slogan in the world: "We must secure the existence of our people and a future for white children." Eric Dolan, "'Please delete your account': Sarah Palin Slammed for Using 'Neo-Nazi' Slogan to Praise Trump," Raw Story, July 7, 2017.

17. Franz Fanon, *Black Skin, White Masks* (London: Pluto Press, 2008), 25.

18. George Yancy, *Look, a White! Philosophical Essays on Whiteness* (Philadelphia: Temple University Press, 2012), 24–25.

19. Lloyd Bitzer, "The Rhetorical Situation," *Philosophy & Rhetoric* 1(1) (1968): 1.

20. Jennifer Edbauer, "Unframing Models of Public Distribution: From Rhetorical Situation to Rhetorical Ecologies," *Rhetoric Society Quarterly* 35(4) (2005): 4.

21. Franchesca Ramsey, "The Surprisingly Racist History of 'Caucasian.'" MTV News. April 15, 2016.

22. Lee Bebout, "Onward into the Discomfort: Teaching for Racial Justice in an Era of Media Outrage, the Alt-right, and the Neoliberal University," in Philathia Bolton et al., eds., *Teaching with Tension: Race, Resistance, and Reality in the Classroom* (Evanston, IL: Northwestern University Press, 2019), 166.

23. Charles W. Mills, *The Racial Contract* (Ithaca, NY: Cornell University Press, 1997), 127. Italics in original.

24. bell hooks, "The Other: Desire and Resistance," in *Black Looks: Race and Representation* (Boston: South End Press, 1992), 21–39.

25. Ruth Frankenberg, *White Women, Race Matters: The Social Construction of Whiteness* (Minneapolis: University of Minnesota Press, 1993), 17. Italics in original.

26. Yancy, *Look, a White!*, 20.

27. Kenneth Burke, *Language as Symbolic Action* (Berkeley: University of California Press, 1966), 22.

28. Thomas K. Nakayama and Robert L. Krizek, "Whiteness as a Strategic Rhetoric," *Quarterly Journal of Speech* 81 (1995): 293.

29. Alexis Shotwell, *Against Purity: Living Ethically in Compromised Times* (Minneapolis: University of Minnesota Press, 2016), 25–26, 55.

30. Mills, *The Racial Contract*, 3.

31. W. E. B. Du Bois, *Black Reconstruction: An Essay toward a History of the Past which Black Folk Played in an Attempt to Reconstruct Democracy in America* (Harcourt, Brace, 1934), 700.

32. Fanon, 131.

33. Kenneth Burke, ed., *The Philosophy of Literary Form* (Berkeley: University of California Press, 1941), 9.

34. In this reference, the "Other" may be compared to McGee's notion of "the people," an amorphous construct used to extend beyond individual audience to a group to legitimize a collective identity.

35. Kimberlé Crenshaw, "Race, Reform, and Retrenchment: Transformation and Legitimation in Antidiscrimination Law." In Crenshaw et al., eds., *Critical Race Theory: The Key Writings That Formed the Movement* (New York: New Press, 1995), 112.

36. I use "nonwhite" in this case because categorizing people together in one racial group problematically reduces people who racially identify differently into one category opposite to "white" (Crenshaw, "Race, Reform, and Retrenchment," 113). This limited categorization also does not account for the unique experiences of racism experienced by people who identify as different socially constructed race categories (Black, African American, Latinx, Mexican, Hmong, Korean, Chinese, Indian, etc.).

37. Teresa J. Guess, "The Social Construction of Whiteness: Racism by Intent, Racism by Consequence," *Critical Sociology* 32(4) (2006): 654.

38. Patricia Hill Collins, *Black Feminist Thought: Knowledge, Empowerment and Consciousness* (New York: Routledge, 2000), 4.

39. W. O. Brown, "The Nature of Race Consciousness." *Social Forces* 10(1) (1931): 94.

40. Don, "OK Symbol," Part of a series on Emoji, Know Your Meme, March 4, 2019. https://knowyourmeme.com/memes/ok-symbol-%F0%9F%91%8C.

41. Taylor Telford and Eli Rosenberg, "A Coast Guard Officer on Florence Duty Made a Hand Gesture on TV. Some Saw a White-power Sign," *Washington Post*, September 14, 2018. https://www.washingtonpost.com/nation/2018/09/15/coast-guard-officer-ousted-florence -duty-after-viewers-claim-he-made-white-power-sign-tv/?arc404=true

42. Stuart Hall, "The Whites of Their Eyes," in G. Dines and J. M. Humez, eds., *Gender, Race and Class: A Media Reader* (Thousand Oaks, CA: Sage, 1995), 20.

43. Hall, 20.

44. Eduardo Bonilla-Silva, "The Linguistics of Color Blind Racism: How to Talk Nasty about Blacks without Sounding 'Racist,'" *Critical Sociology* 28(1–2) (2002): 41.

45. Sara Ahmed, "Declarations of Whiteness: The Non-performativity of Anti-racism," *Borderlands* 3(2) (2004). http://www.borderlands.net.au/vol3no2_2004/ahmed_declarations.htm.

46. Eddo, 86–87.

47. Lisa Nakamura, *Cybertypes: Race, Ethnicity, and Identity on the Internet* (New York: Routledge, 2002), 78.

48. Lisa A. Flores, "Between Abundance and Marginalization: The Imperative of Racial Rhetorical Criticism," *Review of Communication* 16.1 (2016): 4.

49. Flores, 5.

50. Sally Kitch, *The Specter of Sex: Gendered Foundations of Racial Formation in the United States* (Albany: State University of New York Press, 2009), 21–23.

51. Kitch, 18.

52. Catarina Kinnvall, "Globalization and Religious Nationalism: Self, Identity, and the Search for Ontological Security," *Political Psychology* 25(5) (2004): 762; Kitch, 4.

53. Marshall McLuhan, *The Medium Is the Massage: An Inventory of Effects* (Corte Madera, CA: Gingko Press, 1967), 8, 31.

54. Nicholas Negroponte, "Negroponte: Internet Is Way to World Peace," CNN Interactive, November 25, 1997. http://www.cnn.com/TECH/9711/25/internet.peace.reut/.

55. Lisa Gitelman, *Always Already New: Media, History, and the Data of Culture* (Cambridge, MA: MIT Press, 2006), 84.

56. Hall, 20.

57. Safiya U. Noble, *Algorithms of Oppression: How Search Engines Reinforce Racism* (New York: New York University Press, 2018).

58. Lawrence Lessig, *Code and Other Laws of Cyberspace* (New York: Basic Books, 2000).

59. Alexander R. Galloway, *Protocol: How Control Exists after Decentralization* (Cambridge, MA: MIT Press, 2004), xii; Thomas Rickert, "Tarrying with the <head>: The emergence of control through protocol," In Bradley Dilger and Jeff Rice, eds., *From A to A: Keywords of Markup* (Minneapolis: University of Minnesota Press, 2010), 2.

60. Noble, *Algorithms of Oppression*, 82.

61. David Roberts, "Donald Trump and the Rise of Tribal Epistemology," Vox, May 19, 2017.

62. "Blue Feed Red Feed," *Wall Street Journal.* http://graphics.wsj.com/blue-feed-red-feed/. Accessed May 20, 2017.

63. Lisa Nakamura, "Watching White Supremacy on Digital Video Platforms: 'Screw Your Optics, I'm Going In.'" *Film Quarterly* 72(3) (Spring 2019): 19. doi:10.1525/fq.2019.72.3.19.

64. Nancy Fraser, "Rethinking the Public Sphere: A Contribution to the Critique of Actually Existing Democracy," *Social Text* 25/26 (1990): 63.

65. By rhetorics I mean not only traditional "content" such as language and symbols (values, ideologies, classifications); I also seek to reassert critical contemplation of the digital forms of rhetoric, in which the medium makes an argument by the way its users engage in dissemination of information and interact with other users/audiences.

66. Alt-right as an identity label is a structural byproduct of racism. I have chosen not to put the term in quotes because using quotations undermines the historical development of the term and assigns an ephemerality of the group rather than recognizing the historic reiteration of racism; it also undermines the value, ideological, and classificatory proximity to the conservative right, which is at the crux of my argument. Other classifications, like "alt-lite" (see Hayden, "Alt-right Women Asked to 'Choose Submission' to Grow Political Movement"), have been used to define the white women seeking a whites-only culture, but, due to the similar ways these groups facilitate white supremacy and contain the agency of women, I refer to them as alt-right rather than "alt-right."

67. Zeus Leonardo, "The Color of Supremacy: Beyond the Discourse of 'White Privilege,'" *Educational Philosophy and Theory* 36(2) (2004): 37.

68. Robin DiAngelo, "White Fragility," *International Journal of Critical Pedagogy* 3(3) (2011): 54–70.

69. Judith Butler, "Performativity, Precarity, and Sexual Politics." *Revista de Antropología Iberoamericana* 4(3) (2009): i.

70. By critical race theory I mean the tradition forged by critical BIPOC scholars to recognize how the power of institutional racism is established and continued through the procedures of our legal and organizational institutions to detail the roots of white supremacy and embody social justice as detailed in Rachel A. Griffin, "Critical Race Theory as a Means to Deconstruct, Recover and Evolve in Communication Studies," *Communication Law Review* 10(1) (2018): 2; Richard Delgado and Jean Stefancic, Introduction, in Richard Delgado and Jean Stefancic, eds., *Critical Race Theory: An Introduction* (New York: New York University Press, 2001), 11.

71. "Fighting Words." Cornell University Law School. N.d. https://www.law.cornell.edu /wex/fighting_words. Accessed February 13, 2017.

72. Kimberlé Crenshaw, Neil Gotanda, Gary Peller, and Charle Inglis, Introduction, in Kimberlé Crenshaw, Neil Gotanda, Gary Peller, and Charle Inglis, eds., *Critical Race Theory: The Key Writings That Formed the Movement* (New York: New Press, 1995), xix.

73. Donna Haraway, "Situated Knowledges: The Science Question in Feminism and the Privilege of a Partial Perspective," *Feminist Studies* 14(3) (Autumn 1988): 595–96; Sandra Harding, *Whose Science? Whose Knowledge? Thinking from Women's Lives* (Ithaca, NY: Cornell University Press, 1991), 138; Patricia Hill Collins, *Black Feminist Thought: Knowledge, Consciousness, and the Politics of Empowerment* (New York: Routledge, 1990), 11–12.

74. Rachel Dolezal was a woman whose parents both identified themselves and her as white, who identified herself as "black" as she progressed in her career at Eastern Washington Universities as she taught courses related to African American culture. See Lisa R. France, "Rachel Dolezal on Being Black: 'I Didn't Deceive Anybody,'" CNN, July 20, 2015. http://www.cnn.com/2015/07/20/us/rachel-dolezal-vanity-fair-feat/. Accessed May 22, 2017.

75. Laura Brownson, *The Rachel Divide* (Netflix, 2018); Ijeoma Oluo, "The Heart of Whiteness: Ijeoma Oluo Interviews Rachel Dolezal, the White Woman Who Identifies as Black," *The Stranger*, April 19, 2017. https://www.thestranger.com/features/2017/04/19/25082450/the-heart-of-whiteness-ijeoma-oluo-interviews-rachel-dolezal -the-white-woman-who-identifies-as-black.

76. bell hooks, "Eating the Other: Desire and Resistance," in *Black Looks: Race and Representation* (Boston: South End Press, 1992).

77. Krista Radcliffe, *Rhetorical Listening: Identification, Gender, Whiteness* (Carbondale: Southern Illinois University Press, 2005), 7, 76–77.

78. Radcliffe argues that the significance of listening metonymically to the commonalities as well as the differences between others is as a means to limit racial and gendered reductions and stereotypes (76, 78–88).

79. Lisa Corrigan, "On Rhetorical Criticism, Performativity, and White Fragility," *Review of Communication* 16(1) (2016): 87, 88. doi:10.1080/15358593.2016.1183886.

80. Jona Olsson, "Detour-spotting for White Anti-racists," Cultural Bridges to Justice, updated January 2011. http://www.culturalbridgestojustice.org/resources/written/detour. Accessed February 12, 2018.

81. One challenge I faced when conducting this research and writing this book is that I wanted to keep my feminist ideology intact as I critiqued women's rhetoric. The clear voices of these white women demonstrated individual empowerment, which is culturally significant. However, I would be remiss not to note how these white women's voices served white, affluent men's interests, which may be a mitigating factor as to why we hear them so clearly. I hope that my research gives credence to the importance of their voices, yet offers critique of the ideological purpose and outcomes of their rhetoric.

82. Hall, 20, italics in original.

83. Kimberlé Crenshaw, "Mapping the Margins: Intersectionality, Identity Politics, and Violence against Women of Color," *Stanford Law Review* 43 (1991): 1241–99. http://social difference.columbia.edu/files/socialdiff/projects/Article__Mapping_the_Margins_by _Kimblere_Crenshaw.pdf. Accessed December 15, 2016.

84. Audre Lorde, "The Master's Tools Will Never Dismantle the Master's House," In *Sister Outsider: Essays and Speeches* (Berkeley, CA: Crossing Press, 2007), 110–14. Found on Collectiveliberation.org. http://collectiveliberation.org/wp-content/uploads/2013/01/Lorde _The_Masters_Tools.pdf. Accessed January 2, 2016.

85. Ange-Marie Hancock, *Intersectionality: An Intellectual History* (Oxford: Oxford University Press, 2016), 60; Bonnie Thornton Dill, "Race, Class, and Gender: Prospects for an All-Inclusive Sisterhood," *Feminist Studies* 9(1) (Spring 1983): 148. https://www.jstor.org /stable/3177687.

86. Crenshaw et al., xxxi.

87. In hopes that I do not use intersectionality as a means to "'lift up' non-intersectional scholarship" (Hancock, *Intersectionality*, 2), I see my use of "intersectionality" as a way to meaningfully challenge problematic reductions of white nationalists' use of "diversity" and conservative use of [white] "feminism." I ground "contained agency" in Black feminist thought and women's studies work through meaningful conversation with authors like Lorde, Crenshaw, Collins, and Hancock to ensure I honor the intellectual roots of this discussion as well as add to how an academic discipline, like communication studies, contributes to the discussion.

88. I first developed the concept of contained agency with a graduate school colleague, Juliette Ludeker, within a gaming context as we recognized the limits facing players when they are not part of a design team. We ended up changing the original term to "constrained agency"; however, the implications of this concept seem larger, which is why I develop them here.

89. Hancock, *Intersectionality*, 7; Devon W. Carbado, "Intersectionality: Theorizing Power, Empowering Theory," *Signs* 38(4) (2013): 811–45. https://www.jstor.org/stable/10.1086/669666.

90. Hancock, *Intersectionality*, 10.

91. Karma R. Chávez and Cindy L. Griffin, "Power, Feminisms, and Coalitional Agency: Inviting and Enacting Difficult Dialogues." *Women's Studies in Communication* 32(1) (2009): 2.

92. Cynthia S. Lin, Alisa A. Pyketta, Constance Flanagana, and Karma R. Chávez, "Engendering the Prefigurative: Feminist Praxes That Bridge a Politics of Prefiguration and Survival," *Journal of Social and Political Psychology* 4(1) (2016): 305. doi:10.5964/jspp.v4i1.537.

93. Lisa M. Corrigan, *Prison Power: How Prison Influenced the Movement for Black Liberation* (Jackson: University Press of Mississippi, 2017), 5.

94. Crenshaw, "Race, Reform, and Retrenchment," 109. Italics mine.

95. Michel Foucault, *Discipline and Punishment: The Birth of the Prison* (New York: Vintage Books, 1995).

96. Bonilla-Silva, *Racism without Racists*, 83.

97. Scott A. Hunt, Robert D. Benford, and David A. Snow, "Identity Fields: Framing Processes and the Social Construction of Movement Identities," in E. Larana, H. Johnston, and J. R. Gusfield, eds., *New Social Movements: From Ideology to Identity* (Philadelphia: Temple University Press, 1994), 186.

98. Hancock, *Intersectionality*, 60.

99. Sheryl Sandberg, *Lean In: Women, Work, and the Will to Lean.* New York: Knopf, 2013.

100. Crenshaw, et al., Introduction, xv.

101. Angela Helm, "Trump Suggests Certain Federal Financing for HBCUs May Be Unconstitutional," *The Root*, May 5, 2017.

102. Anya Kamenetz, "DeVos to Rescind Obama-Era Guidance on School Discipline," *All Things Considered*, NPR, December 18, 2018; Kate Reilly, "The Biggest Controversies in Betsy DeVos' First Year," *Time*, December 14, 2017.

103. Carrie Crenshaw, "Resisting Whiteness' Rhetorical Silence," *Western Journal of Communication* 61(3) (1997): 253; Charlotte Hogg, "Including Conservative Women's Rhetorics in an 'Ethics of Hope and Care,'" *Rhetoric Review* 34(4) (2015): 393.

104. Bonilla-Silva has noted a form of color-blindness associated with only reflecting racism (*Racism without Racists*, 140–43). By providing illustrations as to how white people can critically engage in conversations, I hope to provide further dialogue concerning dialectical engagement of racism.

105. George Yancy, *White Self-Criticality beyond Anti-racism: How Does It Feel to Be a White Problem?* (Lanham, MD: Lexington Books, 2015), xii.

106. Sharon Tettegah, Brian P. Bailey, and Kona Taylor, "Clover: Narratives and Simulations in Virtual Environments," *Journal of Negro Education* 76(1) (2007): 43.

107. In this study, I analyze ten individual and ten organizational websites, five organizational discussion pages, and five individual blogs on April 10, 2007, by and/or for women who identify themselves as "Pro-White," highlight the "white" race, or call for a focus on "nationalism" and chosen due to the high number of links from individual white nationalists and their organizations and/or based on their "authority" (credibility assigned to a particular website based on the number of incoming links from other websites) as determined by Technorati. com (approximately 1,000 pages of printed text). The number of links to a particular blog over the last six months calculates authority (http://technorati.com/what-is-technorati-authority/). See original dissertation (Wendy K. Z. Anderson, "The Context of Power and Race in Online Social Movement Rhetoric: An Analysis of White Nationalist Cyber-rhetoric by/towards Women and Girls," diss., Purdue University, 2009) for link statistics.

108. Catherine Squires *The Post-Racial Mystique: Media and Race in the Twenty-First Century* (New York: New York University Press, 2014), 190; Carol Swain, *The New White Nationalism in America* (Cambridge: Cambridge University Press, 2002), 4.

109. Michelle Alexander, *The New Jim Crow: Mass Incarceration in the Age of Color-blindness* (New York: New Press, 2012).

110. Laura Grattan, *Populism's Power: Radical Grassroots Democracy in America* (New York: Oxford University Press, 2016), 4–5.

111. In the first few chapters, I use [] to indicate an implied white identity. The roots of the identity reside in a color-blind ideology that forwards whiteness, which is clarified in chapter 2.

112. Paul R. Carr, "Whiteness and White Privilege: Problematizing Race and Racism in a 'Color-blind' World, and in Education," *International Journal of Critical Pedagogy* 7(1) (2016): 51–73.

113. Bonilla-Silva, "The Linguistics of Color Blind Racism," 41–64.

114. An ideograph is an ordinary-language term that represents a collective commitment to an abstract or vague normative goal, which "warrants the use of power, excuses behavior and belief which might otherwise be perceived as eccentric or antisocial, and guides behavior and belief into channels easily recognized by a community as acceptable and laudable." Michael Calvin McGee, "The 'Ideograph': A Link Between Rhetoric and Ideology," *Quarterly Journal of Speech* 66 (1980): 15.

115. "< >" are used throughout this book to denote ideographs.

116. Anna M. Zajicek, "Race Discourses and Antiracist Practices in a Local Women's Movement," *Gender and Society* 16(2) (2002): 156. http://www.jstor.org/stable/3081859.

117. Jo Reger, "Drawing Identity Boundaries: The Creation of Contemporary Feminism," in Jo Reger, Daniel J. Myers, and Rachel L. Einwohner, eds., *Identity Work in Social Movements* (Minneapolis: University of Minnesota Press, 2008), 116.

118. Wendy K. Z. Anderson and Kittie E. Grace, "'Taking Mama Steps' Toward Authority, Alternatives, and Advocacy," *Feminist Media Studies* 15:6 (2015): 943.

119. DiAngelo, "White Fragility," 58.

120. Vlog stands for video blog, on YouTube or an online radio station.

121. Carolyn Miller, "What Can Automation Tell Us about Agency?" *Rhetoric Society Quarterly* 37(2) (2007): 141.

122. DiAngelo, "White Fragility," 66.

123. Karma Chávez, "Doing Intersectionality: Power, Privilege, and Identities in Political Activist Communities," in Nilanjana Bardhan and Mark P. Orbe, eds., *Identity Research and Communication: Intercultural Reflections and Future Directions* (Lanham, MD: Lexington Books, 2012), 31–32.

Chapter 1: Safety for White People Only through Nationalism: Decoding Rhetorical Refinement of White Supremacist Values

An earlier version of this research was entitled "(De)coding Whiteness: Appropriations of White Nationalist Women's Inferential Racism as Coded Rhetoric in U.S. Politics" published in Meta G. Carstarphen, Kathleen E. Welch, Wendy K. Z. Anderson, Davis W. Houck, Mark L. McPhail, David A. Frank, Rachel C. Jackson, James Alexander McVey, Christopher J. Gilbert, Patricia G. Davis, and Lisa M. Corrigan, Rhetoric, Race, and Resentment: Whiteness and the New Days of Rage, *Rhetoric Review* 36(4) (2017): 263–72. doi: 0.1080/07350198.201 7.135519110.1080/07350198.2017.1355191. The material is reprinted by permission of Taylor & Francis Group, https://www.tandfonline.com/.

1. Aaron Blake, "Yes, You Can Blame the Millennials for Hillary Clinton's Loss." *Washington Post*, December 2, 2016; Matthew Green, "How Millennials Voted in the Presidential Election (with Lesson Plan)," KQED News: Politics & Elections. November 15, 2016; Ryan Kartje, "Did Millennial Apathy Propel Trump Election?" *Orange County Register*, November 12, 2016.

2. Kerry Flynn, "Nearly Half of Americans Didn't Vote—Not Even for Harambe," Mashable, November 9, 2016. http://mashable.com/2016/11/09/voting-poll-numbers/#NM lMLGNCZqqI. Accessed December 15, 2016.

3. Damon Young, "I Will Never Underestimate White People's Need to Preserve Whiteness Again," The Root, November 9, 2016. http://verysmartbrothas.com/i-will-never-underesti mate-white-peoples-need-to-preserve-whiteness-again/. Accessed December 15, 2017.

4. Samhita Mukhhopadhyay and Kate Harding, eds., *Nasty Women: Feminism, Resistance, and Revolution in Trump's America* (New York: Picador, 2017), 4–5.

5. Marcie Bianco, "White Women Voted for Trump in 2016 because They Still Believe White Men Are Their Saviors," *Quartz*, November 14, 2016. http://qz.com/835567/election-2016-white-women-voted-for-donald-trump-in-2016-because-they-still-believe-white-men}

-are-their-saviors/. Accessed December 15, 2016;Elizabeth Grattan, "The Decent White Woman Who Voted for Trump," *Medium*, November 12, 2016. https://medium.com/@ elizabethgrattan/the-decent-white-woman-who-voted-for-trump-ffcd4eedf90d#. vez65p307. Accessed December 15, 2016; Katie McDonough, "The Silent Majority: The Quiet Racism behind the White Female Trump Voter," *Fusion*, November 17, 2016. http://fusion. net/story/370440/white-women-racism-donald-trump/. Accessed December 15, 2016; Suzanne Moore, "Why Did Women Vote for Trump? Because Misogyny Is Not a Male-only Attribute," *The Guardian,* November 16, 2016; Alex Orlov, "More White Women Voted for Donald Trump than Hillary Clinton." *Mic*, November 9, 2016; Ali Tharrington, What Happened When I Took a 'White Women Elected Trump' Sign to the Women's March," Vox. January 24, 2017. http://www.vox.com/first-person/2017/1/24/14369914/donald-trump -womens-march-sign; Kate Harding, "Are Women Persons?" in Mukhhopadhyay et al., *Nasty Women*, 14.

6. CNN. "Exit polls." CNN Politics: Election 2016. November 23, 2016.http://www .cnn.com/election/results/exit-polls/national/president. Accessed December 15, 2017; Katie Rogers, "White Women Helped Elect Donald Trump," *New York Times*, November 9, 2016.

7. Jonathan Allen, "Alabama's Women Wrote the Verdict on Roy Moore," NBC News, December 13, 2017. https://www.nbcnews.com/storyline/2017-elections/alabama-s-women -wrote-verdict-roy-moore-n829186.

8. "Exit Poll Results: How Different Groups Voted in Alabama," *Washington Post*, December 13, 2017; Summer Meza, "Who Voted for Doug Jones? White Women back Roy Moore," *Newsweek*, December 13, 2017.

9. In this case, I do not specify only white people since BIPOC can internalize oppression to become powerful tools of racist code enforcement.

10. Southern Poverty Law Center, "Fringe Racists, Conspiracy Theorists Make Bids for Office," August 3, 2016.

11. Alexander, *The New Jim Crow*, 2; George Lipsitz, *The Possessive Investment in Whiteness: How White People Profit from Identity Politics*, rev. and expanded ed. Philadelphia: Temple University Press, 2006, 15; Bonilla-Silva, *Racism without Racists*, 2; Michael Brown et al., *Whitewashing Race: The Myth of a Color-blind Society* (Berkeley: University of California Press, 2005), 13–15; J. B. W. Tucker, "The Ultimate White Privilege Statistics and Data Post," 2015. http://www.jbwtucker.com/ultimate-white-privilege-statistics/; Ibram X. Kendi, *Stamped from the Beginning: The Definitive History of Racist Ideas in America* (New York: Nation Books, 2016), 1–2.

12. Swain, *The New White Nationalism*, 2.

13. In my initial research I analyzed texts initially for five sets of values (see Wendy K. Z. Anderson, "The Context of Power and Race in Online Social Movement Rhetoric: An Analysis of White Nationalist Cyber-rhetoric by/towards Women and Girls," diss., Purdue University, 2009) identified by Rokeach, Steele and Redding, and Stewart and Cash as core values (with corresponding sub-values) dominant in U.S. culture (see Appendix 1). Milton Rokeach, *Beliefs, Attitudes, and Values* (San Francisco: Jossey-Bass, 1968), 124; Edward Steele and William Redding, "The American Value System: Premises for Persuasion," *Western Speech* 26(2) (1962): 86–91; Charles Stewart and William Cash, "The Persuasive Interview: The Persuader," in Charles Stewart and William Cash, eds., *Interviewing: Principles and Practices* (269–99) (New York: McGraw-Hill 2006).

14. J. M. Berger, "Nazis vs. ISIS on Twitter: Comparative Study of White Nationalist and ISIS Online Social Media Networks," *Program on Extremism* (2016): 3–4, 10, 18. George Washington University. Web.

15. Raymie McKerrow, "Critical Rhetoric: Theory and Praxis," *Communication Monographs* 56 (1989): 100; Thomas K. Nakayama and Robert L. Krizek, "Whiteness as a Strategic Rhetoric," *Quarterly Journal of Speech* 81 (1995): 299–300.

16. I assessed Donald Trump's campaign rhetoric in 2015 and 2016 as well as rhetoric by Donald Trump that was revisited during the campaign itself (such as his interviews on *The View* many years earlier).

17. The lack of recognition of one's own bias may lead people to embody unwitting resistance, or resistance "not intended as resistance by the actor yet is recognized as threatening by targets and other observers," concerning race politics. Jocelyn Hollander and Rachel Einwohner, "Conceptualizing Resistance," *Sociological Forum* 19(4) (2004): 545.

18. Mitch Berbrier, "'Half the Battle': Cultural Resonance, Framing Processes, and Ethnic Affectations in Contemporary White Supremacist Rhetoric," *Social Problems* 45 (1998): 432. Accessed August 29, 2006. doi:10.2307/3097206; Kathleen Blee, *Women of the Klan: Racism and Gender in the 1920s* (Los Angeles: University of California Press, 1991); Denise M. Bostdorff, "The Internet Rhetoric of the Ku Klux Klan: A Case Study in Website Community Building Run Amok." *Communication Studies* 55(2) (2004): 340–61; Margaret E. Duffy, "Web of Hate: A Fantasy Theme Analysis of the Rhetorical Vision of Hate Groups Online. *Journal of Communication Inquiry* 27 (2003): 291–312. doi:10.1177/0196859903252850; Tamara V. Ford and Genève Gill, "Radical Internet Use," In J. D. H. Downing, ed., *Radical Media: Rebellious Communication and Social Movements*, 201–34 (Thousand Oaks, CA: Sage, 2001); Mary Marcel, "The Zapatistas and Cyberspace," paper presented at National Communication Association Convention, Seattle, Washington, 2000; Charles Stewart, "White Aryan Resistance on the Internet: A Rhetorical Assault on Conventional Rhetorical Wisdom," paper presented at National Communication Association convention, Seattle, Washington, 2000; Southern Poverty Law Center, "Active Hate Groups in the United States in 2015." https://www.splcenter.org/fighting-hate/intelligence-report/2016/active-hate-groups-united -states-2015; Michael Waltman, "Stratagems and Heuristics in the Recruitment of Children into Communities of Hate: The Fabric of Our Future Nightmares," *Southern Communication Journal* 69(1) (2003): 22–36.

19. Mark Potok, "The Year in Hate and Extremism," Southern Poverty Law Center, February 17, 2016. Web.

20. Todd Schroer, "Technical Advances in Communication: The Example of White Racialist 'Love Groups' and 'White Civil Rights Organizations,'" in Jo Reger et al., eds., *Identity Work in Social Movements*, 77–99 (Minneapolis: University of Minnesota Press, 2008).

21. Blee, "Women of the Klan," 3, 102; Bostdorff, 246.

22. Blee, "Women of the Klan," 3.

23. Kathleen M. Blee, *Inside Organized Racism: Women and Men in the Hate Movement* (Los Angeles: University of California Press, 2002), 130, 147.

24. Linda Kerber, "The Republican Mother: Women and the Enlightenment—An American Perspective," *American Quarterly* 28(2) (1976): 188–96.

25. Kerber, 202.

26. Rita Felski, *Beyond Feminist Aesthetics: Feminist Literature and Social Change* (Cambridge, MA: Harvard University Press, 1989), 12, 164; Sarah Jackson and Sonja

Banaszczyk, "Digital Standpoints: Debating Gendered Violence and Racial Exclusion in the Feminist Counterpublic," *Journal of Communication Inquiry* 40(4) (2016): 393.

27. Blee, "Inside Organized Racism," 9, 133.

28. Blee, "Inside Organized Racism," 116–20; Robert Futrell and Pete Simi, "Free Spaces, Collective Identity, and the Persistence of U.S. White Power Activism," *Social Problems* 51(1) (February 2004): 18. http://www.jstor.org/stable/4148758.

29. Blee, "Inside Organized Racism," 120–22; Berbrier, 432.

30. Blee, "Inside Organized Racism," 136–37, 141, 143; Bostdorff, 353.

31. Bostdorff, 353.

32. Paige P. Edley, "Entrepreneurial mothers' balance of Work and Family," in Patrice M. Buzzanell et al., eds., *Gender in Applied Communication Contexts* (Thousand Oaks, CA: Sage, 2004), 259; Lisa Nakamura, "Pregnant Sims: Avatars and the Visual Reproduction of Motherhood on the Web," in Chris Berry, Soyoung Kim, Lynn Spigel, eds., *Electronic Elsewheres: Media, Technology, and the Experience of Social Space* (Minneapolis: University of Minnesota Press, 2009); "Latest Trends: Usage over Time," Pew Internet and American Life Project, June 2005. http://www.pewintemet.org/trends.asp. Accessed January 12, 2006; Allucquère R. Stone, *The War of Desire and Technology and the Close of the Mechanical Age* (Cambridge, MA: MIT Press, 1996), 88.

33. Kenneth Burke, "Definition of Man," *Hudson Review* 16(4) (1963): 498.

34. Hall, 20.

35. Berbrier; Blee, "Women of the Klan"; Bostdorff; Crenshaw, "Resisting Whiteness' Rhetorical Silence"; Waltman, 30.

36. Federal Bureau of Investigation, "2017 Hate Crime Statistics Released," November 13, 2018. https://www.fbi.gov/news/stories/2017-hate-crime-statistics-released-111318; Niall McCarthy, "U.S. Hate Crimes Rise for Third Straight Year," Statista, November 12, 2018. https://www.statista.com/chart/16100/total-number-of-hate-crime-incidents-recorded-by-the-fbi/.

37. Jessie Daniels, *Cyberracism: White Supremacy Online and the New Attack on Civil Rights* (New York: Rowman & Littlefield, 2009), 6.

38. Bonilla-Silva, *Racism without Racists*, 3.

39. Berbrier, 431.

40. Rian Dundon, "Klan Family Values: How Baby-toting, Robed-and-Hooded Moms Paved the Way for Today's White Hate Groups," Timeline, January 24, 2018. https://timeline.com/klan-family-values-539be2ff7f55; Patricia Hill Collins, "It's All in the Family: Intersections of Gender, Race, and Nation," *Hypatia* 13(3) (1998): 62–82. www.jstor.org/stable/3810699.

41. Nancy S. Love, *Trendy Fascism: White Power Music and the Future of Democracy* (Albany: State University of New York Press, 2016), 74–86; Collins, "It's All in the Family," 64–77.

42. Futrell and Simi, "Free Spaces, Collective Identity," 24.

43. Swain, 4.

44. Julian Hattem, "Obama Signs NSA bill, renewing Patriot Act Powers," *The Hill*, June 2, 2015. https://thehill.com/policy/national-security/243850-obama-signs-nsa-bill-renewing-patriot-act-powers; Jacqueline Stevens, *States without Nations: Citizenship for Mortals* (New York: Columbia University Press, 2010), xiv. One point to note is that, regardless of political affiliation, politicians have consistently become more conservative concerning immigration polities. See Stevens, xv, for further clarification.

45. Kinnvall, 741–42. Concerns about the lessened potential for more open borders with Mexico began in December 2001 and continued as Bush focused policy on comprehensive immigration reform. See Tim Weiner and Ginger Thompson, "Mexico Lower on Bush's List Since September 11," *New York Times*, December 29, 2001. http://www.nytimes.com/2001 /12/29/world/mexico-lower-on-bush-s-list-since-sept-11.html.

46. Robert T. Carter and A. Lin Goodwin, "Racial Identity and Education," *Review of Research in Education* 20 (1994): 312. http://www.jstor.org/stable/1167387. Accessed July 28, 2008; Michael Billig, "Humour and Hatred: The Racist Jokes of the Ku Klux Klan," *Discourse and Society* 12(3) (2001): 269; Teun A. van Dijk, "Discourse and the Denial of Racism," *Discourse and Society* 3 (1992): 105.

47. Lipsitz, 19.

48. Catherine Squires, "Post-Racial News Covering the 'Joshua Generation,'" in *The Post-Racial Mystique: Media and Race in the Twenty-First Century* (New York: New York University Press, 2014), 2.

49. Swain, 2.

50. Squires, 2; Kendi, 483; Michael G. Lacy and Kent A. Ono, Introduction, in Michael G. Lacy and Kent A. Ono, eds., *Critical Rhetorics of Race* (New York: New York University Press, 2011), 1.

51. Lipsitz, 23.

52. Lipsitz, xiv.

53. L. Grattan, 34.

54. L. Grattan, 10.

55. Lipsitz, 16.

56. Rokeach, 124; Steele and Redding, 86–91; Stewart and Cash, 269–99.

57. Alyssa Rosenberg, "'Politically Incorrect' Ideas Are Mostly Rude, Not Brave," *Washington Post*, August 11, 2016.

58. Jean Baudrillard, *Simulacra and Simulation* (Ann Arbor: University of Michigan Press, 1994), 20; Burke, "The Rhetoric of Hitler's 'Battle,'" 194.

59. Women for Aryan Unity and Friends, Homefront Publications, 2007. http://www. homefrontpublications.com/. Accessed April 10, 2007; "kirkwomen," New Banner Arm Women, 2007. http://kelticklankirk.com/womens_auxiliaries_arm.htm. Accessed April 10, 2007; National Socialist Movement Women's Division, NSM Women's Division Voices of Victory Archive, 2007. https://web.archive.org/web/20070212232708/http://www.nsm88 womensdivision.com:80/Radio/index.html.

60. National Alliance, National Alliance Main Page. http://www.natvan.com/. Accessed April 10, 2007.

61. "kirkwomen," New Banner Arm Women.

62. Paul Solotaroff, "Trump Seriously: On the Trail with the GOP's Tough Guy," *Rolling Stone*, September 9, 2015. https://www.rollingstone.com/politics/politics-news/trump -seriously-on-the-trail-with-the-gops-tough-guy-41447/. Accessed March 23, 2016.

63. "Donald Trump Nearly Casually Remarks about Incest with Daughter Ivanka," YouTube, June 11, 2016. https://www.youtube.com/watch?v=D2nPXdtYYtk.

64. "Trump Calls Ivanka and Pompeo 'Beauty and the Beast,'" *The Guardian*, July 1, 2019. https://www.theguardian.com/us-news/video/2019/jul/01/trump-calls-ivanka-and-pompeo -beauty-and-the-beast-video.

65. Julia Ioffe, "Melania Trump on Her Rise, Her Family Secrets, and Her True Political Views: 'Nobody Will Ever Know,'" *GQ*, April 27, 2016. https://www.gq.com/story

/melania-trump-gq-interview_; Evgenia Peretz, "Inside the Trump Marriage: Melaina's Burden," *Vanity Fair*, May 2017. https://www.vanityfair.com/news/2017/04/donald-melania -trump-marriage.

66. By their own articulation, the Internet Association is "the only trade association that exclusively represents leading global internet companies on matters of public policy. . . . Our mission is to foster innovation, promote economic growth, and empower people through the free and open internet." https://internetassociation.org/.

67. Internet Association, "Internet Association to Honor House Speaker Nancy Pelosi and Advisor to the President Ivanka Trump at Sixth Annual Charity Gala," April 25, 2019. https:// internetassociation.org/internet-association-to-honor-house-speaker-nancy-pelosi-and -advisor-to-the-president-ivanka-trump-at-sixth-annual-charity-gala/.

68. Jack Morse, "The White House's Social Media 'Bias' Survey Has a Terrible Media Privacy Policy," Mashable, May 15, 2019. https://mashable.com/article/trump-social-media -bias-survey-privacy-policy/.

69. National Socialist Movement Women's Division. "Photo Gallery." NSM Women's Division Voices of Victory Archive, 2007. https://web.archive.org/web/20070212233346 /http://www.nsm88womensdivision.com:80/Photos/index.html.

70. Dean Obeidallah, "Donald Trump's horrifying words about Muslims." CNN, November 20, 2015.

71. "Donald Trump Announces a Presidential Bid," *Washington Post*, June 16, 2015.

72. "Donald Trump Transcript: 'Our Country Needs a Truly Great Leader,'" Washington Wire, June 16, 2015.

73. Although Trump uses the term "America," he limits his boundaries to claims of United States as a nation rather than referring to the Americas or even North America. His boundaries on the term are most evident when considering his claims about building a wall between the United States and Mexico.

74. Bonilla-Silva writes about this type of racial preferencing argument in *Racism without Racists*, 135–38.

75. Candace Epps-Robertson, "The Race to Erase Brown v. Board of Education: The Virginia Way and the Rhetoric of Massive Resistance," *Rhetoric Review* 35(2) (2016): 109.

76. "Trump Ends DACA, Calls on Congress to Act," National Public Radio, September 5. 2017. https://www.npr.org/2017/09/05/546423550/trump-signals-end-to-daca-calls-on -congress-to-act.

77. Jason Thompson, "Magic for a People Trained in Pragmatism: Kenneth Burke, Mein Kampf, and the Early 9/11 Oratory of George W. Bush," *Rhetoric Review* 30(4) (2011): 358–59.

78. Angry White Female, Home page, 2007. http://www.angrywhitefemale.net/. Accessed April 10, 2007.

79. Snow White, "Snow White & the Cheshire Cat: 1984—Animal Farm-The Matrix and the global hive-mind . . . what they have in mind for you!" 2007. http://web.archive.org/web /20070630122813/http://snowwhitecheshirecat.blogspot.com/.

80. Astead W. Herndon, "Elizabeth Warren Stands by Her DNA Test. But Around Her, Worries Abound," *New York Times*, December 6, 2018.

81. Elena Haskins, "Wake Up or Die.," 2007. http://web.archive.org/web/20090414225247/ http://wakeupordie.com/index2.html.

82. Nakayama and Krizek, 301.

83. Cheryl Harris, "Whiteness as Property," *Harvard Law Review* 106(8) (1993): 1736.

84. Donald Trump, "Democracy in Action," Iowa Freedom Summit, January 24, 2015. Web.

85. Alberto A. Martinez, "The Media Needs to Stop Telling This Lie about Donald Trump. I'm a Sanders Supporter—and Value Honesty," Salon, December 21, 2015. https://www.salon.com/2015/12/21/the_media_needs_to_stop_telling_this_lie_about_donald_trump_im_a_sanders_supporter_and_value_honesty/.

86. Thompson, 360.

87. Brian Fehler, "Reading, Writing, and Redemption: Literacy Sponsorship and the Mexican-American Settlement Movement in Texas," *Rhetoric Review* 29(4) (2010): 349; Love, 4.

88. Donald Trump, "Foreign Policy Remarks," *New York Times*, April 27, 2016.

89. Kenneth Burke, *Language as Symbolic Action* (Berkeley: University of California Press, 1966), 282; Thompson, 366.

90. Brenda Walker, Immigration's Human Cost [blog], 2007. http://www.immigrationshumancost.org/. Accessed January 8, 2013.

91. Although on the graphic user interface of her site Angry White Female does not name herself, in the html and CSS code, she uploaded an image from "Elisha Strom's computer," leading me to believe that she was in fact Elisha Strom (Anderson, "The Context of Power"). By asking rhetorical questions about digital form such as when was a program created, why was it created, how was this program created and by whom, what are the representations or language used to develop its code, and what adaptations are possible through the program, people can contextualize and critically analyze programmatic development.

92. Angry White Female, "About Me," 2007. http://www.angrywhitefemale.net/about-me.html. Accessed April 20, 2007.

93. Eddo, 98.

94. Tucker.

95. DiAngelo, 54–55.

96. Colin Campbell, "'Get a Job!': Donald Trump rally Rocked by Hecklers as He Complains about Their 'Gentle' Treatment," *Business Insider*, March 11, 2016.

97. Jeremy Diamond, "Donald Trump on Protester: 'I'd Like to Punch Him in the Face,'" CNN, February 23, 2016.

98. Pamela Engel, "CNN's Jake Tapper Hammers Donald Trump over the Violent 'Tone' of His Rallies," *Business Insider*, March 10, 2016.

99. Southern Poverty Law Center, "Ten Days After: Harassment and Intimidation in the Aftermath of the Election," November 29, 2016; Yan et al., "'Make American White Again': Hate Speech and Crimes Post-election," CNN, November 29, 2016.

100. Love, 4.

101. Sarah Kendzior, "Donald Trump and His Followers Could Destroy America Even If He Loses," The Pied Piper, August 5, 2016.

Chapter 2: <Freedom of Speech> without Responsibility: Unmasking a Privilege Filter of Color-Blind Racism as a White Supremacist Ideograph

1. Hall, 20.

2. Charles W. Mills, "Global White Ignorance," in *Routledge International Handbook of Ignorance Studies* (2015), 219. doi:10.4324/9781315867762.

3. Bostdorff, 53.

4. Lipsitz, 46.

5. Wendy K. Z. Anderson, "Classifying Whiteness: Unmasking White Nationalist Women's Digital Design through an Intersectional Analysis of Contained Agency," Special Issue on Media and the Extreme Right, *Communication, Culture, and Critique* 11(1) (March 2018): 116–32. https://doi.org/10.1093/ccc/tcy002; Anderson, "The Context of Power"; Anderson, "(De)coding Whiteness"; Berbrier; Blee, "Inside Organized Racism," "Women of the Klan"; Bostdorff; Crenshaw, "Resisting Whiteness' Rhetorical Silence"; Waltman.

6. Hall, 19.

7. George Lakoff, *Don't Think of an Elephant: Know Your Values and Frame the Debate* (White River Junction, VT: Chelsea Green Publishing, 2004), xv.

8. McGee, 15.

9. Crenshaw, "Resisting Whiteness' Rhetorical Silence," 256; italics added.

10. McGee, 4.

11. Hall, 10.

12. Crenshaw, "Race, Reform, and Retrenchment," 106.

13. As noted in the introductory chapter, staggering racial discrepancies exist regarding legal enforcement (police), drug laws, mass incarceration, criminal justice, education, employment, economic security, career advancement, civil rights, media access, and housing as noted by Alexander, *The New Jim Crow*, 2; Lipsitz, 15; Tucker; Kendi, 1–2; Sharon Tettegah, "The Racial Consciousness Attitudes of White Prospective Teachers and Their Perceptions of the Teachability of Students from Different Racial/Ethnic Backgrounds: Findings from a California Study," *Journal of Negro Education* 65(2) (Spring 1996): 151–63. https://www.jstor.org/stable/2967310.

14. Bonilla-Silva, "The Linguistics of Color Blind Racism," 61.

15. Bonilla-Silva, "The Linguistics of Color Blind Racism," 41.

16. Bonilla-Silva, "The Linguistics of Color Blind Racism," 41.

17. Bonilla-Silva, *Racism without Racists*, 5.

18. bell hooks, "Representing Whiteness in the Black Imagination," in Lawrence Grossberg, Cary Nelson, and Paula A. Treichler, eds., *Cultural Studies* (New York: Routledge, 1992), 345–46.

19. Carol Lynne D'Arcangelis, "Revelations of a White Settler Woman Scholar-Activist: The Fraught Promise of Self-Reflexivity," *Cultural Studies Critical Methodologies* 18(5) (October 2018): 342–43. doi:10.1177/1532708617750675.

20. John L. Lucaites, Celeste Michelle Condit, and Sally Caudill, eds., *Contemporary Rhetorical Theory: A Reader* (New York: Guilford Press, 1999), 458.

21. Fanon, 9–11.

22. Collins, vii.

23. Joe R. Feagin, *The White Racial Frame: Centuries of Racial Framing and Counter-framing* (New York: Routledge, 2010), xi.

24. Mills, 219.

25. McGee, 15.

26. John L. Lucaites and Celeste M. Condit, "Reconstructing <Equality>: Culturetypal and Counter-cultural Rhetorics in the Martyred Black Vision," *Communication Monographs* 57 (1990): 18. EBSCOhost.

27. Kenneth Burke, *Permanence and Change: An Anatomy of Purpose*, 3rd ed. (Berkeley: University of California Press, 1935), 14.

28. Donaldo Macedo, *Introduction*, in Paolo Freire, ed., *Pedagogy of the Oppressed* (New York: Continuum International Publishing, 1970), 11.

29. Crenshaw, "Resisting Whiteness' Rhetorical Silence," 272.

30. Dana Cloud, "The Rhetoric of <Family Values>: Scapegoating, Utopia, and the Privatization of Social Responsibility," *Western Journal of Communication* 62(4) (1998): 387–419. doi:10.1080/10570319809374617; Hall; Lucaites and Condit; McGee.

31. Cloud, "The Rhetoric of <Family Values>," 390, 392.

32. Cloud, "The Rhetoric of <Family Values>"; Robert Ivie, "The Ideology of Freedom's 'Fragility' in American Foreign Policy Argument," *Journal of the American Forensic Association* 24 (1987): 27–36; Lucaites and Condit.

33. Breanna Bevens, VDare.com: Blog Articles » Bryanna Bevens. 2007. http://blog.vdare.com/. Accessed April 10, 2007.

34. Brenda Walker, "New Postings of Victims and Criminals. . . ," 2007. https://www.immigrationshumancost.org/archives.html. Accessed July 5, 2020.

35. Angry White Female, "Links," 2007. http://www.angrywhitefemale.net/links.html. Accessed April 20, 2007.

36. Christopher Brown, "WWW.HATE.COM: White Supremacist Discourse on the Internet and the Construction of Whiteness Ideology," *Howard Journal of Communications* 20 (2009): 196, 198. doi:10.1080/10646170902869544.

37. "American," *Concise Oxford English Dictionary*, 11th ed. 2008.

38. "American," *Oxford English Dictionary*, 11th ed. 2009.

39. Philip H. Herbst, *The Color of Words: An Encyclopaedic Dictionary of Ethnic Bias in the United States* (Yarmouth, ME: Intercultural Press, 1997), 9.

40. Athena Kerry, VDare.com: Blog Articles » Athena Kerry, 2007. http://blog.vdare.com/archives/author/athena_kerry/. Accessed April 20, 2007.

41. "Multiracial in America. Chapter 1: Race and Multiracial Americans in the U.S. Census," Pew Internet & American Life Project, 2015. http://www.pewsocialtrends.org/2015/06/11/chapter-1-race-and-multiracial-americans-in-the-u-s-census/. Accessed June 11, 2015.

42. Angry White Female, "About Me."

43. Haskins. Since no title is provided on this page, I identify Haskins's first page (as web designers do) as a *splash page.*

44. Angry White Female, "About Me"; Haskins; Walker.

45. Although used by white nationalists, I choose not to use the popular term "minority" to describe people of African American, Hispanic, Indigenous, and Pacific Islander descent in that the term reinforces a group's minority status. The term "minority" lumps many people into one "victim" category, which perpetuates hierarchical thought concerning racial agency, where racial credibility is lost in that a "minority" concern represents only a small group of people. The term "minority" further perpetuates a white/nonwhite dichotomy, dissolving racial uniqueness by ignoring over five hundred years of oppression toward specific races.

46. Haskins, "Wake Up or Die."

47. Haskins, splash page.

48. Walker.

49. Walker.

50. Angry White Female. "About Me."

51. Nakamura, *Cybertypes* 78.

52. "Diversity." *Concise Oxford English Dictionary*. 11th ed. 2008.

53. Burke, "Definition of Man," LASA. I use LASA in accordance with the abbreviation used by Burkean scholars to signify *Language of Symbolic Action*.

54. Herbst, 70.

55. Hélène Cixous, "The Laugh of the Medusa," *Signs* 1(4) (1976): 876. http://www.jstor .org/stable/3173239. Accessed June 1, 2016.

56. Vidhya Shanker, "A Look at Language Week: Tidying Evaluation of 'Diversity' and 'Culture,'" American Evaluation Association, June 24, 2019. https://aea365.org/blog/a-look -at-language-week-tidying-evaluation-of-diversity-culture-by-vidhya-shanker/.

57. Snow White. In this quotation I preserve the all-capital letters from original text.

58. Carol A. Valentine, Public Action: A News and News Analysis Service, 2007. http:// www.public-action.com/. Accessed April 20, 2007.

59. Thomas L. Tedford and Dale A. Herbeck, *Freedom of Speech in the United States*, 8th ed. (State College, PA: Strata, 2017), 201.

60. Bevens.

61. "Freedom of Speech," *Concise Oxford English Dictionary*, 11th ed. 2008.

62. Steve Martinot, *The Machinery of Whiteness: Studies in the Structure of Racialization* (Philadelphia: Temple University Press, 2010), 62.

63. Ronald C. Arnett, Janie Harden Fritz, and Leanne M. Bell, *Communication Ethics Literacy: Dialogue and Difference* (Thousand Oaks, CA: Sage, 2009), 109.

64. Prussian Blue, "Home," 2007. http://web.archive.org/web/20070406182925/www .prussianbluestore.com/11/24/08. Accessed April 20, 2007.

65. Casey R. Kelly, "Chastity for Democracy: Surplus Repression and the Rhetoric of Sex Education," *Quarterly Journal of Speech* 102(4) (2016): 363.

66. Karen Brodkin, *How Jews Became White Folks and What That Says about Race in America* (Piscataway, NJ: Rutgers University Press, 1999); Noel Ignatiev, *How the Irish Became White* (New York: Routledge, 2008).

67. "Unity," *Concise Oxford English Dictionary*, 11th ed. 2008.

68. See France, "Rachel Dolezal on Being Black."

69. Hancock, 110.

70. Olsson.

71. Nakamura, *Cybertypes*, 78.

72. Donald Trump [@realDonaldTrump], "If U.C. Berkeley does not allow free speech and practices violence on innocent people with a different point of view—NO FEDERAL FUNDS?" Twitter, February 2, 2017. twitter.com/realdonaldtrump/status/8271126332245442 56?lang=en.

73. Helm.

74. Herbst, 154.

Chapter 3: Classifying Whiteness as "Contained Agency": Decrypting White Nationalist Women's Digital Design through Understanding Intersectional Analysis

Material appearing in this chapter from Anderson, Wendy K. Z., "Classifying Whiteness: Unmasking White Nationalist Women's Digital Design through an Intersectional Analysis of Contained Agency." Special Issue on Media and the Extreme Right in *Communication, Culture, and Critique* 11, no. 1: 116–32 (March 2018), is used by permission of Oxford University Press.

1. Michael L. Dertouzos, *What Will Be: How the New World of Information Will Change Our Lives* (New York: HarperCollins, 1997), 283.

2. McLuhan, 8, 31.

3. David Bolter and Richard Grusin, *Remediation: Understanding New Media* (Cambridge, MA: MIT Press, 1999), 246; Dertouzos, 283; McLuhan, 8, 31; Negroponte.

4. Andrew Feenberg, *Transforming Technology: A Critical Theory Revisited* (New York: Oxford University Press, 2002), 14–15; Gitelman, 84.

5. Deborah Fallows, "How Women and Men Use the Internet," Pew Research Center, December 28, 2005. http://www.pewinternet.org/Reports/2005/How-Women-and-Men-Use -the-Internet.aspx. Accessed January 8, 2013; Kathryn Zickuhr and Aaron Smith, "Digital Difference," Pew Internet & American Life Project, April 13, 2012. http://pewinternet.org /Reports/2012/Digital-differences/Overview.aspx. Accessed October 3, 2012.

6. Children's Partnership, "Online Content for Low Income and Underserved Americans," 2000. http://www.childrenspartnership.org/pub/low_income. Accessed June 8, 2007; Logan Hill, "Beyond Access: Race, Technology, Community," in Alondra Nelson et al., eds., *Technicolor: Race, Technology, and Everyday Life* (New York: New York Press, 2001), 23; Steven McLaine, "Ethnic Online Communities: Between Profit and Purpose," in M. McCaughey and M. Ayers, eds., *Cyberactivism: Online Activism in Theory and Practice* (New York: Routledge, 2003); Nakamura, *Cybertypes*, 3, 13, 32, 34.

7. Nakamura, *Cybertypes*, 115.

8. Charlotte Ryan, Kevin M. Carragee, and William Meinhofer, "Theory into Practice: Framing, the News Media, and Collective Action," *Journal of Broadcasting and Electronic Media* 45 (2001): 176; Stewart, Smith, and Denton, 63.

9. André Brock, "Beyond the Pale: The Blackbird Web Browser's Critical Reception," *New Media and Society* 13 (2011): 1094, 1096. doi:10.1177/1461444810397031.

10. Harris, "Whiteness as Property."

11. Anderson, "The constructs of power and race"; Anderson, "(De)coding whiteness"; Berbrier, "Half the Battle"; Mitch Berbrier, "Making Minorities: Cultural Space, Stigma Transformation Frames, and the Categorical Status," *Sociological Forum* 17(4) (2002): 553–91; Blee, *Inside Organized Racism*, 2002; Bostdorff; Castells; Crenshaw, "Resisting Whiteness' Rhetorical Silence"; Jessie Daniels, "Cloaked Websites: Propaganda, Cyber-racism and Epistemology in the Digital Era," *New Media Society* 11(5) (2009): 659–83. doi:10.1177/1461444809105345; Daniels, *Cyberracism*; Kevin M. DeLuca and Jennifer Peeples, "From Public Sphere to Public Screen: Democracy, Activism, and the 'Violence' of Seattle," *Critical Studies in Media Communication* 19(2) (2002): 125–51. doi:10.1080/07393180216559; Mario Diani, "Social Movement Networks Virtual and Real," *Information, Communication, and Society* 3(3) (2000): 386–401. doi:10.1080/13691180051033333; Duffy; Peter Van Aelst and Stefaan Walgrave, "New Media, New Movements? The Role of the Internet in Shaping the 'Anti-globalization' Movement," *Information, Communication and Society* 5(4) (2002): 465–93. doi:10.1080/13691180208538801; Waltman.

12. Berger, 3.

13. Schroer.

14. Hall, 20.

15. Anderson, "The Constructs of Power and Race"; Anderson, "(De)coding Whiteness"; Elizabeth Kiefer, "How the Women of the KKK Helped Architect a Hate Movement," Refinery29, October 18, 2017. http://www.refinery29.com/2017/10/176864/white

-supremacy-ku-klux-klan-women; Michelle Legro, "How Can Alt-right Women Exist in a Misogynistic Movement?" Longreads, 2017. https://longreads.com/2017/08/22/how-can-alt-right-women-exist-in-a-misogynistic-movement/.

16. CNN, "Exit Polls"; Shamira Ibrahim, "Once Again, Black Women Did the Work which White Women Refused To," *The Root*, November 9, 2016; David Roberts, "Donald Trump and the Rise of Tribal Epistemology," Vox, May 19, 2017. Retrieved from https://www.vox.com/policy-and-politics/2017/3/22/14762030/donald-trump-tribal-epistemology. Accessed May 20, 2017.

17. Daniels, "Cloaked Websites," 678.

18. Kimberlé Crenshaw, "Demarginalizing the Intersection of Race and Sex: A Black Feminist Critique of Antidiscrimination Doctrine, Feminist Theory and Antiracist Politics," *University of Chicago Legal Forum* 1(8) (1989). http://chicagounbound.uchicago.edu/uclf/vol1989/iss1/8140.

19. Crenshaw, "Demarginalizing the Intersection of Race and Sex," 141–43; Crenshaw, "Mapping the Margins," 1250.

20. Crenshaw, "Demarginalizing the Intersection of Race and Sex," 148.

21. Hancock, 110.

22. Crenshaw, "Demarginalizing the Intersection of Race and Sex," 139; Crenshaw, "Mapping the Margins," 1241.

23. Crenshaw, "Demarginalizing the Intersection of Race and Sex," 144.

24. Frankenburg, 17, italics in original; Stephanie E. Jones-Rogers, "Epilogue: Lost Kindred, Lost Cause," *They Were Her Property: White Women as Slave Owners in the American South* (New Haven and London: Yale University Press, 2019), 205.

25. Burke, *LASA*.

26. Nakayama and Krizek, 293.

27. John Cheney-Lippold, *We Are Data: Algorithms and the Making of Our Digital Selves* (New York: New York University Press, 2017), 7.

28. Squires, 4; Swain, 4.

29. Alexander; Tucker.

30. Jeff Goodwin and James M. Jasper, eds., *The Social Movements Reader: Cases and Concepts* (Malden, MA: Blackwell Publishing, 2003); Jenna N. Hanchey, "Agency beyond Agents: Aid Campaigns in Sub-Saharan Africa and Collective Representations of Agency," *Communication, Culture and Critique* 9 (2016): 13; Gayatri C. Spivak, "Subaltern Studies: Deconstructing Historiography," in R. Guha and G. C. Spivak, eds., *Selected Subaltern Studies* (New York: Oxford University Press, 1988), 14.

31. Miller, 149.

32. Marilyn Cooper, "Rhetorical Agency as Emergent and Enacted," *College Composition and Communication* 62(3) (February 2011): 425.

33. Cooper, 426.

34. Rebecca Aanerud, "Humility and Whiteness: 'How Did I Look without Seeing, Hear without Listening?'" in Yancy, ed., *White Self-criticality beyond Anti-racism*, 102.

35. Hancock, *Intersectionality*, 110.

36. Collins, *Black Feminist Thought*, 253; Crenshaw, "Demarginalizing the Intersection of Race and Sex," 140, 149.

37. Anna M. Hancock, *Solidarity Politics for Millennials: A Guide to Ending the Oppression Olympics* (New York: Palgrave, 2011); Elizabeth Martinez, "Beyond Black/White: The Racisms of Our Times," *Social Justice* 20(1/2) (1993): 22–34.

38. Douglas Walton and Fabrizio Macagno, "Reasoning from Classifications and Definitions," *Argumentation* 23 (2009): 81–107. doi:10.1007/s10503-008-9110-2.

39. Fanon, 20.

40. Cheney-Lippold, 7.

41. Lev Manovich, *The Language of New Media* (Cambridge, MA: MIT Press, 2000), 63.

42. Noble, *Algorithms of Oppression*, 63.

43. Walton and Macagno, 82.

44. Ian Bogost, *Persuasive Games: The Expressive Power of Videogames* (Cambridge, MA: MIT Press, 2007), 3.

45. Nakamura, *Cybertypes*, 101–35.

46. Jennifer Baumgardner and Amy Richards, *Manifesta: Young Women, Feminism, and the Future* (New York: Farrar, Straus, and Giroux, 2000), 51; Maddy Costa, "Le Tigre: Girl Power Burns Bright with Le Tigre," *The Guardian*, December 1, 2000, 27; Rebecca Walker, "Being Real: An Introduction," in Rebecca Walker, ed., *To Be Real: Telling the Truth and Changing the Face of Feminism* (New York: Anchor Books, 1995); Julia T. Wood, *Gendered Lives: Communication, Gender, and Culture*, 3rd ed. (Belmont, CA: Wadsworth, 1999).

47. Jessica Massa, Kirsten King, and Izzy Francke, "How Much of a Feminist Are You?" Buzzfeed, July 29, 2017. https://www.buzzfeed.com/jessicamassa1/how-much-of-a-feminist -are-you?utm_term=.fx16W1ae4#.uu3Wr1wDd.

48. Crenshaw, "Mapping the Margins"; bell hooks, *Talking Back: Thinking Feminist, Thinking Black* (Boston: South End Press, 1989).

49. Ron Howard, "The Vernacular Web of Participatory Media," *Critical Studies in Media Communication* 25(5) (2008): 490–513. doi:10.1080/15295030802468065; Kent Ono and John M. Sloop, "The Critique of Vernacular Discourse," *Communication Monographs* 62 (March 1995): 20.

50. Daniels, "Cloaked Websites."

51. Daniels, *Cyberracism*; Safiya U. Noble, "Missed Connections: What Search Engines Say about Women," *Bitch* 54 (2012): 36–41. https://safiyaunoble.files.wordpress.com/2012/03/54 _search_engines.pdf; Safiya Noble, "Challenging the Algorithms of Oppression," YouTube, June 15, 2016. https://www.youtube.com/watch?v=iRVZozEEWlE. As of January 2018, martinlutherking.org was no longer publicly available.

52. Bonilla, Yamar, et al., "#Ferguson: Digital Protest, Hashtag Ethnography, and the Racial Politics of Social Media in the United States," *American Ethnologist* 42(1) (2015): 5.

53. Berger, 3–4.

54. See Anderson, "The Context of Power and Race," 114–22.

55. First I used close textual analysis to understand the framing of classifications as "political discourse." I analyzed texts for salient classifications, which were unique to the women's sites. I extended Brock's Critical Technocultural Discourse Analysis (CTDA) to include not only user interface and a close reading of the blog posts, but also an analysis of how a website's architecture (hyperlinks provided, gateway and splash page structures, and options for community interaction) illustrated a designer's intended mode of "dialogue" or communication with users, in order to understand the argument inherent in a website's structural design. Norman Fairclough, "Critical Discourse Analysis," *International Advances in Engineering and Technology* 7 (2012): 453. http://scholarism.net/FullText/2012071.pdf.

56. Angry White Female, "About Me."

57. Women for Aryan Unity, "Women for Aryan Unity," 2007. http://www.w-a-u.net/.

58. Women for Aryan Unity, "WAU-FAQ," 2007. http://www.rac-usa.org/wau/waufaq.html.

59. April Gaede, APRILGAEDESBLOG, 2007. http://aprilgaedesblog.blogspot.com/. Accessed April 20, 2007.

60. Angry White Female, "About Me"; Angry White Female "Poisoning Our Preschoolers," 2007; Haskins, Splash Page; kirkwomen, "New banner arm women"; NSM Women's Division; Snow White; Women for Aryan Unity.

61. Love, 5–6.

62. Dyck, Kirsten *Reichsrock: The International Web of White-power and Neo-Nazi Hate Music* (New Brunswick, NJ: Rutgers University Press, 2017), 6–12.

63. Laura C. Prividera and John W. Howard III, "Masculinity, Whiteness, and the Warrior Hero: Perpetuating the Strategic Rhetoric of U.S. Nationalism and the Marginalization of Women," *Women and Language* 29(2) (2006): 31.

64. Anderson, "The Constructs of Power and Race," 192–93.

65. Nakayama and Krizek, 302.

66. Angry White Female. "SPLC's War on Women," 2007. http://web.archive.org/web/20070202070529/http://www.angrywhitefemale.net/splc-war.html.

67. Angry White Female, "Feminism: A Reality Check," 2007. http://web.archive.org/web/20070202070455/http://www.angrywhitefemale.net/feminism.html.

68. Lakoff, 3.

69. Women for Aryan Unity, "WAU mission statement," 2007. http://www.rac-usa.org/wau/missionstatement.html.

70. Stormfront, "Blog Post by SPOON!" 2007. http://www.stormfront.org/forum/

71. Haskins, splash page.

72. Women for Aryan Unity.

73. Women for Aryan Unity and Friends, Homefront Publications, 2007. http://www.homefrontpublications.com/.

74. Cheney-Lippold, xiii.

75. Haskins, splash page.

76. Elena Haskins, "Wake Up or Die: Heads Up, Please!" 2007. https://web.archive.org/web/20060116030825/http://www.wakeupordie.com:80/html/gateway1.html. Accessed April 20, 2007; Elena Haskins, "Wake Up or Die: Sleeper Awake!" 2007. https://web.archive.org/web/20060116030340/http://www.wakeupordie.com:80/html/slprwht.html. Accessed April 20, 2007.

77. Elena Haskins, "Wake Up or Die: Your Choice," 2007. http://web.archive.org/web/20070219033927/http://www.wakeupordie.com/html/choice.html. Accessed April 20, 2007.

78. Haskins, "Wake Up or Die: Zombie."

79. Sigrdrifa, "About," 2007. http://web.archive.org/web/20100921125742/http://www.sigrdrifa.net/about.shtml.

80. Angry White Female, "Poisoning Our Preschoolers."

81. Sigrdrifa, "Sigrdrifa Publications," 2007. http://web.archive.org/web/20070527144419/http://www.sigrdrifa.net/publications.shtml.

82. Stormfront.

83. Elena Haskins, "Wake Up or Die: Love Watch," 2007. https://web.archive.org/web/20070808201349/http://www.wakeupordie.com/html/lovewa1.html. Accessed April 20, 2007.

84. Prussian Blue's Blog, "Prussian Blue," 2007. http://prussianbluefan.blogspot.com/.

85. Women for Aryan Unity, "WAU—Membership," 2007. http://www.rac-usa.org/wau/membership.html.

86. "WAU Membership."

87. Cristina Marcos, "House Dems Press Trump on Paid Leave Plan," *The Hill*, July 10, 2017. http://thehill.com/policy/finance/341343-house-dems-press-trump-on-paid-leave-plan.

88. Emma Bowman and Ian Stewart, "The Women behind The 'Alt-Right,'" *Weekend Edition*, NPR, August 20, 2017. http://www.npr.org/2017/08/20/544134546/the-women-behind -the-altright. Accessed September 6, 2017;Seyward Darby, "The Rise of the Valkyries: In the Alt-right, Women Are the Future, and the Problem," *Harper's*, August 24, 2017. https://harpers. org/archive/2017/09/the-rise-of-the-valkyries/7/; Caroline Kitchener, "The Women behind the 'Alt-right,'" *The Atlantic*, August 18, 2017. https://www.theatlantic.com/politics /archive/2017/08/the-women-behind-the-alt-right/537168/.

89. Legro.

90. Anderson, "(De)coding Whiteness."

91. Ono and Sloop, 23, 22.

92. Howard, 493–94.

93. Haskins, "Wake Up or Die."

94. Evette Dionne, "Women's Suffrage Leaders Left Out Black Women," *Teen Vogue*, August 18, 2017. https://www.teenvogue.com/story/womens-suffrage-leaders-left-out-black -women.

95. Shaymus McLaughlin, "YouTuber Lauren Southern's University of Minnesota Event met with 200 Protesters," *GoMN*, October 26, 2017. https://www.gomn.com/news/youtuber -lauren-southerns-university-of-minnesota-event-met-with-200-protesters.

96. Cooper, 426.

97. Southern Poverty Law Center, "The Alt-right on Campus: What Students Need to Know," 2017. https://www.splcenter.org/20170810/alt-right-campus-what-students-need -know.

98. Dana Cloud, "Responding to Right-Wing Attacks," *Inside Higher Education*, 2017. https://www.insidehighered.com/advice/2017/11/07/tips-help-academics-respond-right -wing-attacks-essay; Jessie Daniels and Arlene Stein, "Protect Scholars against Attacks from the Right," Rutgers Today, 2017. https://news.rutgers.edu/sites/medrel/files/news-clips /Why%20institutions%20should%20shield%20academics%20who%20are%20being%20 attacked%20by%20conservative%20groups%20%28essay%29.pdf; Southern Poverty Law Center "The alt-right on campus."

99. Mark Potok and Laurie Wood, "Leaving White Nationalism." Southern Poverty Law Center, August 21, 2013. https://www.splcenter.org/fighting-hate/intelligence-report/2013 /leaving-white-nationalism.

100. Dyck, 120–22.

101. Saul Levmore and Martha C. Nussbaum, *The Offensive Internet: Speech, Privacy, and Reputation* (Cambridge, MA: Harvard University Press, 2012), 4.

102. Daniels, *Cyberracism*.

103. Crenshaw, "Resisting Whiteness' Rhetorical Silence," 253.

104. Katie Mettler and Avi Selk, "GoDaddy—then Google—Ban Neo-Nazi Site Daily Stormer for Disparaging Charlottesville Victim," *Washington Post*, August 14, 2017. https:// www.washingtonpost.com/news/morning-mix/wp/2017/08/14/godaddy-bans-neo -nazi-site-daily-stormer-for-disparaging-woman-killed-at-charlottesville-rally/?utm_ term=.6a902cc6be5b.

105. Anderson, "(De)coding Whiteness," 265.

106. "Twitter Announces New Measures to Tackle Abuse and Harassment," *The Guardian* February 7, 2017. https://www.theguardian.com/technology/2017/feb/07/twitter -abuse-harassment-crackdown.

107. Chris Morris, "All the Companies Who Say Hate Groups Can't Use Their Services," *Fortune*, August 17, 2017.

http://fortune.com/2017/08/17/hate-groups-google-godaddy-apple-paypal/; Love, 6.

108. Manuel Castells, *The Power of Identity* (Hoboken, NJ: Blackwell Publishing, 1997); Daniels, *Cyberracism*; Diani; Raka Shome, "'Global Motherhood': The Transnational Intimacies of White Femininity," *Critical Studies in Media Communication* 28 (2011): 388–406. doi:10.1080/15295036.2011.589861; Dietrich Soyez, "Anchored Locally—Linked Globally, Transnational Social Movement Organizations in a (Seemingly) Borderless World," *GeoJournal* 52 (2000): 7–16. doi:10.1023/A:1013191329715.

109. See Anderson and Grace.

110. Daniel A. Bell Jr., *Faces at the Bottom of the Well: The Permanence of Racism* (New York: Basic Books, 1992).

Chapter 4: White Outsiderism as White Identity Politics: Situating Tea Party Rhetoric as Uncivil Testing Grounds

1. Janice Schuetz and Rachel Stohr, "Cyberadvocacy and the Evolution of the Tea Party Movement," Conference Proceedings, National Communication Association/American Forensic Association (Alta Conference on Argumentation, 2011), 655, 659.

2. Maegan Stephens et al., "The Life of the Tea Party: Differences between Tea Party and Republican Media Use and Political Variables," *Atlantic Journal of Communication* 24 (3) (2016): 160. doi.org/10.1080/15456870.2016.1184665.

3. Vanessa Williamson et al., "The Tea Party and the Remaking of Republican Conservatism," *Perspectives on Politics* 9(1) (March 2011): 35. https://www.jstor.org/stable/41622724.

4. Grattan, 146–51; Christopher Phillips, "A Good Coalition," *M/C Journal* 13(6) (2010): 10.

5. McVeigh, et al., "Educational Segregation, Tea Party Organizations, and Battles over Distributive Justice," *American Sociological Review* 79(4) (2014): 636, 640. http://www.jstor.org/stable/43187557.

6. L. Grattan, 147.

7. Schuetz and Stohr, 659.

8. Tea Party Patriots, "Mission," March 26, 2010. https://web.archive.org/web/20100326080834/http://www.teapartypatriots.org:80/Mission.aspx.

9. Tea Party Patriots.

10. Tea Party Patriots.

11. Tea Party Patriots.

12. Brittany H. Bramlett and Toni Miles, "Aged Migration, Communities, and Support for the Tea Party in Statewide Elections," *Phylon* 52(2) (2015): 71. http://www.jstor.org/stable/43681954. Accessed January 9, 2018.

13. McVeigh et al., 635, 646.

14. McVeigh et al., 632–33.

15. Mark Lilla, "The Tea Party Jacobins," *New York Review of Books*, May 27, 2010. http://www.nybooks.com.ezp1.lib.umn.edu/articles/2010/05/27/tea-party-jacobins/. Accessed January 9, 2018.

16. McVeigh et al., 633.

17. William A. Gamson, *Talking Politics* (Cambridge: Cambridge University Press, 1992); Doug McAdam, *Political Process and the Development of Black Insurgency, 1930–1970*

(Chicago: University of Chicago Press, 1982); David A. Snow et al., "Frame Alignment Processes, Micromobilization, and Movement Participation," *American Sociological Review* 51(4) (1986): 454–81.

18. McVeigh et al., 630.

19. McVeigh et al., 647.

20. Stephens et al., 159.

21. Schuetz and Stohr, 658; Wideman, 12.

22. McVeigh et al., 362.

23. Schuetz and Stohr, 658; Wideman, 12.

24. Lilla, 53; "Beyond Red vs. Blue: Political Typology," Pew Research Center, 2011, 7. http://people-press.org/files/legacy-pdf/Beyond-Red-vs-Blue-The-Political-Typology.pdf; Schuetz and Stohr, 658; Stephens et al., 159; Clarence Walker, "'We're Losing Our Country': Barack Obama, Race and the Tea Party," *Daedalus* 140(1) (2011): 126. http://www.jstor.org /stable/25790447. Accessed January 9, 2018.

25. Bramlett and Miles, 76; Wideman, 12.

26. Deckman, 2.

27. Stephens et al., 159.

28. Frank Newport, "U.S., Negative View of the Tea Party Rise to New High," Gallup, April 28, 2011. http://news.gallup.com/poll/147308/negative-views-tea-party-rise-new-high .aspx. Accessed January 22, 2018; McVeigh et al., 633, 634.

29. Melissa Deckman, *Tea Party Women: Mama Grizzlies, Grassroots Leaders, and the Changing Face of the American Right* (New York: New York University Press, 2016), 1–2.

30. Stephanie L. Wideman, "An American Carnival: The Tea Party and Sarah Palin," *The Forensic of Pi Kappa Delta* 96(2) (2011): 12.

31. New York Times/CBS Poll, "National Poll of Tea Party Supporters," April 2010. https:// www.nytimes.com/interactive/projects/documents/new-york-timescbs-news-poll -national-survey-of-tea-party-supporters.

32. Stephens et al., 158.

33. Stephens et al., 157.

34. Schuetz and Stohr, 659; Stephens et al., 157.

35. McVeigh et al., 639.

36. Mikhail Bakhtin, *Rabelais and His World*, trans. Helene Iswolsky (Bloomington: Indiana University Press, 1984), 159.

37. Ronnee Schreiber, "Dilemmas of Representation: Conservative and Feminist Women's Organizations React to Sarah Palin," in Kathleen M. Blee and Sandra McGee Deutsch, eds., *Women of the Right: Comparisons and Interplay across Borders* (University Park: Pennsylvania State University Press, 2012), 274.

38. Walker, 126.

39. Cecilia Ridgeway and Lynn Smith-Lovin, "The Gender System and Interaction," *Annual Review of Sociology* 25 (1999): 209. Accessed November 22, 2005.

40. Kirsten Delegard, "'It Takes Women to Fight Women': Woman Suffrage and the Genesis of Female Conservatism in the United States," in Kathleen M. Blee and Sandra McGee Deutsch, *Women of the Right: Comparisons and Interplay across Borders.* University Park: Pennsylvania State University Press, 2012), 213.

41. Walker, 126.

42. Walker, 126.

43. Wideman, 11.

44. Nakayama and Krizek, 302.

45. McVeigh et al., 644.

46. Kay S. Hymowitz, "Sarah Palin and the Battle for Feminism," *City Journal*. https://www .city-journal.org/html/sarah-palin-and-battle-feminism-13348.html. Accessed January 22, 2018.

47. Deckman, 2.

48. Peter Roff, "The Tea Party Movement Is a Women's Movement," *U.S. News*, September 23, 2010. https://www.usnews.com/opinion/blogs/peter-roff/2010/09/23/the-tea-party-move ment-is-a-womens-movement. Accessed January 9, 2018.

49. hooks, *Ain't I a Woman*, 150.

50. Laris Karklis and Emily Badger, "Every Term the Census Has Used to Describe America's Racial and Ethnic Groups since 1790," *Washington Post*, November 4, 2015. https:// www.washingtonpost.com/news/wonk/wp/2015/11/04/every-term-the-census-has-used-to -describe-americas-racial-groups-since-1790/?utm_term=.12c46ce9d992. Accessed October 16, 2017.

51. Matthew Frye Jacobson, *Whiteness of a Different Color: European Immigrants and the Alchemy of Race* (Cambridge, MA: Harvard University Press, 1999), 7–10, 13–14, 16–22.

52. Alexander, 24, 25; Sherley A. Williams, "Some Implications of Womanist Theory," *Callaloo* 27 (Spring 1986): 303–4. http://www.jstor.org/stable/2930649.

53. Nakayama and Krizek, 293.

54. Noel Ignatiev, *How the Irish Became White* (New York: Routledge, 1995); Jacobson; Haney Lopéz, *White by Law: The Legal Construction of Race* (New York: New York University Press, 1996).

55. Crenshaw, "Resisting Whiteness' Rhetorical Silence," 264.

56. Rachel Einwohner, "Identity Work and Collective Action in a Repressive Context: Jewish Resistance on the 'Aryan Side' of the Warsaw Ghetto," *Social Problems* 53(1) (2006): 51.

57. Grace Kao, "Group Images and Possible Selves among Adolescents: Linking Stereotypes to Expectations by Race and Ethnicity," *Sociological Forum* 15(3) (2000): 409.

58. Foucault, 198.

59. Kendi, 3, 9.

60. Feliks Garcia, "White Men radicalised Online Were amongst the 'Silent Majority' Who Chose Donald Trump," November 14, 2016. http://www.independent.co.uk/news/world /americas/us-elections/donald-trump-white-men-online-radicalization-reddit-twitter-alt -right-latest-a7417296.html. Accessed February 28, 2018.

61. Love, 31–32.

62. Nicolle Wallace, "Sarah Palin, Rage Whisperer," *New York Times*, January 25, 2016. https://www.nytimes.com/2016/01/26/opinion/sarah-palin-rage-whisperer.html.

63. Burke, "The Rhetoric of Hitler's 'Battle,'" 194; Judith Butler, "Subversive Bodily Acts," in *Gender Trouble: Feminism and the Subversion of Identity* (New York: Routledge, 1990), 131, 136.

64. Sarah Palin, "Vice President Presidential candidate Governor Sarah Palin (AK) Full speech at the RNC," C-Span, September 3, 2008. https://www.youtube.com/watch?v=UCD xXJSucF4.

65. Palin, "Vice President Presidential candidate Governor Sarah Palin."

66. Sarah Palin, *State of the Union*, Fox News, April 27, 2017. http://video.foxnews.com/v /4500318/?#sp=show-clips.

67. Palin, *State of the Union*.

68. Palin, *State of the Union*.

69. Kellyanne Conway, "Kellyanne Conway's full speech at CPAC 2017," *Washington Post*, February 23, 2017. https://www.washingtonpost.com/videopolitics/kellyanne-conways-full -speech-at-cpac-2017/2017/02/23/67ddfb90-f9dd-11e6-aa1e-5f735ee31334_video.html?utm _term=.fafa25324754

70. Palin, Sarah. "Palin Campaigns for Trump. Reuters," *New York Times*, February 1, 2016. https://www.nytimes.com/video/us/politics/100000004181714/palin-stumps-for-donald -trump-in-iowa.html.

71. "Race and Ethnicity in the Midwest," Statistical Atlas. https://statisticalatlas.com/region /Midwest/Race-and-Ethnicity. Accessed February 28, 2018.

72. Palin, "Palin Campaigns for Trump."

73. Palin, "Palin Campaigns for Trump."

74. Hymowitz; Cecily Devereux, "New Woman, New World: Maternal Feminism and the New Imperialism in the White Settler Colonies," *Women's Studies International Forum* 22(2) (1999): 175.

75. Devereux, 178.

76. Anderson and Grace, 943.

77. Devereux, 178.

78. Marta Alice Gabriel Soares, "The Problem That Has a Name: On "Mama Grizzlies" and Conservative Feminism. *e-cadernos Ces* 14 (2011). http://journals.openedition.org/ eces/890; doi:10.4000/eces.890. Accessed March 7, 2018.

79. Palin, "Vice President Presidential candidate Governor Sarah Palin."

80. Palin, "Vice President Presidential candidate Governor Sarah Palin."

81. Sarah Palin, "Sarah Palin Remarks on Pro-Life Agenda," C-Span, May 14, 2010. http:// www.c-spanvideo.org/program/293509–1. Accessed October 1, 2011.

82. Rebecca Traister, "Sarah Palin's Feminist Revolution," Salon, September 13, 2010. https://www.salon.com/2010/09/13/big_girls_dont_cry_traister_palin/.

83. Butler, "Subversive Acts," 136.

84. Miller, 145.

85. Richard Adams, "Sarah Palin: Conservative Feminist," *The Guardian*, May 15, 2010. https://www.theguardian.com/world/richard-adams-blog/2010/may/15/sarah-palin -feminism-abortion.

86. Deckman, 18.

87. Soares; Schrieber, 274.

88. Palin, "Vice President Presidential candidate Governor Sarah Palin."

89. "Sarah Palin are you a feminist?" YouTube, October 24, 2008. https://www.youtube .com/watch?v=QJzuDEnJcxM.

90. "Sarah Palin are you a feminist?"

91. Governor Sarah Palin, "Palin on Sexism in Politics," Fox News Mobile, YouTube, November 12, 2008. https://www.youtube.com/watch?v=1Gwn2BSp6Bo.

92. Palin, "Sarah Palin Remarks on Pro-Life Agenda."

93. Tracy Clark-Flory, "Is Sarah Palin really a Feminist?" Salon, May 20, 2010. https:// www.salon.com/2010/05/20/sarah_palin_feminism/.

94. Soares.

95. Wideman, 14.

96. Dawn M. Szymanski, Arpana Gupta, Erika R. Carr, and Destin Stewart, "Internalized Misogyny as a Moderator of the Link between Sexist Events and Women's Psychological Distress," *Sex Roles* 61 (2009): 101–3. doi:10.1007/s11199-009-9611-y.

97. Combahee River Collective, "The Combahee River Collective Statement." https://americanstudies.yale.edu/sites/default/files/files/Keyword%20Coalition_Readings.pdf.

98. hooks, *Ain't I a Woman*, 157.

99. Michelle E. Carreon and Valentine M. Moghdam, "'Resistance Is Fertile': Revisiting Maternalist Frames across Cases of Women's Mobilization," *Women's Studies International Forum* 51 (2015): 19.

100. Deckman, 2.

101. Conway, "Kellyanne Conway's full speech at CPAC 2017."

Chapter 5: Reckoning with White Fragility by Alt-Right Shield Maidens: Disassembling "Contained Agency" of the Alt-Right

1. John Gramlich, "Most Americans Haven't Heard of the 'Alt-right,'" Pew Internet Center, December 12, 2016. http://www.pewresearch.org/fact-tank/2016/12/12/most-americans-havent-heard-of-the-alt-right/.

2. ABC News/Washington Post Poll, "Trump Charlottesville. Trump Approval Is Low but Steady; On Charlottesville, Lower Still," August 21, 2017. http://www.langerresearch.com/wp-content/uploads/1190a1TrumpandCharlottesville.pdf.

3. Ipsos Public Affairs, "Reuters/Ipsos/UVA Center for Politics Race Poll," September 11, 2017. http://www.centerforpolitics.org/crystalball/wp-content/uploads/2017/09/2017-Reuters-UVA-Ipsos-Race-Poll-9–11–2017.pdf.

4. Nikhil Sonnad et al., "The Alt-right Is Creating Its Own Dialect. Here's a Complete Guide," Quartz, November 30, 2017. https://qz.com/1092037/the-alt-right-is-creating-its-own-dialect-heres-a-complete-guide/.

5. Southern Poverty Law Center, "Alt-right." https://www.splcenter.org/fighting-hate/extremist-files/ideology/alt-right. Accessed March 4, 2018.

6. McLaughlin.

7. Cloud, "Responding to Right-Wing Attacks."

8. SPLC, "The Alt-Right on Campus."

9. Bowman and Stewart; Darby; Kitchener.

10. The conversation/interview between Brittany Pettibone and Tara McCarthy with Lana Lokteff was posted by "Virtue of the West w/ Tara McCarthy," but since the "#1 Virtue of the West" video with Lauren Southern was posted by Brittany Pettibone, I find it reasonable to assume that Brittany Pettibone posted the other "Virtue of the West" video as well.

11. Out of all four people, Southern might be the only one resistant to labeling herself as white nationalist or alt-right, yet she is included in this study due to her chosen proximity to and the similarities of her views. Scholars like Robert Howard Glenn have discussed using pseudonyms for their interview subjects when interrogating structural racism (McKinnon et al., 4), yet due to the nature of the self-published online materials, I found it important to use the names of the people whose rhetoric I studied to clarify rhetorical accountability of how white women promote and protect structural racism. Sara L. McKinnon, et al., "Rhetoric and Ethics Revisited: What Happens When Rhetorical Scholars Go into the Field," *Cultural Studies Critical Methodologies* 1 (2016): 1–11. doi:10.1177/1532708616659080. Accessed August 22, 2016.

12. I provided the brackets to illustrate how Spencer tries to use color-blind ideology to invisibilize his interest in forwarding white (racial construction based on skin) interests, not ethnic ones.

13. Paul Gottfried, "The Decline and Rise of the Alternative Right," Taki's Magazine, December 1, 2008. http://takimag.com/article/the_decline_and_rise_of_the_alternative_right#axzz4jzfoQiP3.

14. Hatewatch staff, "Identitarian Ideology," October 12, 2015. https://www.splcenter.org/hatewatch/2015/10/12/american-racists-work-spread-%E2%80%98identitarian%E2%80%99-ideology.

15. Richard Spencer, "The Purpose and Meaning of the Alt-right Movement," December 21, 2016. https://www.geopolitica.ru/en/video/richard-spencer-purpose-and-meaning-alt-right-movement; Annie Kelly, "The Alt-right: Reactionary Rehabilitation for White Masculinity," Soundings 66 (2017): 68. doi.org/10.3898/136266217821733688.

16. According to Vox, paleoconservatism is a group of people who "adhere to the normal conservative triad of nationalism, free markets, and moral traditionalism, but they put greater weight on the nationalist leg of the stool — leading to a more strident form of anti-immigrant politics that often veers into racism, an isolationist foreign policy rather than a hawkish or dovish one, and a deep skepticism of economic globalization that puts them at odds with an important element of the business agenda." Dylan Matthews, "Paleoconservatism, the Movement that Explains Donald Trump, Explained," Vox, May 6, 2016. https://www.vox.com/2016/5/6/11592604/donald-trump-paleoconservative-buchanan.

17. Gottfried.

18. George Hawley, Making Sense of the Alt-right (New York: Columbia University Press, 2017), 4.

19. Brian McLaren, "The 'Alt-right' has Created Alt-Christianity," Time, August 25, 2017. http://time.com/4915161/charlottesville-alt-right-alt-christianity/.

20. Alt-right..com, "On Women in the Alt-right," Altright.com, March 4, 2018. https://altright.com/2017/12/13/on-women-in-the-alt-right/.

21. Joe Carter, "What Christians Should Know about the Alt-right," Ethics and Religious Liberty Commission of the Southern Baptist Convention, June 14, 2017. https://erlc.com/resource-library/articles/what-christians-should-know-about-the-alt-right.

22. Cheney-Lippold, 7.

23. Hawley, 11.

24. Sydney Ember, "News Outlets Rethink Usage of the Term 'Alt-right,'" New York Times, November 28, 2016. https://www.nytimes.com/2016/11/28/business/media/news-outlets-rethink-usage-of-the-term-alt-right.html; Rebecca Lewis, Alternative Influence: Broadcasting the Reactionary Right on YouTube (Data and Society, 2018). https://datasociety.net/wp-content/uploads/2018/09/DS_Alternative_Influence.pdf.

25. Garcia.

26. Sarah Posner, "How Donald Trump's New Campaign Chief Created an Online Haven for White Nationalists," Mother Jones, August 22, 2016. https://www.motherjones.com/politics/2016/08/stephen-bannon-donald-trump-alt-right-breitbart-news/.

27. Carter; Gottfried.

28. Spencer.

29. Andrew Boge, "A Rhetoric of Intellectual Racism: The National Policy Institute's Epistemology of Strategic Whiteness," Race and Pedagogy National Conference, Tacoma, Washington, September 2018.

30. George Michael, "The Rise of the Alt-right and the Politics of Polarization in America," Skeptic, 9. www.skeptic.com/reading_room/rise-of-alt-right-politics-of-polarization-in-america/. Accessed March 4, 2018; SPLC, "Alt-right."

31. Kelly, 69.

32. I have chosen to use the quotation marks around "alt-right" in this section because, of the women I studied, at least one would not identify herself with the term. That noted, due to the way she identifies herself and articulates her values, ideologies, and (other) classifications like "traditionalism," she signals or simulates similar to the "alt-right."

33. Luzilda Carrillo Arciniega, "Diversity and Inclusion and the Rise of the Alt-right," *Anthropology News* 58(1) (January/February 2017): 175–79. https://doi.org/10.1111/AN.332; Carter; Masood Farivar, "U.S. White Nationalists Barred by Facebook Find Haven on Russian Site," Voice of America, April 10, 2019. https://www.voanews.com/a/american-white-nationalists-barred-by-facebook-find-friendly-haven-on-russia-s-vk-website-/4871044.html; Robert Futrell and Pete Simi, "The [Un]surprising Alt-right," *Contexts* 16(2) (2017): 76. doi:10.1177/1536504217714269; Gramlich; A. Kelly; Kelly McEvers, "'We're Not Going Away': Alt-Right Leader on Voice in Trump Administration," *All Things Considered*. NPR, November 17, 2016. https://www.npr.org/2016/11/17/502476139/were-not-going-away-alt-right-leader-on-voice-in-trump-administration; McLaren.

34. Lana Lokteff, "Virtues of the West," hosted by Brittany Pettibone and Tara McCarthy YouTube, March 2, 2017. https://www.youtube.com/watch?v=58mdlRSoHrs.

35. Laura Smith, "The Truth about Women and White Supremacy." The Cut, *New York*, August 13, 2017. https://www.thecut.com/2017/08/charlottesville-attack-women-white-supremacy.html.

36. Sarah Ditum, "Why Are We So Desperate to Blame White Supremacy on Women?" New Statesman, August 21, 2017. https://www.newstatesman.com/world/north-america/2017/08/why-are-we-so-desperate-blame-white-supremacy-women.

37. Michael Edison Hayden, "Alt-right Women Asked to 'Choose Submission' to Grow Political Movement," *Newsweek*, November 16, 2017. http://www.newsweek.com/alt-right-women-asked-choose-submission-grow-political-movement-705655; Michael E. Hayden, "Women Shouldn't Have the Right to Vote Says 'Alt-right' Leader Richard Spencer," *Newsweek*, October 14, 2017. https://www.newsweek.com/alt-right-leader-richard-spencer-isnt-sure-if-women-should-be-allowed-vote-685048.

38. DiAngelo, 56.

39. DiAngelo, 55.

40. DiAngelo, 57.

41. Radcliffe, 88–89.

42. Tedford and Herbeck, 128.

43. DiAngelo, 58–59.

44. DiAngelo, 59.

45. DiAngelo, 60–61.

46. DiAngelo, 61.

47. DiAngelo, 62.

48. DiAngelo, 62–63.

49. DiAngelo, 63.

50. Lokteff, "Virtue of the West."

51. @LanaLokteff, "Ethnically #Russian. Wife of a Swedish Viking. Mother. Producer of #Identitarian#Nationalist Media for @redicetv Founder of @reallanasllama organic clothing," Twitter. https://twitter.com/LanaLokteff. Accessed February 28, 2018.

52. Lokteff, "Virtue of the West."

53. Lokteff, "Virtue of the West."

54. Red Ice TV, "About Lana Lokteff." https://redice.tv/about.

55. Lana Lokteff, "How the Left is Betraying Women," YouTube. https://www.youtube.com/watch?v=BjnH99slHmE.

56. Tara McCarthy, "Tara McCarthy Was a Socialist, Anti-natalist, Feminist in 2015," YouTube, December 5, 2017. https://www.youtube.com/watch?v=OqR-phb3Wkk.

57. Tara McCarthy, "What It Is Like Being a Mixed Race Ethno-nationalist," Archive.org, May 15, 2015. https://archive.org/details/youtube-lgthyxE6D04.

58. McCarthy, "What It Is Like Being a Mixed Race Ethno-nationalist."

59. McCarthy, "What It Is Like Being a Mixed Race Ethno-nationalist."

60. McCarthy, "Virtue of the West."

61. Tara McCarthy, "Irreplaceable: How and Why We Must Save the West, by Tara McCarthy." http://www.irreplaceablebook.com/.

62. Tara McCarthy, "Virtue of the West," hosted by Brittany Pettibone and Tara McCarthy, March 2, 2017. https://www.youtube.com/watch?v=58mdlRS0Hrs.

63. Tara McCarthy, "Tara McCarthy on Ethno Nationalism," YouTube. https://www.youtube.com/watch?v=tTNfiNh5Nic.

64. @BrittPettibone, "Award-winning Sci-fi Author, Catholic," Twitter, February 28, 2018.

65. Brittany Pettibone, "American Identitarianism (Martin Sellner, Brittany Pettibone, and James Allsup) Part 1," YouTube, January 8, 2018. https://www.youtube.com/watch?v=mJO_PkLJUHU.

66. T.S. Pettibone, "About Us," T.S. Pettibone. http://tspettibone.com/about-us/. Accessed February 28, 2018; Tara McCarthy, YouTube, March 2, 2017. https://www.youtube.com/watch?v=58mdlRS0Hrs.

67. Brittany Pettibone, "Virtue of the West," hosted by Brittany Pettibone and Tara McCarthy, YouTube. https://www.youtube.com/channel/UCesrUK_dMDBZAf7cnjQPdgQ/about.

68. Pettibone, "American Identitarianism (Martin Sellner, Brittany Pettibone, and James Allsup) Part 1."

69. @Lauren_Southern, "Best Selling Author. Lover of hedgehogs and Freedom. Retweets ≠ endorsement," Twitter. Accessed February 28, 2018.

70. Lauren Southern, "Return of the Traditional Woman," YouTube, May 27, 2017. https://www.youtube.com/watch?v=HFW0z0Y5TR4.

71. Southern, "Return of the Traditional Woman."

72. Hayden, "Alt-right Women Asked to 'Choose Submission.'"

73. Lauren Southern, "I Was Wrong About Identity Politics?" YouTube, June 8, 2017. https://www.youtube.com/watch?v=LE5AyRPZK8Q.

74. Southern, "I Was Wrong About Identity Politics?"

75. McLaughlin.

76. Southern, "Return of the Traditional Woman."

77. Southern, Lauren. "To those who care." Archive.today. Originally published in Medium. http://archive.is/E60KP. Accessed July 3, 2020.

78. Lokteff, "How the Left Is Betraying Women."

79. Lokteff, "How the Left Is Betraying Women."

80. Lokteff, "How the Left Is Betraying Women."

81. Lokteff, "How the Left Is Betraying Women."

82. McCarthy, "Virtue of the West."

83. McCarthy, "Virtue of the West."

84. McCarthy, "Virtue of the West."

85. Lauren Southern [@Lauren_Southern], "Diversity literally just means less white peo-ple lmao," Twitter, February 14, 2017.

86. Lana Lokteff, "Oprah #MeToo #TimesUp Movement Ignores "Migrant" Gang Rapists Who Walk Free," Red Ice TV, January 16, 2018. https://redice.tv/red-ice-tv/oprah-metoo-timesup-movement-ignores-migrant-gang-rapists-who-walk-free.

87. Elisabeth G. McRae, *Mothers of a Massive Resistance: White Women and the Politics of White Supremacy* (Oxford: Oxford University Press, 2018), 6.

88. Harris, 1714.

89. Mills.

90. Lokteff, "Virtue of the West."

91. Lokteff, "Virtue of the West."

92. Pettibone, "Virtue of the West."

93. Lokteff, "How the Left Is Betraying Women."

94. Lokteff, "How the Left Is Betraying Women."

95. Lokteff, "Virtue of the West."

96. Lokteff, "How the Left Is Betraying Women."

97. Lokteff, "How the Left Is Betraying Women."

98. Lokteff, "How the Left Is Betraying Women."

99. Blee, "Women of the Klan."

100. McCarthy, "Virtue of the West."

101. Hayden, "Women Shouldn't Have the Right to Vote."

102. Lokteff, "How the Left Is Betraying Women."

103. Lokteff, "Intersectional Feminism Wages War on White Women."

104. Richard Dyer, *White* (New York: Routledge, 1997), 10.

105. Rebecca, "A Chat with Blonde in the Belly of the Beast," hosted by Brittany Pettibone and Tara McCarthy, YouTube, March 16, 2017. https://www.youtube.com/watch?v=QkTvRFuXomE.

106. McCarthy, "Virtue of the West."

107. Lokteff, "Virtue of the West."

108. Kitch, 54–56.

109. Pettibone, "Virtue of the West."

110. Lokteff, "Virtue of the West"; McCarthy, "Virtue of the West"; Pettibone, "Virtue of the West."

111. Lokteff, "Virtue of the West."

112. Lokteff, "How the Left Is Betraying Women."

113. McCarthy, in Rachel Leah, "'Alt-right' Women Are Upset That 'Alt-right' men Are Treating Them Terribly," Salon, December 4, 2017. https://www.salon.com/2017/12/04/alt-right-women-are-upset-that-alt-right-men-are-treating-them-terribly/.

114. Leah.

115. Following this event, McCarthy removed her statements from her YouTube and Twitter content and tweeted that it was time for her to leave Twitter for a while. @TaraMcCarthy444, "It's that time again where I am taking a break from Twitter. Be kind. Stay strong. Question the things you're not allowed to question," Twitter, January 30, 2018. https://twitter.com/TaraMcCarthy444/status/958345082519871496.

116. Lauren Southern, "Why I'm not married," YouTube, November 23, 2017. https://www.youtube.com/watch?v=P-UKPpmQlys.

117. Southern, "Why I'm not married."

118. Southern, "Why I'm not married."

119. Southern, "Why I'm not married."

120. Southern is now making documentary films.

121. "Media: On women of the alt-right," altright.com. https://altright.com/2017/12/13/on-women-in-the-alt-right/. Accessed July 5, 2020.

122. Southern, "Why I'm not married."

123. Southern, "Return of the Traditional woman."

124. Anderson and Grace, 943.

125. Lokteff, "How the Left Is Betraying Women."

126. Southern, "Return of the Traditional woman."

127. Southern, "Return of the Traditional woman."

128. Lokteff, "How the Left Is Betraying Women."

129. Pettibone, "Virtue of the West."

130. Pettibone, "Virtue of the West."

131. Lokteff, "Virtue of the West."

132. Pettibone, "Virtue of the West."

133. Lana Lokteff, "Intersectional Feminism Wages War on White Women," Red Ice TV, February 3, 2018. https://www.youtube.com/watch?v=HgmXDbsd-fQ.

134. Lokteff. "Oprah #MeToo #TimesUp Movement Ignores 'Migrant' Gang Rapists Who Walk Free."

135. DiAngelo, 54–55.

136. DiAngelo, 60–61.

137. DiAngelo, 62.

138. Glenn Eric Singleton and Curtis Linton, *Courageous Conversations about Race: A Field Guide for Achieving Equity in Schools* (Thousand Oaks, CA: Corwin Press, 2006).

139. Anderson and Grace, 943.

140. DiAngelo, 63.

141. Jessica Taylor, "Laptops and Playpens: 'Mommy Bloggers' and Visions of Household Work," in In L. Adkins and M. Dever, eds., *The Post-Fordist Sexual Contract* (London: Palgrave Macmillan, 2016), 109, 115; Mari Lehto, "Bad Is the New Good: Negotiating Bad Motherhood in Finnish Mommy Blogs," *Feminist Media Studies* 19(5) (2019). doi:10.1080/14680777.2019.16422242.

142. DiAngelo, 62–63.

143. Potok and Wood.

144. Blee, "Inside Organized Racism," 115–16, 118–20.

145. Blee, "Inside Organized Racism," 120–22.

146. Laura Smith, "The KKK Might Have Died in Obscurity If this Sinister, Racist Woman Didn't Come Along," Timeline, December 11, 2017. https://timeline.com/did-you-know-that-the-brains-behind-the-kkk-was-a-woman-a23d7d361d1d; Smith, "The Truth about Women and White Supremacy"; Blee, "Women of the Klan," 1.

Chapter 6: Responsibility of a White "Privilege Filter": Dismantling Conservative White Women as Color-Blind Maiden Shields

1. Crenshaw, "Demarginalizing the Intersection of Race and Sex," 151–52.

2. Rachel Butt, "America's Shrinking Middle Class Is Killing the Economy," Business Insider, June 28, 2016. http://www.businessinsider.com/americas-shrinking-middle-class

-hurts-economy-2016–6; Richard Fry and Rakesh Kochhar, "The Shrinking Middle Class in U.S. Metropolitan Areas: 6 Key Findings," Pew Research Center. May 12, 2016. http://www .pewresearch.org/fact-tank/2016/05/12/us-middle-class-metros-takeaways/; Phillip Wallach, "Why America's Response to the Financial Crisis Brought us to the Edge of Political Crisis," Brookings Institution, April 21, 2015. https://www.brookings.edu/blog/fixgov/2015/04/21 /why-americas-responses-to-the-financial-crisis-brought-us-to-the-edge-of-political-crisis/. Accessed February 14, 2018.

3. Ali Vitali, "The White House Women Who've Got Trump's Back," NBC News, September 18, 2017. https://www.nbcnews.com/politics/white-house/white-house-women -who-ve-got-trump-s-back-n799646.

4. Kelsey Harkness, "Hope Hicks Shows Accomplishments for Women, by Women, Count Only If You're a Democrat," Daily Signal, September 14, 2017. http://dailysignal.com /2017/09/14/hope-hicks-shows-accomplishments-for-women-by-women-only-count-if -youre-a-democrat/. Accessed February 24, 2018; Vitali; Patrice Lee Onwuka, "Hope Brings Another Woman to Trump Leadership Circle," International Women's Forum August 17, 2017. http://iwf.org/blog/2804564/Hope-Brings-Another-Woman-to-Trump-Leadership -Circle. Accessed February 23, 2018.

5. Radcliffe, 31.

6. Baumgardner and Richards, 51; Charlotte Krolokke and Anne S. Sorensen, *Gender Communication Theories and Analyses* (Thousand Oaks, CA: Sage, 2006), 1–7.

7. Elsa B. Brown, "Womanist Consciousness: Maggie Lena Walker and the Independent Order of Saint Luke," *Signs* 14(3) (1989): 612; Carol Chehade, *Big Little White Lies: Our Attempt to White-out America* (Kearney, NE: Nehmarche Publications, 2001), 136; Dill, 135–38; K. Harding, 16–22.

8. Rochelle Gurstein, "Emma Goldman and the Tragedy of Modern Love," *Salmagundi* 135 (2002): 68.

9. hooks, *Ain't I a Woman*, 145–58.

10. Paul Smith, "Responsibilities," in *Discerning the Subject* (Minneapolis: University of Minnesota Press, 1988), 153.

11. Combahee River Collective.

12. Adrienne Rich, "Disloyal to Civilization: Feminism, Racism, Gynephobia" (1978). http://chainsofblocks.com/kindle/download/id=188848&type=file

13. Mariana Ortega, "Being Lovingly, Knowingly Ignorant: White Feminism and Women of Color," *Hypatia* 21(3) (2006): 58.

14. Bonilla-Silva, "The Linguistics of Color Blind Racism." 63.

15. Abigail Geiger and Lauren Kent, "Number of Women Leaders Around the World Has Grown, but They're Still a Small Group," Pew Internet Research Center, March 8, 2017. http:// www.pewresearch.org/fact-tank/2017/03/08/women-leaders-around-the-world/. Accessed February 23, 2018.

16. Kelly Dittmar et al., "Black Women in American Politics: 2017 Status Update," Rutgers Center for American Women and Politics, 2.

17. "Women in the U.S. Congress 2018," Center for American Women and Politics, 2018. http://www.cawp.rutgers.edu/women-us-congress-2018. Accessed February 24, 2018.

18. "Women of Color in Elective Office 2018," Center for American Women and Politics, 2018. http://www.cawp.rutgers.edu/women-color-elective-office-2018. Accessed February 24, 2018.

19. Kelly Dittmar et al., "Representation Matters: Women in the U.S. Congress," Rutgers Center for American Women and Politics, 4.

20. "Women in the U.S. Congress 2019," Center for American Women and Politics, 2019. https://cawp.rutgers.edu/women-us-congress-2019. Accessed March 27, 2019.

21. "Women of Color in Elective Office 2019."

22. Kelly Dittmar, "Candidates Matter: Gender Differences in Election 2016," Rutgers Center for American Women and Politics, February 14, 2017. http://www.cawp.rutgers.edu/sites/default/files/resources/closer_look_candidates_matter_2.14.17.pdf. Accessed February 28, 2018.

23. Dittmar et al., "Black Women in American Politics," 2.

24. Dittmar et al., "Women of Color in Elective Office 2019."

25. D'vera Cohn and Gretchen Livingston, "Americans' Views of Women as Political Leaders Differ by Gender," Pew Internet Research Center, May 19, 2016. http://www.pewresearch.org/fact-tank/2016/05/19/americans-views-of-women-as-political-leaders-differ-by-gender/.

26. Emily Harmer, Heather Saving, and Orlanda Ward, "'Are you Tough Enough?' Performing Gender in the UK Leadership Debates 2015," Media, Culture, and Society 29(7) (2016): 962. doi:10.1177/0163443716682074; Sarah Pedersen, "Press Response to Women Politicians," Journalism Studies 19(5) (2018): 709–10.

27. Richard L. Fox and Jennifer L. Lawless, "Reconciling Family Roles with Political Ambition: The New Normal for Women in Twenty-first Century U.S. Politics," Journal of Politics 76(2) (2014): 398, 403.

28. Edda Humprecht and Frank Esser, "A Glass Ceiling in the Online Age? Explaining the Underrepresentation of Women in Online Political Newspapers," European Journal of Communication 35(5) (2017): 448–49.

29. Fox and Lawless, 402.

30. Fox and Lawless, 403.

31. Republican Party, "Restoring the American Dream." https://www.gop.com/platform/restoring-the-american-dream/.

32. "Republican Platform 2016," Committee on Arrangements for the 2016 Republican National Convention, i. https://prod-cdn-static.gop.com/media/documents/DRAFT_12_FINAL%5B1%5D-ben_1468872234.pdf. Accessed February 28, 2018.

33. "Republican Platform 2016," i.

34. Love, 3; Rory McVeigh, "Structured Ignorance and Organized Racism in the United States," Social Forces 82(3) (2004): 895–936. doi.org/10.1353/sof.2004.0047.

35. Even though Manigault and Hicks resigned in 2017 and 2018, respectively, their appointments in office were significant.

36. Alexandra Desanctis, "The Progressive Double Standard on Feminism," National Review, September 19, 2017. https://www.nationalreview.com/2017/09/conservative-women-double-standard-victims/. Accessed February 24, 2018; Harkness; Ginny Montalbano, "Feminist Snipes at Melania Are Unfair. She's a Fine First Lady," Newsweek, January 25, 2018. http://www.newsweek.com/feminist-snipes-melania-are-unfair-shes-fine-first-lady-790765 Accessed February 24, 2018; Conway, quoted in Vitali.

37. Burke, "The Rhetoric of Hitler's 'Battle,'" 141.

38. Lindsay Meeks and David Domke, "When Politics Is a Woman's Game: Party and Gender Ownership in Woman-versus-Woman Elections," Communication Research 4(7) (2016): 897. doi:10.1177/0093650215581369; Karrin V. Anderson, "Presidential Pioneer or Campaign Queen?: Hillary Clinton and the First-time Frontrunner Double Bind," Rhetoric and Public Affairs 20(3) (2017): 525.

39. Michelle Brunetti Post, "Kellyanne Conway Played Key Role in Trump's Road to Presidency," *Press of Atlantic City*, November 9, 2016. http://www.pressofatlanticcity.com/news/trump-strategist-kellyanne-conway-has-deep-roots-in-south-jersey/article_59853be4-6e5a-5e9c-bdf7-cfc18fb1647e.html.

40. Michael Sebastian, "Who Is Kellyanne Conway? 20 Things to Know about Donald Trump's Presidential Counselor," *Cosmopolitan*, June 5, 2017. http://www.cosmopolitan.com/politics/news/a62994/kellyanne-conway-trump-new-campaign-manager/.

41. Don Van Natta and Jill Abramson, "The Presidential Trial: The Lawsuit; Quietly a Team of Lawyers Kept the Jones' Case Alive," *New York Times*, January 24, 1999. http://www.nytimes.com/1999/01/24/us/president-s-trial-lawsuit-quietly-team-lawyers-kept-paula-jones-s-case-alive.html; Sarah Jacobs, "How Kellyanne Conway Makes and Spends Her $39 Million Fortune," *Business Insider*, April 28, 2017. http://www.businessinsider.com/how-kellyanne-conway-became-rich-2017-4.

42. Jacobs; "Kellyanne Conway's full speech at CPAC 2017."

43. Jacobs; Sebastian.

44. "Kellyanne Conway's full speech at CPAC 2017"; Sebastian.

45. Jacobs.

46. "Ivanka Trump," Archives of Women's Political Communication, Iowa State University.

47. Erika Harwood, "Ivanka Trump's Forgotten Modeling Years," *Vanity Fair*, October 19, 2017. https://www.vanityfair.com/style/photos/2017/10/ivanka-trump-modeling-years.

48. Max Greenwood, "Spicer: Ivanka Trump's White House Role Is 'to Be Helpful and Provide Input,'" *The Hill*, February 23, 2017. http://thehill.com/blogs/blog-briefing-room/news/320903-sean-spicer-ivanka-trumps-white-house-role-is-to-be-helpful-and.

49. Javier Panzar, "Melania Trump's RNC Speech Is Strikingly Similar to Michelle Obama's 2008 Convention Speech," *Los Angeles Times*, July 18, 2016. http://www.latimes.com/nation/politics/trailguide/la-na-republican-convention-2016-live-melania-trump-s-rnc-speech-appears-to-1468901655-htmlstory.html.

50. Abby Phillip, "Embassies Court Ivanka Trump to Build a Relationship with Her Father's Administration," *Washington Post*, May 19, 2017.

51. Shelbi Austin, "10 Things You Did Not Know about Sarah Huckabee Sanders," October 25, 2017. https://www.usnews.com/news/politics/articles/2017-10-25/10-things-you-didnt-know-about-sarah-huckabee-sanders.

52. Austin; Eliza Relman, "The Rise of Sarah Huckabee Sanders, the New Star of the Trump Administration," *Business Insider*, June 30, 2017. http://www.businessinsider.com/sarah-huckabee-sanders-bio-photos-white-house-press-2017-6#ever-since-stephanie-grisham-now-melania-trumps-communications-director-and-mike-dubke-the-former-white-house-communications-director-left-trumps-communication-team-sanders-has-become-more-visible-and-is-considered-a-top-candidate-to-take-over-spicers-job-if-his-responsibilities-change-6.

53. "Ivanka Trump—Motherhood," advertisement for Donald J. Trump for President, YouTube, September 30, 2016. https://www.youtube.com/watch?v=b9SfVSa4zZc; Emily Jane Fox, "Ivanka Trump's Post-election Playbook," *Vanity Fair*, October 4, 2016. https://www.vanityfair.com/news/2016/10/ivanka-trump-ad-post-election-playbook; Christina Cauterucci, "Mother Is a Woman's Most Important Job," *Slate*, October 3, 2016.

54. Frank Pallotta, "The 'P-word' Problem: Trump's Comments Pose Issue for News Outlets," CNN. September 7, 2016. http://money.cnn.com/2016/10/07/media/vulgar-comments-donald-trump-headlines/index.html.

55. Julia Carpenter, "Forget the 'Glass Ceiling.' Women of Color Face a 'Concrete Ceiling,'" CNN Money, August 8, 2018. https://money.cnn.com/2018/08/06/pf/women-of-color-ceos /index.html.

56. "Women in the Trump Administration: Kellyanne Conway," #WomenRule Summit, Politico, December 5, 2017. https://www.politico.com/video/2017/12/05/women-in-the-trump -administration-kellyanne-conway-064518.

57. Prividera and Howard, 31.

58. "Kellyanne Conway's full speech at CPAC 2017."

59. "Kellyanne Conway's full speech at CPAC 2017."

60. Ivanka Trump, "An Exclusive Excerpt from Ivanka Trump's New Book, 'Women Who Work,'" *Fortune*, May 1, 2017. http://fortune.com/2017/05/01/ivanka-trump-book -women-who-work/.

61. Masha Gessen, "The Degrading Ritual of Sarah Huckabee Sanders's Pre-Thanksgiving Press Briefing," *The New Yorker*, November 21, 2017. https://www.newyorker.com/news /our-columnists/degrading-ritual-sarah-huckabee-sanders-pre-thanksgiving-press-briefing.

62. Prividera and Howard, 31.

63. Erik Wemple, "You're a Parent: Reporter Presses Sarah Huckabee Sanders on Immigration," *Washington Post*, June 14, 2018. https://www.washingtonpost.com/blogs/erik -wemple/wp/2018/06/14/youre-a-parent-reporter-presses-sarah-huckabee-sanders-on -immigration/.

64. Anderson and Grace, 943.

65. Conway, "Kellyanne Conway's full speech at CPAC 2017."

66. Trump, "An Exclusive Excerpt from Ivanka Trump's New Book, 'Women Who Work.'"

67. Conway, "Kellyanne Conway's full speech at CPAC 2017."

68. Conway, "Kellyanne Conway's full speech at CPAC 2017."

69. Conway, "Women in the Trump Administration: Kellyanne Conway."

70. Hamilton Carroll, *Affirmative Reaction: New Formations of White Masculinity* (Durham, NC: Duke University Press, 2011), 9; Kate Lockwood Harris and Jenna N. Hanchey, "(De)stabilizing Sexual Violence Discourse: Masculinization of Victimhood, Organizational Blame, and Labile Imperialism," *Communication and Critical/Cultural Studies* 11(40) (December 2014): 324–25.

71. Harmer et al., 972.

72. Conway, "Kellyanne Conway's full speech at CPAC 2017."

73. Conway, "Kellyanne Conway's full speech at CPAC 2017."

74. "Women in the Trump Administration: Kellyanne Conway."

75. Zajicek, 156.

76. Jaclyn Reiss, "Kellyanne Conway Says Anderson Cooper's Eye Roll Was 'Possibly Sexist,'" *Boston Globe*, May 14, 2017. https://www.bostonglobe.com/news/politics/2017 /05/14/kellyanne-conway-says-anderson-cooper-eye-roll-was-possibly-sexist/3UsNcT24 uw610AP52JylYO/story.html.

77. Edward Luce, "Ivanka Trump's G20 Performance Puzzles World Leaders," *Irish Times*, July 1, 2019. https://www.irishtimes.com/news/world/us/ivanka-trump-s-g20-performance- puzzles-world-leaders-1.3942812; Susan Moore, "We Laugh at Ivanka Trump—Because to Take Her Seriously Is Frightening," *The Guardian*, July 1, 2019. https://www.theguardian .com/commentisfree/2019/jul/01/ivanka-trump-g20-ghastly-spectacle-rise-unelected.

78. Ivanka Trump, CBS Interview, April 5, 2017 https://www.youtube.com/watch?v=XRL dnBpEMAA.

79. "White House Press Secretary Sarah Huckabee Sanders Calls For Journalist To Be Fired," MSNBC. September 13, 2017. https://www.youtube.com/watch?v=FOwAtWXe6fo.

80. Anushay Hossain, "Sarah Sanders and the Sexism of Women," CNN Opinion, February 1, 2018. https://www.cnn.com/2018/02/01/opinions/sarah-sanders-and-the-sexism-of-women-hossain/index.html.

81. Wendy K. Z. Anderson and Patrice M. Buzzanell, "'Outcast among Outcasts': Identity, Gender, and Leadership in a Mac Users Group," *Women and Language* 30(1) (2007): 34; Cathryn Johnson, "Gender, Legitimate Authority, and Leader-Subordinate Conversations," *American Sociological Review* 59(1) (1994): 123. doi:10.2307/2096136.

82. Butler, "Subversive Acts," 131.

83. Madeline Conway, "Conway Asked How She Justified Trump and Sexual Assault Allegations," Politico, November 30, 2016. https://www.politico.com/story/2016/11/kellyanne-conway-trump-sexual-assault-232002.

84. Madeline Conway, "Conway Asked How She Justified Trump and Sexual Assault Allegations," Politico, November 30, 2016. https://www.politico.com/story/2016/11/kellyanne-conway-trump-sexual-assault-232002.

85. Aimee Picci, "Kellyanne Conway on Ivanka's Brand: 'Go Buy It Today,'" *Moneywatch*, CBS News, February 9, 2017. https://www.cbsnews.com/news/kellyanne-conway-on-ivankas-brand-go-buy-it-today/.

86. "Women in the Trump Administration: Kellyanne Conway."

87. Conway, "Kellyanne Conway's full speech at CPAC 2017."

88. "Ivanka Trump on Her New White House Role," *CBS This Morning*, April 5, 2017. https://www.youtube.com/watch?v=XRLdnBpEMAA.

89. "Sarah 'Huckabee' Sanders FIERCE response when asked on Trump's 'SH!thole countries' comments," YouTube, January 16, 2018. https://www.youtube.com/watch?v=k-K4NnrbUc4.

90. Tucker.

91. Noble, 84.

92. "Sarah Huckabee Sanders Holds Her First White House Daily Briefing As Deputy Press Secretary," YouTube, May 5, 2017. https://www.youtube.com/watch?v=vcPihsiD8ng.

93. "Trump's 3 Statements On Charlottesville," YouTube, August 15, 2017. https://www.youtube.com/watch?v=jHzbo5xvaY8.

94. Conway, "Kellyanne Conway's full speech at CPAC 2017."

95. Sarah Huckabee Sanders, "White House: 'Pocahontas' Not a Racial Slur," CNN, November 27, 2017. https://www.youtube.com/watch?v=jxLkSiAzqwo.

96. Jemele Hill [@jemelehill], "Donald Trump is a white supremacist who has largely surrounded himself w/ other white supremacists," Twitter, September 11, 2017. twitter.com/jemelehill/status/907391978194849793?lang=en.

97. Jemele Hill [@jemelehill], "Trump is the most ignorant, offensive president of my lifetime. His rise is a direct result of white supremacy. Period," Twitter, September 11, 2017. twitter.com/jemelehill/status/907392882155425793?lang=en.

98. "White House Press Secretary Sarah Huckabee Sanders Calls for Journalist to Be Fired," MSNBC, September 13, 2017. https://www.youtube.com/watch?v=FOwAtWXe6fo.

99. Radcliffe, 91.

100. Bob Fredricks, "Trump Can't Be Racist Because He Had a TV Show: Sanders," *New York Post*, January 16, 2018. https://nypost.com/2018/01/16/trump-cant-be-racist-because-he-had-a-tv-show-sanders/.

101. "Sarah 'Huckabee' Sanders FIERCE response when asked on Trump's 'SH!thole countries' comments."

102. "KellyAnne Conway's Racist Barack Obama Slur," YouTube, March 8, 2008. https://www.youtube.com/watch?v=qD113L3h1cQ.

103. "Sarah Huckabee Sanders Holds Her First White House Daily Briefing As Deputy Press Secretary."

104. Ivanka Trump [@IvankaTrump], "1:2 There should be no place in society for racism, white supremacy and neo-nazis," Twitter, August 13, 2017. twitter.com/IvankaTrump /status/896705195228381187?ref_src=twsrc%5Etfw&ref_url=http%3A%2F%2Ffortune .com%2F2017%2F08%2F13%2Fivanka-trump-response-charlottesville-virginia-rally%2F.

105. Fox and Lawless, 413.

106. Karma Chávez, "The Body: An Abstract and Actual Rhetorical Concept," *Rhetoric Society Quarterly* 48(3) (May 2018): 244. doi:10.1080/02773945.2018.1454182; Cheryl Glenn, "Sex, Lies, and Manuscript: Refiguring Aspasia in the History of Rhetoric," *College Composition and Communication* 45(2) (May 1994): 180.

107. Shotwell, *Against Purity*, 8–9.

108. Kevin Neuhouser, "'If I Had Abandoned My Children': Community Mobilization and Commitment to the Identity of Mother in Northeast Brazil," *Social Forces* 77(1) (1998): 347, 358–59. http://www.jstor.org/stable/3006020. Accessed March 8, 2018.

109. Cloud, "The rhetoric of <family values>," 398.

110. Anderson and Grace, 943.

111. Kate Lockwood Harris, "'Compassion' and Katrina: Reasserting Violent White Masculinity after the Storm," *Women and Language* 34(1) (2011): 22.

112. "The Ivanka Trump Guide to Being a Modern Mom," *People*, October 14, 2016. http://people.com/babies/ivanka-trump-quotes-on-motherhood/get-some-me-time-before -mom-time/.

113. Will Drabold, "Read Michelle Obama's Emotional Speech at the Democratic Convention," *Time*, July 26, 2016. http://time.com/4421538/democratic-convention-michelle -obama-transcript/.

114. McRae.

115. Michelle Obama, "TRANSCRIPT: Michelle Obama's Speech On Donald Trump's Alleged Treatment Of Women," NPR, October 13, 2016. https://www.npr.org/2016/10/13 /497846667/transcript-michelle-obamas-speech-on-donald-trumps-alleged-treatment -of-women.

116. Maya Oppenheimer, "Ivanka Trump's New Book on Being a Working Mother Struggling to Fit In Massages," *The Independent*, May 2, 2017. http://www.independent.co.uk /news/world/americas/ivanka-trump-new-book-no-time-for-massages-superwoman-myth -working-mother-debunk-first-daughter-a7713546.html.

117. Ivanka Trump, "The Trump Card: Playing to Win in Work and Life." Google Books. https://books.google.com/books?id=Ag_vs9qt6U4C&pg=PT11&dq=%22in+truth,+the+ only+advantage+is+psychological%22&hl=en&sa=X&ved=0ahUKEwitkLCAs8TZAhW F30MKHRsdDq0Q6AEIJzAA#v=onepage&q=%22in%20truth%2C%20the%20only%20 advantage%20is%20psychological%22&f=false.

118. Radcliffe, 88–89.

119. Jennifer Wright, "Men Are Responsible for Mass Shootings: How Toxic Masculinity Is Killing Us," *Harper's Bazaar*, February 16, 2018. https://www.harpersbazaar.com/culture /politics/a18207600/mass-shootings-male-entitlement-toxic-masculinity/.

120. Conway, "Kellyanne Conway's full speech at CPAC 2017."

121. Nina M. Lozano-Reich and Dana L. Cloud, "The Uncivil Tongue: Invitational Rhetoric and the Problem of Inequality," *Western Journal of Communication* 73(2) (2009): 221–24. doi:10.1080/10570310902856105.

122. Hannah Karolak and Craig T. Maier, "From 'Safe Spaces' to 'Communicative Spaces': Semiotic Labor, Authentic Civility and the Basic Communication Course," *Journal of the Association for Communication Administration* 34(2) (2015): 93.

123. Audre Lorde, "The Uses of Anger: Women Responding to Racism," Keynote presentation at the National Women's Studies Association Conference, Storrs, Connecticut, 1981. http://www.blackpast.org/1981-audre-lorde-uses-anger-women-responding-racism.

124. Lonnae O'Neal, "Ibram Kendi, One of the Nation's Leading Scholars of Racism, Says Education and Love Are Not the Answer," *The Undefeated*, September 20, 2017. https://theundefeated.com/features/ibram-kendi-leading-scholar-of-racism-says-education-and-love-are-not-the-answer/.

Epilogue: Amplifying Intersectionality as an Ethical Response

1. Radcliffe, 96.

2. Colleen Clemens, "Ally or Accomplice? The Language of Activism," Teaching Tolerance, June 5, 2017. https://www.tolerance.org/magazine/ally-or-accomplice-the-language-of-activism.

3. George Yancy, "Introduction," in *Black Bodies, White Gazes: The Continuing Significance of Race.* (Lanham, MD: Rowman & Littlefield 2008), 98.

4. George Yancy, "Musings: On autobiography and Africana Philosophy," *in Across Black Spaces: Essays and Interviews from an American Philosopher* (Lanham, MD: Rowman & Littlefield Publishers, 2020), 231.

5. Marilyn Frye, "White Woman Feminist," in *Willful Virgin: Essays in Feminism* (Berkeley, CA: Crossing Press, 1992), 151.

6. Barbara Applebaum, "Flipping the Script . . . and Still a Problem: Staying in the Anxiety of Being a Problem," in Yancy, *White Self-criticality beyond Anti-racism,* 2–3, 9.

7. Reuters/Ipsos/UVA Center for Politics Race Poll.

8. Michael Norton and Samuel R. Sommers, "Whites See Racism as a Zero-Sum Game That They Are Now Losing," *Perspectives on Psychological Science* 6(3) (2011): 217. https://www.jstor.org/stable/41613491.

9. Nakayama and Krizek, 301.

10. Emily Heil, "'Be Kind to Each Other': Melania Trump Continues Anti-bullying Campaign," *Washington Post*, October 23, 2018. https://www.washingtonpost.com/arts-entertainment/2018/10/23/be-kind-each-other-melania-trump-continues-anti-bullying-campaign/?noredirect=on&utm_term=.3bddaa269ac4.

11. Mills, *The Racial Contract,* 4.

12. Daniels and Stein.

13. "Taking a Stand Against Harassment, Part of the Broader Threat to Higher Education," American Association of University Professors. https://www.aaup.org/taking-stand-against-harassment-part-broader-threat-higher-education.

14. Daniels and Stein.

15. Daniels and Stein.

16. Tedford and Herbeck, 26.

17. Combahee River Collective.

18. Combahee River Collective.

19. Bradley Dilger and Jeff Rice, *From A to A: Keywords of Markup* (Minneapolis: University of Minnesota Press, 2010).

20. Mikhail M. Bakhtin, *The Dialogic Imagination: Four Essays by M. M. Bakhtin*, transl. M. Holquist (Austin: University of Texas Press, 2000), 91.

21. "Standards," W3C. http://www.w3.org/standards/.

22. T. L. Taylor, "Multiple Pleasures: Women and Online Gaming," *Convergence* 9 (2003): 21–46. doi:10.1177/135485650300900103.

23. Janice D. Hamlet, "Word! The African American Oral Tradition and its Rhetorical Impact on American Popular Culture," *Black History Bulletin* 74(1) (2011): 27. http:// people.morrisville.edu/~reymers/readings/SOCI101/African%20Americans%20and%20 Popular%20Culture.pdf.

24. Cheris Kramarae and Paula A. Treichler, *A Feminist Dictionary* (Champaign: University of Illinois Press, 1996).

25. "New Policy: Do Not Post in Support of Trump or His Administration," Ravelry, June 23, 2019. https://www.ravelry.com/content/no-trump.

26. Ravelry, "New Policy."

27. "New Ban: Do Not Post in Support of Trump or His Administration," RPG.com. October 29, 2018. https://forum.rpg.net/index.php?threads/ new-ban-do-not-post-in-support-of-trump-or-his-administration.835849/.

28. United States District Court: Southern District Court of New York, *Knight First Amendment Institute v. Trump, Hicks, Sanders, and Scavino*, Case 1:17-cv-05205-NRB Document 72 Filed 23 May 2018. 1–75. HeinOnline. https://www-heinonline-org.ezp2.1ib .umn.edu/HOL/CaseLawAuth?cid=12720317&native_id=12720317&rest=1&collection= fastcasefull.

29. Micah Emmel-Duke, "How the University of Minnesota Hides Its Professors' Sexual Harassment," *City Pages*, May 2, 2018. http://www.citypages.com/news/how-the-university- of-minnesota-hides-its-professors-sexual-harassment/481408991; "Sexual Harassment, Sexual Assault, Stalking and Relationship Violence," University of Minnesota Administrative Policy. https://policy.umn.edu/hr/sexharassassault; Mila Koumpilova, "University of Minnesota Ramps Up Sexual Misconduct Prevention Program," *Star Tribune*, February 9, 2018. http://www.startribune.com/u-ramps-up-sexual-misconduct-program/473605633/.

30. Blee; Frankenberg; Frye; Stephanie Jones-Rogers, "Introduction: Mistresses of the Market," in *They Were Her Property: White Women as Slave Owners in the American South* (New Haven and London: Yale University Press, 2019), ix–xxii; bell hooks, "Sisterhood: Political Solidarity between Women," *Feminist Review* 23, Socialist-Feminism: Out of the Blue (Summer 1986): 125–38. doi:10.2307/1394725; Lorde, "The Uses of Anger," 278–85; Audre Lorde, "Age, Race, Class and Sex: Women Redefining Difference," paper delivered at the Copeland Colloquium, Amherst College, April 1980; reproduced in *Sister Outsider* (Berkeley, CA: Crossing Press, 1984); McRae, "Mothers of Massive Resistance."

31. Anderson and Grace, 943.

32. Kenneth Jones and Tema Okun, "The Characteristics of White Supremacy Culture," in *Dismantling Racism: A Workbook for Social Change Groups.* (Social up for Social Justice, 2001). https://www.showingupforracialjustice.org/white-supremacy-culture-characteristics.html.

33. Butler, "Performativity, Precarity, and Sexual Politics," x.

34. Ijeoma Oluo, Twitter, July 14, 2019. https://twitter.com/IjeomaOluo/status/1150565193 832943617?s=20.

35. Yancy, *Black Bodies, White Gazes*, 229.

36. Tina Askanius, "Studying the Nordic Resistance Movement: Three Urgent Questions for Researchers of Contemporary Neo-Nazis and Their Media Practices," *Media, Culture and Society* 41(6) (2019): 1–11.

37. Askanius, 7–9.

38. Karen Teel, "Feeling White, Feeling Good: 'Antiracist' White Sensibilities," in Yancy, *White Self-criticality beyond Anti-racism*, 21–35.

39. Dyer, 10–11. On a personal note, I find myself considering how, during my research for this book, I became emotionally stagnant and communicatively frozen after making a comment to a professor of color that I hadn't even recognized as racist before I had made it. Although she immediately and graciously forgave me, I sat within that guilt for years. By sitting in that guilt, I not only buried my relationship with that brilliant professor, but I also intellectually stagnated by recentering the interaction on myself as victim.

40. Reuters/Ipsos/UVA Center for Politics Race Poll.

41. Kinnvall, 762.

42. "Republican Platform 2016."

43. Baudrillard.

44. "Immigration Offenders in the Federal Justice System, 2010," Bureau of Justice Statistics, U.S. Department of Justice, October 22, 2013, 9, 28. https://www.bjs.gov/content /pub/pdf/iofjs10.pdf; "Departments of Justice and Homeland Security Release Quarterly Alien Incarceration Report Highlighting the Negative Effects of Illegal Immigration and the Need for Border Security," U.S. Department of Homeland Security, June 7, 2018. https:// www.dhs.gov/news/2018/06/07departments-justice-and-homeland-security-release -quarterly-alien-incarceration.

45. Michael T. Light and Ty Miller, "Does Undocumented Immigration Increase Violent Crime?" *Criminology* 56(2) (May 2017): 370–401. https://www.ncbi.nlm.nih.gov/pmc /articles/PMC6241529/; Graham C. Ousey and Charis E. Kubrin, "Immigration and Crime: Assessing a Contentious Issue," *Annual Review of Criminology* 1 (June 2017): 63–84. doi .org/10.1146/annurev-crimnol-032317-0920226.

46. John Gramlich, "5 Facts about Crime in the U.S.," Pew Research Center, January 3, 2019. https://www.pewresearch.org/fact-tank/2019/01/03/5-facts-about-crime-in-the-u-s/.

47. Rita K. Whillock, "The Use of Hate as a Stratagem for Achieving Political and Social Goals," in Rita K. Whillock and David Slayden, eds., *Hate Speech* (Thousand Oaks, CA: Sage, 1995), 31.

48. Shanker.

49. "The Alt-right on Campus."

50. Avery Anapol, "Tennessee Legislature Kills Resolution Condemning Neo-Nazis as terrorists," *The Hill*, March 15, 2018. https://www.msn.com/en-us/news/us/tennessee -legislature-kills-resolution-condemning-neo-nazis-as-terrorists/ar-BBKdOnN.

51. Anne Branigin, "Florida Middle School Teacher Outed as 'Unapologetic' White Supremacist," The Root, March 4, 2018. https://www.theroot.com/florida-middle-school -teacher-outed-as-unapologetic-whi-1823497416.

52. Foucault, 194.

53. Ryan Cooper, "The Subtle Racism of Centrist Democrats," *The Week*, March 9, 2018. http://theweek.com/articles/759789/subtle-racism-centrist-democrats.

54. Angela Davis, "Civil Liberties and Women's Rights: Twenty Years On," *Irish Journal of American Studies* 3 (1993): 24–27. https://www.jstor.org/stable/30003220.

55. Paulo Freire, *Pedagogy of the Oppressed* (New York: Continuum International Publishing, 1970), 44.

56. Lorde, "The Uses of Anger," 285.

57. Aanerud, 101–13.

58. Rachel Griffin, "Whitening Intersectionality at Play: A Call for Re-Race(ing) Intercultural Communication," National Communication Association Convention 2018, Salt Lake City, Utah, November 8, 2018. https://www.natcom.org/sites/default/files/annual -convention/NCA_Convention_Archives_2018_Program.pdf.

59. "#rhetoricsowhite: Addressing Racial, Gender, Language, and Nationality Bias in Publications, Editorships, Reviews, and Citation Patterns in Rhetorical Studies," panel at National Communication Association Convention 2018, Salt Lake City, Utah, November 9, 2018. https://www.natcom.org/sites/default/files/annual-convention/NCA_Convention _Archives_2018_Program.pdf.

60. Ta-Nehisi Coates, "The Good, Racist People," *New York Times*, March 6, 2013. http:// www.nytimes.com/2013/03/07/opinion/coates-the-good-racist-people.html?_r=0.

61. D'Arcangelis, 343; Sara Ahmed, "Declarations of Whiteness: The Non-performativity of Anti-racism," *Borderlands* 3(2) (2004). http://www.borderlands.net.au/vo13no2_2004 /ahmed_declarations.htm.

62. James McWilliams, "Bryan Stevenson on What Well-meaning White People Need to Know about Race," Pacific Standard February 6, 2018. https://psmag.com/magazine/bryan -stevenson-ps-interview.

63. Donna Haraway, "A Cyborg Manifesto: Science, Technology and Socialist-Feminism in the Late Twentieth Century," in D. Bell and B. M. Kennedy, eds., *The Cybercultures Studies Reader*, 291–324 (London: Routledge, 2000).

Bibliography

Aanerud, Rebecca. "Humility and Whiteness: 'How Did I Look without Seeing, Hear without Listening?'" In George Yancy, *White Self-criticality beyond Anti-racism: How Does It Feel to Be a White Problem?*, 101–13. New York: Lexington Books, 2015.

ABC News/Washington Post Poll. "Trump Charlottesville. Trump Approval Is Low but Steady; On Charlottesville, Lower Still." August 21, 2017. http://www.langerresearch.com/wp-content/uploads/1190a1TrumpandCharlottesville.pdf.

Adams, Richard. "Sarah Palin: conservative feminist." *The Guardian*. https://www.theguardian.com/world/richard-adams-blog/2010/may/15/sarah-palin-feminism-abortion.

Ahmed, Sara. "Declarations of Whiteness: The Non-performativity of Anti-racism." *Borderlands* 3(2) (2004). http://www.borderlands.net.au/vol3no2_2004/ahmed_declarations.htm.

Alexander, Michelle. *The New Jim Crow: Mass Incarceration in the Age of Color-blindness*. New York: New Press, 2012.

Allen, Jonathan. "Alabama's Women Wrote the Verdict on Roy Moore." NBC News, December 13, 2017. https://www.nbcnews.com/storyline/2017-elections/alabama-s-women-wrote-verdict-roy-moore-n829186.

"American." *Concise Oxford English Dictionary*. 11th ed. 2008.

"American." *Oxford English Dictionary*. 11th ed. 2009.

Anapol, Avery. "Tennessee Legislature Kills Resolution Condemning Neo-Nazis as Terrorists." *The Hill*. March 15, 2018. https://www.msn.com/en-us/news/us/tennessee-legislature-kills-resolution-condemning-neo-nazis-as-terrorists/ar-BBKdOnN.

Anderson, Karrin V. "Presidential Pioneer or Campaign Queen?: Hillary Clinton and the First-time Frontrunner Double Bind." *Rhetoric and Public Affairs* 20(3) (2017): 525–38.

Anderson, Wendy K. Z. "Classifying Whiteness: Unmasking White Nationalist Women's Digital Design through an Intersectional Analysis of Contained Agency." Special Issue on Media and the Extreme Right, *Communication, Culture, and Critique* 11(1) (March 2018): 116–32. https://doi.org/10.1093/ccc/tcy002.

Anderson, Wendy K. Z. "The Context of Power and Race in Online Social Movement Rhetoric: An Analysis of White Nationalist Cyber-rhetoric by/towards Women and Girls." Diss., Purdue University. 2009. ProQuest 3402278.

Anderson, Wendy K. Z. "(De)coding Whiteness: Appropriations of White Nationalist Women's Inferential Racism as Coded Rhetoric in U.S. Politics." In Meta G. Carstarphen, Kathleen E. Welch, Wendy K. Z. Anderson, Davis W. Houck, Mark L. McPhail, David A. Frank, Rachel C. Jackson, James Alexander McVey, Christopher J. Gilbert, Patricia G. Davis, and Lisa M. Corrigan, Rhetoric, Race, and Resentment: Whiteness and the New Days of Rage, *Rhetoric Review* 36(4) (2017): 263–72. doi: 0.1080/07350198.2017.135519110 .1080/07350198.2017.1355191.

Anderson, Wendy K. Z., and Patrice M. Buzzanell. "'Outcast among Outcasts': Identity, Gender, and Leadership in a Mac Users Group." *Women and Language* 30(1) (2007): 32–45.

Anderson, Wendy K. Z., and Kittie E. Grace. "'Taking Mama Steps' Toward Authority, Alternatives, and Advocacy." *Feminist Media Studies* 15(6) (2015): 942–59. Taylor and Francis.

Applebaum, Barbara. "Flipping the Script . . . and Still a Problem: Staying in the Anxiety of Being a Problem." In George Yancy, *White Self-criticality beyond Anti-racism: How Does It Feel to Be a White Problem?*, 1–9, New York: Lexington Books, 2015.

Arciniega, Luzilda Carrillo. "Diversity and Inclusion and the Rise of the Alt-right." *Anthropology News* 58(1) (January/February 2017): 175–79. https://doi.org/10.1111/AN.332.

Arnett, Ronald C., Janie Harden Fritz, and Leanne M. Bell. *Communication Ethics Literacy: Dialogue and Difference.* Thousand Oaks, CA: Sage, 2009.

Askanius, Tina. "Studying the Nordic Resistance Movement: Three Urgent Questions for Researchers of Contemporary Neo-Nazis and Their Media Practices." *Media, Culture & Society* (2019): 1–11.

Austin, Shelbi. "10 Things You Didn't Know about Sarah Huckabee Sanders." *US News and World Report.* October 25, 2017. https://www.usnews.com/news/politics/articles/2017 -10-25/10-things-you-didnt-know-about-sarah-huckabee-sanders.

Bakhtin, Mikhail M. *The Dialogic Imagination: Four Essays by M. M. Bakhtin.* Trans. M. Holquist. Austin: University of Texas Press, 2000.

Bakhtin, Mikhail. *Rabelais and His World.* Trans. Helene Iswolsky. Bloomington: Indiana University Press, 1984.

Baudrillard, Jean. *Simulacra and Simulation.* Ann Arbor: University of Michigan Press, 1994.

Baumgardner, Jennifer, and Amy Richards. *Manifesta: Young Women, Feminism, and the Future.* New York: Farrar, Straus, and Giroux, 2000.

Bebout, Lee. "Onward into the Discomfort: Teaching for Racial Justice in an Era of Media Outrage, the Alt-right, and the Neoliberal University." In Philathia Bolton et al., eds., *Teaching with Tension: Race, Resistance, and Reality in the Classroom*, 163–78. Evanston, IL: Northwestern University Press, 2019.

Bell, Daniel A., Jr. *Faces at the Bottom of the Well: The Permanence of Racism.* New York: Basic Books, 1992.

Berbrier, Mitch. "'Half the Battle': Cultural Resonance, Framing Processes, and Ethnic Affectations in Contemporary White Supremacist Rhetoric." *Social Problems* 45 (1998): 431–50. Accessed August 29, 2006. doi:10.2307/3097206.

Berbrier, Mitch. "Making Minorities: Cultural Space, Stigma Transformation Frames, and the Categorical Status." *Sociological Forum* 17(4) (2002): 553–91. http://www.jstor.org.ezp1.iib .umn.edu/stable/3070360. Accessed December 10, 2012.

Berger, J. M. "Nazis vs. ISIS on Twitter: Comparative Study of White Nationalist and ISIS Online Social Media Networks." *Program on Extremism* (2016): 1–31, 10, 18. George Washington University. Web.

"Beyond Red vs. Blue: Political Typology." *Pew Internet & American Life Project*. 2011. 7. http://people-press.org/files/legacy-pdf/Beyond-Red-vs-Blue-The-Political-Typology.pdf.

Bianco, Marcie. "White Women Voted for Trump in 2016 because They Still Believe White Men Are Their Saviors." *Quartz*. November 14, 2016. http://qz.com/835567/election-2016 -white-women-voted-for-donald-trump-in-2016-because-they-still-believe-white-men -are-their-saviors/. Accessed December 15, 2016.

Billig, Michael. "Humour and Hatred: The Racist Jokes of the Ku Klux Klan." *Discourse and Society* 12(3) (2001): 267–89. http://citeseerx.ist.psu.edu/viewdoc/download?doi=10.1.1.483 .1916&rep=rep1&type=pdf.

Bitzer, Lloyd. "The Rhetorical Situation." *Philosophy and Rhetoric* 1(1) (1968): 1–15.

Black, Edwin. "Secrecy and Disclosure as Rhetorical Forms." *Quarterly Journal of Speech* 74(2) (1988): 133–50. doi.org/10.1080/00335638809383833.

Blake, Aaron. "Yes, You Can Blame the Millennials for Hillary Clinton's Loss." *Washington Post*, December 2, 2016. https://www.washingtonpost.com/news/the-fix/wp/2016/12/02/yes -you-can-blame-millennials-for-hillary-clintons-loss/?utm_term=.28d8f421abed. Accessed December 15, 2016.

Blee, Kathleen M. *Inside Organized Racism: Women and Men in the Hate Movement*. Los Angeles: University of California Press, 2002.

Blee, Kathleen. *Women of the Klan: Racism and Gender in the 1920s*. Los Angeles: University of California Press, 1991.

"Blue Feed Red Feed." *Wall Street Journal*. http://graphics.wsj.com/blue-feed-red-feed/. Accessed May 20, 2017.

Boge, Andrew. "A Rhetoric of Intellectual Racism: The National Policy Institute's Epistemology of Strategic Whiteness." Race and Pedagogy National Conference. Tacoma, Washington. September 2018.

Bogost, Ian. *Persuasive Games: The Expressive Power of Videogames*. Cambridge, MA: MIT Press, 2007.

Bolter, David, and Richard Grusin. *Remediation: Understanding New Media*. Cambridge, MA: MIT Press, 1999.

Bonilla, Yamar, et al. "#Ferguson: Digital Protest, Hashtag Ethnography, and the Racial Politics of Social Media in the United States." *American Ethnologist* 42(1) (2015): 4–17.

Bonilla-Silva, Eduardo. "The Linguistics of Color Blind Racism: How to Talk Nasty about Blacks without Sounding 'Racist.'" *Critical Sociology* 28(1–2) (2002): 41–64. Sage. Accessed May 22, 2017. https://doi.org/10.1177/08969205020280010501.

Bonilla-Silva, Eduardo. *Racism with Racists: Color-blind Racism and the Persistence of Racial Inequality in America*. New York: Rowman & Littlefield, 2014.

Boryczka, Jocelyn M. "Intersectionality for the Global Age." *New Political Science* 37(4) (2015): 447–57. doi.org/10.1080/07393148.2015.1090137.

Bostdorff, Denise M. "The Internet Rhetoric of the Ku Klux Klan: A Case Study in Website Community Building Run Amok." *Communication Studies* 55(2) (2004): 340–61. Accessed August 26, 2016. doi:10.1080/10510970409388623.

Bowman, Emma, and Ian Stewart. "The Women behind The 'Alt-Right.'" *Weekend Edition*. NPR. August 20, 2017. http://www.npr.org/2017/08/20/544134546/the-women-behind-the -altright. Accessed September 6, 2017.

Bramlett, Brittany H., and Toni P. Miles. "Aged Migration, Communities, and Support for the Tea Party in Statewide Elections." *Phylon* 52(2) (2015): 68–86. http://www.jstor.org/stable /43681954. Accessed January 9, 2018.

Branigin, Anne. "Florida Middle School Teacher Outed as 'Unapologetic' White Supremacist." *The Root*. March 4, 2018. https://www.theroot.com/florida-middle-school-teacher-outed -as-unapologetic-whi-1823497416.

Brock, André. "Beyond the Pale: The Blackbird Web Browser's Critical Reception." *New Media and Society* 13(7) (2011): 1085–1103. doi:10.1177/1461444810397031.

Brodkin, Karen. *How Jews Became White Folks and What That Says about Race in America.* Piscataway, NJ: Rutgers University Press, 1999.

Brown, Christopher. "WWW.HATE.COM: White Supremacist Discourse on the Internet and the Construction of Whiteness Ideology." *Howard Journal of Communications* 20(2) (2009): 189–208. doi:10.1080/10646170902869544.

Brown, Elsa B. "Womanist Consciousness: Maggie Lena Walker and the Independent Order of Saint Luke." *Signs* 14(3) (1989): 610–33.

Brown, Michael, et al. *Whitewashing Race: The Myth of a Color-blind Society.* Berkeley: University of California Press, 2005.

Brown, W. O. "The Nature of Race Consciousness." *Social Forces* 10(1) (1931): 90–97.

Brownson, Laura. *The Rachel Divide*. Netflix. 2018.

Bureau of Justice Statistics. "Immigration Offenders in the Federal Justice System, 2010." U.S. Department of Justice. October 22, 2013. https://www.bjs.gov/content/pub/pdf/iofjs10.pdf.

Burke, Kenneth. "Definition of Man." Hudson Review 16(4) (1963): 498.

Burke, Kenneth. *Language as Symbolic Action* [LASA]. Berkeley: University of California Press, 1966.

Burke, Kenneth. *Permanence and Change: An Anatomy of Purpose.* 3rd ed. Berkeley: University of California Press, 1935.

Burke, Kenneth. "The Rhetoric of Hitler's 'Battle.'" In Kenneth Burke, ed., *The Philosophy of Literary Form*, 192–220. Berkeley: University of California Press, 1941.

Butler, Judith. "Performativity, Precarity, and Sexual Politics." *Revista de Antropología Iberoamericana* 4(3) (2009): i–xiii. https://www.aibr.org/antropologia/04v03/criticos /040301b.pdf.

Butler, Judith. "Subversive Bodily Acts." In *Gender Trouble: Feminism and the Subversion of Identity*, 371–82. New York: Routledge, 1990.

Butt, Rachel. "America's Shrinking Middle Class Is Killing the Economy." *Business Insider*. June 28, 2016. http://www.businessinsider.com/americas-shrinking-middle-class-hurts -economy-2016-6.

Campbell, Colin. "'Get a job!': Donald Trump Rally Rocked by Hecklers as He Complains about Their 'Gentle' Treatment." *Business Insider*. March 11, 2016.

Carbado, Devon W. "Intersectionality: Theorizing Power, Empowering Theory." *Signs* 38(4) (2013): 811–45. https://www.jstor.org/stable/10.1086/669666.

Carpenter, Julia. "Forget the 'Glass Ceiling.' Women of Color Face a 'Concrete Ceiling.'" *CNN Money*. August 8, 2018. https://money.cnn.com/2018/08/06/pf/women-of-color-ceos /index.html.

Carr, Paul R. "Whiteness and White Privilege: Problematizing Race and Racism in a 'Color-blind' World, and in Education." *International Journal of Critical Pedagogy* 7(1) (2016): 51–73.

Carreon, Michelle E,. and Valentine M. Moghdam. "'Resistance Is Fertile': Revisiting Maternalist Frames across Cases of Women's Mobilization." *Women's Studies International Forum* 51 (2015): 19–30. doi.org/10.1016/j.wsif.2015.04.002.

Carroll, Hamilton. *Affirmative Reaction: New Formations of White Masculinity.* Durham, NC: Duke University Press, 2011.

Carter, Joe. "What Christians Should Know about the Alt-right." Ethics and Religious Liberty Commission of the Southern Baptist Convention. June 14, 2017. https://erlc.com/resource-library/articles/what-christians-should-know-about-the-alt-right.

Carter, Robert. T., and A. Lin Goodwin. "Racial Identity and Education." *Review of Research in Education* 20(1) (1994): 291–336. http://www.jstor.org/stable/1167387. Accessed July 28, 2008.

Castells, Manuel. *The Power of Identity*. Hoboken, NJ: Blackwell, 1997.

Chávez, Karma. "The Body: An Abstract and Actual Rhetorical Concept." *Rhetoric Society Quarterly* 48(3) (May 2018): 242–50. doi:10.1080/02773945.2018.1454182.

Chávez, Karma. "Doing Intersectionality: Power, Privilege, and Identities in Political Activist Communities." In Nilanjana Bardhan and Mark P. Orbe, eds., *Identity Research and Communication: Intercultural Reflections and Future Directions*, 21–32. New York: Lexington Books, 2012.

Chávez, Karma R., and Cindy L. Griffin. "Power, Feminisms, and Coalitional Agency: Inviting and Enacting Difficult Dialogues." *Women's Studies in Communication* 32(1) (2009): 2.

Cheney-Lippold, John. *We Are Data: Algorithms and the Making of Our Digital Selves*. New York: New York University Press, 2017.

Chehade, Carol. *Big Little White Lies: Our Attempt to White-out America*. Kearney, NE: Nehmarche Publications, 2001.

Children's Partnership. "Online Content for Low Income and Underserved Americans." 2000. http://www.childrenspartnership.org/pub/low_income. Accessed June 8, 2007.

Cixous, Hélène. "The Laugh of the Medusa." *Signs* 1(4) (1976): 875–93. http://www.jstor.org/stable/3173239. Accessed June 1, 2016.

Clark-Flory, Tracy. "Is Sarah Palin Really a Feminist?" Salon. May 20, 2010. https://www.salon.com/2010/05/20/sarah_palin_feminism/.

Clemens, Colleen. "Ally or Accomplice? The Language of Activism." *Teaching Tolerance*. June 5, 2017. https://www.tolerance.org/magazine/ally-or-accomplice-the-language-of-activism.

Cloud, Dana. "Responding to Right-Wing Attacks." *Inside Higher Education*. 2017. https://www.insidehighered.com/advice/2017/11/07/tips-help-academics-respond-right-wing-attacks-essay.

Cloud, Dana. "The Rhetoric of <Family Values>: Scapegoating, Utopia, and the Privatization of Social Responsibility." *Western Journal of Communication* 62(4) (1998): 387–419. doi:10.1080/10570319809374617.

CNN. "Exit Polls." CNN Politics: Election 2016. November 23, 2016. http://www.cnn.com/election/results/exit-polls/national/president. Accessed December 15, 2017.

Coates, Ta-Nehisi. "The Good, Racist People." *New York Times*. March 6, 2013. http://www.nytimes.com/2013/03/07/opinion/coates-the-good-racist-people.html?_r=0.

Cohn, D'vera, and Gretchen Livingston. "Americans' Views of Women as Political Leaders Differ by Gender." Pew Internet Research Center. May 19, 2016. http://www.pewresearch.org/fact-tank/2016/05/19/americans-views-of-women-as-political-leaders-differ-by-gender/.

Collins, Patricia Hill. *Black Feminist Thought: Knowledge, Empowerment and Consciousness*. New York: Routledge, 2000.

Collins, Patricia Hill. "It's All in the Family: Intersections of Gender, Race, and Nation." *Hypatia* 13(3) (1998): 62–82. www.jstor.org/stable/3810699.

Combahee River Collective. "The Combahee River Collective Statement." https://americanstudies.yale.edu/sites/default/files/files/Keyword%20Coalition_Readings.pdf.

Conway, Madeline. "Conway Asked How She Justified Trump and Sexual Assault Allegations." Politico. November 30, 2016. https://www.politico.com/story/2016/11/kellyanne-conway-trump-sexual-assault-232002.

Cook, Donelda A., and Janet E. Helms. "Visible Racial/Ethnic Group Supervisees Satisfaction with Cross Cultural Supervision as Predicted by Relationship Characteristics." *Journal of Counseling Psychology* 33 (1988): 268–74.

Cooper, Marilyn. "Rhetorical Agency as Emergent and Enacted." *College Composition and Communication* 62(3) (February 2011): 420–49.

Cooper, Ryan. "The Subtle Racism of Centrist Democrats." *The Week*. March 9, 2018. http://theweek.com/articles/759789/subtle-racism-centrist-democrats.

Corrigan, Lisa. M. *Prison Power: How Prison Influenced the Movement for Black Liberation*. Jackson: University Press of Mississippi, 2017.

Corrigan, Lisa. "On Rhetorical Criticism, Performativity, and White Fragility." *Review of Communication* 16(1) (2016): 86–88. doi:10.1080/15358593.2016.1183886.

Costa, Maddy. "Le Tigre: Girl Power Burns Bright with Le Tigre." *The Guardian*. December 1, 2000. 27 Retrieved from LexisNexis Academic.

Crenshaw, Carrie. "Resisting Whiteness' Rhetorical Silence." *Western Journal of Communication* 61(3) (1997): 253–78. doi.org/10.1080/10570319709374577.

Crenshaw, Kimberlé. "Demarginalizing the Intersection of Race and Sex: A Black Feminist Critique of Antidiscrimination Doctrine, Feminist Theory and Antiracist Politics." *University of Chicago Legal Forum* 1(8) (1989): 139–67. http://chicagounbound.uchicago.edu/uclf/vol1989/iss1/8.

Crenshaw, Kimberlé. "Mapping the Margins: Intersectionality, Identity Politics, and Violence against Women of Color." *Stanford Law Review* 43 (1991): 1241–99. doi: 10.2307/1229039. Accessed December 15, 2016.

Crenshaw, Kimberlé. "Race, Reform, and Retrenchment: Transformation and Legitimation in Antidiscrimination Law." In Crenshaw et al., eds., *Critical Race Theory: The Key Writings That Formed the Movement*, 103–26. New York: New Press, 1995.

Crenshaw, Kimberlé, Neil Gotanda, Gary Peller, and Charles Inglis. Introduction. In Kimberlé Crenshaw, Neil Gotanda, Gary Peller, and Charles Inglis, eds., *Critical Race Theory: The Key Writings That Formed the Movement*. New York: New Press, 1995.

Daniels, Jessie. "Cloaked Websites: Propaganda, Cyber-racism and Epistemology in the Digital Era." *New Media Society* 11(5) (2009): 659–83. doi:10.1177/1461444809105345.

Daniels, Jessie. *Cyberracism: White Supremacy Online and the New Attack on Civil Rights*. New York: Rowman & Littlefield, 2009.

Daniels, Jessie, Arlene Stein. "Protect Scholars against Attacks from the Right." *Rutgers Today*. 2017. https://news.rutgers.edu/sites/medrel/files/news-clips/Why%20institutions%20should%20shield%20academics%20who%20are%20being%20attacked%20by%20conservative%20groups%20%28essay%29.pdf.

Darby, Seyward. "The Rise of the Valkyries: In the Alt-right, Women Are the Future, and the Problem." *Harpers*. August 24, 2017. https://harpers.org/archive/2017/09/the-rise-of-the-valkyries/7/.

D'Arcangelis, Carol Lynne. "Revelations of a White Settler Woman Scholar-Activist: The Fraught Promise of Self-Reflexivity." *Cultural Studies Critical Methodologies* 18(5) (October 2018): 339–53. doi:10.1177/1532708617750675.

Davis, Angela. "Civil Liberties and Women's Rights: Twenty Years On." *Irish Journal of American Studies* 3 (1993): 17–29. https://www.jstor.org/stable/30003220.

Davis, Angela. "Women, Race and Class: An Activist Perspective." *Women's Studies Quarterly* 10(4) (1982): 5–9. https://www.jstor.org/stable/40004176.

Deckman, Melissa. *Tea Party Women: Mama Grizzlies, Grassroots Leaders, and the Changing Face of the American Right*. New York: New York University Press, 2016.

Delegard, Kirsten. "'It Takes Women to Fight Women': Woman Suffrage and the Genesis of Female Conservatism in the United States." In Kathleen M. Blee and Sandra McGee Deutsch, eds., *Women of the Right: Comparisons and Interplay across Borders*. University Park: Pennsylvania State University Press, 2012.

Delgado, Richard, and Jean Stefancic. Introduction. In Richard Delgado and Jean Stefancic, eds., *Critical Race Theory: An Introduction*. New York: New York University Press, 2001.

DeLuca, Kevin M., and Jennifer Peeples. "From Public Sphere to Public Screen: Democracy, Activism, and the 'Violence' of Seattle." *Critical Studies in Media Communication* 19(2) (2002): 125–51. doi:10.1080/07393180216559.

Demby, Gene. "It's Gotten a Lot Harder to Act Like Whiteness Doesn't Shape Our Politics." *All Things Considered*. NPR. May 13, 2016. http://www.npr.org/sections/codeswitch/2016/05 /13/477803909/its-gotten-a-lot-harder-to-act-like-whiteness-doesnt-shape-our-politics. Accessed December 15, 2016.

Dertouzos, Michael L. *What Will Be: How the New World of Information Will Change Our Lives*. New York: HarperCollins, 1997.

Desanctis, Alexandra. "The Progressive Double Standard on Feminism." *National Review*. September 19, 2017. https://www.nationalreview.com/2017/09/conservative-women-double -standard-victims/. Accessed February 24, 2018.

Devereux, Cecily. "New Woman, New World: Maternal Feminism and the New Imperialism in the White Settler Colonies." *Women's Studies International Forum* 22(2) (1999): 175–84. https://doi.org/10.1016/S0277-5395(99)00005-9.

Diamond, Jeremy. "Donald Trump on Protester: 'I'd Like to Punch Him in the Face.'" CNN. February 23, 2016. Web. https://www.cnn.com/2016/02/23/politics/donald-trump-nevada -rally-punch/index.html. Accessed September 13, 2016.

DiAngelo, Robin. "White Fragility." *International Journal of Critical Pedagogy* 3(3) (2011): 54–70. https://libjournal.uncg.edu/ijcp/article/viewFile/249/116.

Diani, Mario. "Social Movement Networks Virtual and Real." *Information, Communication, and Society* 3(3) (2000): 386–401. doi:10.1080/13691180051033333.

Dilger, Bradley, and Jeff Rice. *From A to A: Keywords of Markup*. Minneapolis: University of Minnesota Press. 2010.

Dill, Bonnie Thornton. "Race, Class, and Gender: Prospects for an All-Inclusive Sisterhood." *Feminist Studies* 9(1) (Spring 1983): 131–50. https://www.jstor.org/stable/3177687.

Dionne, Evette. "Women's Suffrage Leaders Left Out Black Women." *Teen Vogue*. August 18, 2017. https://www.teenvogue.com/story/womens-suffrage-leaders-left-out-black-women.

Dittmar, Kelly. "Candidates Matter: Gender Differences in Election 2016." Rutgers Center for American Women and Politics. February 14, 2017. http://www.cawp.rutgers.edu/sites/default /files/resources/closer_look_candidates_matter_2.14.17.pdf. Accessed February 28, 2018.

Dittmar, Kelly, et al. "Black Women in American Politics: 2017 Status Update." Rutgers Center for American Women and Politics. http://www.cawp.rutgers.edu/sites/default/files /resources/black-women-in-american-politics-2017-status-update.pdf.

Dittmar, Kelly, et al. "Representation Matters: Women in the U.S. Congress." Rutgers Center for American Women and Politics. 2017.

Ditum, Sarah. "Why Are We So Desperate to Blame White Supremacy on Women?" *New Statesman*. August 21, 2017. https://www.newstatesman.com/world/north-america/2017/08 /why-are-we-so-desperate-blame-white-supremacy-women.

"Diversity." *Concise Oxford English Dictionary*. 11th ed. 2008.

Dizard, Wilson. "Fear and Whiteness on the Campaign Trail." Mondoweiss. July 25, 2016. http://mondoweiss.net/2016/07/whiteness-campaign-trail/. Accessed December 15, 2016.

Dolan, Eric. "'Please Delete Your Account': Sarah Palin Slammed for Using 'Neo-Nazi' Slogan to Praise Trump." Raw Story. July 7, 2017.

Don. "OK Symbol." Part of a series on Emoji. Know Your Meme. March 4, 2019. https://know yourmeme.com/memes/ok-symbol-%F0%9F%91%8C.

Drabold, Will. "Read Michelle Obama's Emotional Speech at the Democratic Convention." *Time.* July 26, 2016. http://time.com/4421538/democratic-convention-michelle-obama-transcript/.

Du Bois, W. E. B. *Black Reconstruction: An Essay toward a History of the Past which Black Folk Played in an Attempt to Reconstruct Democracy in America.* New York: Harcourt, Brace, 1934. http://ouleft.org/wp-content/uploads/2012/blackreconstruction.pdf.

Duffy, Margaret E. "Web of Hate: A Fantasy Theme Analysis of the Rhetorical Vision of Hate Groups Online." *Journal of Communication Inquiry* 27 (2003): 291–312. doi:10.1177/0196859903252850.

Dundon, Rian. "Klan Family Values: How Baby-toting, Robed-and-Hooded Moms Paved the Way for Today's White Hate Groups." Timeline. January 24, 2018. https://timeline.com /klan-family-values-539be2ff7f55.

Dyck, Kirsten. *Reichsrock: The International Web of White-power and Neo-Nazi Hate Music.* New Brunswick, NJ: Rutgers University Press, 2017.

Dyer, Richard. *White.* New York: Routledge, 1997.

Edbauer, Jennifer. "Unframing Models of Public Distribution: From Rhetorical Situation to Rhetorical Ecologies." *Rhetoric Society Quarterly* 35(4) (2005): 5–24. doi.org/10.1080 /02773940509391320.

Eddo-Lodge, Reni. *Why I'm No Longer Talking to White People about Race.* New York: Bloomsbury Circus, 2017.

Edley, Paige P. "Entrepreneurial Mothers' Balance of Work and Family." In Patrice M. Buzzanell et al., eds., *Gender in Applied Communication Contexts,* 255–73. Thousand Oaks, CA: Sage, 2004.

Einwohner, Rachel. "Identity Work and Collective Action in a Repressive Context: Jewish Resistance on the 'Aryan Side' of the Warsaw Ghetto." *Social Problems* 53(1) (2006): 38–56.

Ember, Sydney. "News Outlets Rethink Usage of the Term 'Alt-right.'" *New York Times.* November 28, 2016. https://www.nytimes.com/2016/11/28/business/media/news-outlets -rethink-usage-of-the-term-alt-right.html.

Emmel-Duke, Micah. "How the University of Minnesota Hides Its Professors' Sexual Harassment." *City Pages.* May 2, 2018. http://www.citypages.com/news/how-the-university -of-minnesota-hides-its-professors-sexual-harassment/481408991.

Engel, Pamela. "CNN's Jake Tapper Hammers Donald Trump over the Violent 'Tone' of his Rallies." *Business Insider.* March 10, 2016.

Epps-Robertson, Candace. "The Race to Erase Brown v. Board of Education: The Virginia Way and the Rhetoric of Massive Resistance." *Rhetoric Review* 35(2) (2016): 108–20. doi.org /10.1080/07350198.2016.1142812. Accessed May 20, 2016.

"Exit Poll Results: How Different Groups Voted in Alabama." *Washington Post.* December 13, 2017. https://www.washingtonpost.com/graphics/2017/politics/alabama-exit-polls/?utm _term=.a2a47fe168b8.

Fairclough, Norman. "Critical Discourse Analysis." *International Advances in Engineering and Technology* 7 (2012): 452–85. http://scholarism.net/FullText/2012071.pdf.

Fallows, Deborah. "How Women and Men Use the Internet." Pew Research Center. December 28, 2005. http://www.pewinternet.org/Reports/2005/How-Women-and-Men-Use-the -Internet.aspx. Accessed January 8, 2013.

Fanon, Franz. *Black Skin, White Masks*. London: Pluto Press, 2008.

Farivar, Masood. "U.S. White Nationalists Barred by Facebook Find Haven on Russian Site." Voice of America. April 10, 2019. https://www.voanews.com/a/american-white-nationalists -barred-by-facebook-find-friendly-haven-on-russia-s-vk-website-/4871044.html.

Feagin, Joe R. *The White Racial Frame: Centuries of Racial Framing and Counter-framing*. New York: Routledge, 2010.

Federal Bureau of Investigation. "2017 Hate Crime Statistics Released." November 13, 2018. https://www.fbi.gov/news/stories/2017-hate-crime-statistics-released-111318.

Feenberg, Andrew. *Transforming Technology: A Critical Theory Revisited*. New York: Oxford University Press, 2002.

Fehler, Brian. "Reading, Writing, and Redemption: Literacy Sponsorship and the Mexican-American Settlement Movement in Texas." *Rhetoric Review* 29(4) (2010): 346–63. https://www.jstor.org/stable/40997181. Accessed May 20, 2016.

Felski, R. *Beyond Feminist Aesthetics: Feminist Literature and Social Change*. Cambridge, MA: Harvard University Press, 1989.

Flores, Lisa A. "Between Abundance and Marginalization: The Imperative of Racial Rhetorical Criticism." *Review of Communication* 16(1) (2016): 4–24. doi:10.1080/15358593.2016.1183871.

Flynn, Kerry. "Nearly Half of Americans Didn't Vote—Not Even for Harambe." Mashable. November 9, 2016. http://mashable.com/2016/11/09/voting-poll-numbers/#NMlMLGNCZqqI. Accessed December 15, 2016.

Ford, Tamara V., and Genève Gill. "Radical Internet Use." In J. D. H. Downing, ed., *Radical Media: Rebellious Communication and Social Movements*, 201–34. Thousand Oaks, CA: Sage, 2001.

Foucault, Michel. *Discipline and Punishment: The Birth of the Prison*. New York: Vintage Books, 1995.

Fox, Richard L., Jennifer L. Lawless. "Reconciling Family Roles with Political Ambition: The New Normal for Women in Twenty-first Century U.S. Politics." *Journal of Politics* 76(2) (2014): 398–414. doi:10.1017/s0022381613001473.

France, Lisa R. "Rachel Dolezal on Being Black: 'I Didn't Deceive Anybody.'" CNN. July 20, 2015. http://www.cnn.com/2015/07/20/us/rachel-dolezal-vanity-fair-feat/. Accessed May 22, 2017.

Frankenberg, Ruth. *White Women, Race Matters: The Social Construction of Whiteness*. Minneapolis: University of Minnesota Press, 1993.

Fraser, Nancy. "Rethinking the Public Sphere: A Contribution to the Critique of Actually Existing Democracy." *Social Text* 25/26 (1990): 56–80. doi:10.2307/466240.

Fredricks, Bob. "Trump Can't Be Racist because He Had a TV Show: Sanders." *New York Post*. January 16, 2018. https://nypost.com/2018/01/16/trump-cant-be-racist-because-he-had-a-tv -show-sanders/.

"Freedom of Speech." *Concise Oxford English Dictionary*. 11th ed. 2008.

Freire, Paulo. *Pedagogy of the Oppressed*. New York: Continuum International, 1970.

Fry, Richard, and Rakesh Kochhar. "The Shrinking Middle Class in U.S. Metropolitan Areas: 6 Key Findings." Pew Research Center. May 12, 2016. http://www.pewresearch.org/fact-tank /2016/05/12/us-middle-class-metros-takeaways/.

Frye, Marilyn. "White Woman Feminist." In *Willful Virgin: Essays in Feminism*, 147–69. Freedom, CA: Crossing Press, 1992.

Futrell, Robert, and Pete Simi. "Free Spaces, Collective Identity, and the Persistence of U.S. White Power Activism." *Social Problems* 51(1) (February 2004): 16–42. http://www.jstor .org/stable/4148758.

Futrell, Robert and Pete Simi. "The [Un]surprising Alt-right." *Contexts* 16(2) (2017): 76–76. doi:10.1177/1536504217714269.

Galloway, Alexander R. *Protocol: How Control Exists after Decentralization.* Cambridge, MA: MIT Press, 2004.

Gamson, William A. *Talking Politics.* Cambridge: Cambridge University Press, 1992.

Garcia, Feliks. "White Men Radicalised Online Were amongst the 'Silent Majority' Who Chose Donald Trump." *The Independent,* November 14, 2016. http://www.independent.co.uk /news/world/americas/us-elections/donald-trump-white-men-online-radicalization-reddit -twitter-alt-right-latest-a7417296.html. Accessed February 28, 2018.

Geiger, Abigail, and Lauren Kent. "Number of Women Leaders around the World Has Grown, but They're Still a Small Group." Pew Research Center. March 8, 2017. http://www.pew research.org/fact-tank/2017/03/08/women-leaders-around-the-world. Accessed February 23, 2018.

Gessen, Masha. "The Degrading Ritual of Sarah Huckabee Sanders's Pre-Thanksgiving Press Briefing." *New Yorker.* November 21, 2017. https://www.newyorker.com/news/our -columnists/degrading-ritual-sarah-huckabee-sanders-pre-thanksgiving-press-briefing.

Gitelman, Lisa. *Always Already New: Media, History, and the Data of Culture.* Cambridge, MA: MIT Press, 2006.

Gittens, Rhana A. "'What If I Am a Woman?': Black Feminist Rhetorical Strategies of Intersectional Identification and Resistance in Maria Stewart's Texts." *Southern Communication Journal* 83(5) (2018): 310–21. doi:10.1080/1041794X.2018.1505939.

Glenn, Cheryl. "Sex, Lies, and Manuscript: Refiguring Aspasia in the History of Rhetoric." *College Composition and Communication* 45(2) (May 1994): 180–99. https://www.jstor.org /stable/359005.

Goodwin, Jeff, and James M. Jasper, eds. *The Social Movements Reader: Cases and Concepts.* Malden, MA: Blackwell, 2003.

Gottfried, Paul. "The Decline and Rise of the Alternative Right." Taki's Magazine. December 1, 2008. http://takimag.com/article/the_decline_and_rise_of_the_alternative_right#axzz 4jzfoQiP3.

Gramlich, John. "5 Facts about Crime in the U.S." Pew Research Center. January 3, 2019. https://www.pewresearch.org/fact-tank/2019/01/03/5-facts-about-crime-in-the-u-s/.

Gramlich, John. "Most Americans Haven't Heard of the 'Alt-right.'" Pew Internet Center. December 12, 2016. http://www.pewresearch.org/fact-tank/2016/12/12/most-americans -havent-heard-of-the-alt-right/.

Grattan, Elizabeth. "The Decent White Woman Who Voted for Trump." Medium. November 12, 2016. https://medium.com/@elizabethgrattan/the-decent-white-woman-who-voted-for -trump-ffcd4eedf90d#.vez65p307. Accessed December 15, 2016.

Grattan, Laura. *Populism's Power: Radical Grassroots Democracy in America.* New York: Oxford University Press, 2016.

Green, Matthew. "How Millennials Voted in the Presidential Election (with Lesson Plan)." KQED News: Politics & Elections. November 15, 2016. https://ww2.kqed.org/lowdown /2016/11/14/how-millennials-voted/. December 15, 2016.

Griffin, Rachel A. "Critical Race Theory as a Means to Deconstruct, Recover and Evolve in Communication Studies." *Communication Law Review* 10(1) (2018): 1–9. http://commlaw-review.org/Archives/CLRv10i1/PDFs/Critical_Race_Theory_as_a_Means_to _Deconstruct_Recover_and_Evolve_in_Communication_Studies.pdf.

Griffin, Rachel. "Whitening Intersectionality at Play: A Call for Re-Race(ing) Intercultural Communication." National Communication Association Conference. Salt Lake City, Utah. November 8, 2018. https://www.natcom.org/sites/default/files/annual-convention/NCA_Convention_Archives_2018_Program.pdf.

Guess, Teresa J. "The Social Construction of Whiteness: Racism by Intent, Racism by Consequence." *Critical Sociology* 32(4) (2006): 649–73. https://doi.org/10.1163/156916306779155199.

Gurstein, Rochelle. "Emma Goldman and the Tragedy of Modern Love." *Salmagundi* 135 (2002): 67–89. EbscoHost.

Hall, Stuart. "The Whites of Their Eyes." In G. Dines and J. M. Humez, eds., *Gender, Race and Class: A Media Reader*, 18–22. Thousand Oaks, CA: Sage, 1995.

Hallenbeck, Sarah. "Toward a Posthuman Perspective: Feminist Rhetorical Methodologies and Everyday Practices." *Advances in the History of Rhetoric* 15(1) (2012): 9–27. doi:10.1080/15362426.2012.657044.

Hamlet, Janice D. "Word! The African American Oral Tradition and Its Rhetorical Impact on American Popular Culture." *Black History Bulletin* 74(1) (2011): 27–31. http://people.morrisville.edu/~reymers/readings/SOCI101/African%20Americans%20and%20Popular%20Culture.pdf.

Hanchey, Jenna N. "Agency beyond Agents: Aid Campaigns in Sub-Saharan Africa and Collective Representations of Agency." *Communication, Culture and Critique* 9(1) (2016): 11–29. doi.org/10.1111/cccr.12130.

Hancock, Ange-Marie. *Intersectionality: An Intellectual History*. New York: Oxford University Press, 2016.

Hancock, Ange M. *Solidarity Politics for Millennials: A Guide to Ending the Oppression Olympics*. New York: Palgrave, 2011. https://sites.oxy.edu/ron/csp19/2010/BTOO%20Chapter%201.PDF.

Haraway, Donna. "A Cyborg Manifesto: Science, Technology and Socialist-Feminism in the Late Twentieth Century." In D. Bell and B. M. Kennedy, eds., *The Cybercultures Studies Reader*, 291–324. London: Routledge, 2000.

Haraway, Donna. "Situated Knowledges: The Science Question in Feminism and the Privilege of a Partial Perspective." *Feminist Studies* 14(3) (Autumn 1988): 575–99.

Harding, Kate. "Are Women Persons?" In Samhita Mukhhopadhyay et al., eds., *Nasty Women: Feminism, Resistance, and Revolution in Trump's America*, 10–28. New York: Picador, 2017.

Harding, Sandra. *Whose Science? Whose Knowledge? Thinking from Women's Lives*. Ithaca, NY: Cornell University Press, 1991.

Harkness, Kelsey. "Hope Hicks Shows Accomplishments for Women, by Women, Count Only If You're a Democrat." *Daily Signal*. September 14, 2017. http://dailysignal.com/2017/09/14/hope-hicks-shows-accomplishments-for-women-by-women-only-count-if-youre-a-democrat/. Accessed February 24, 2018.

Harmer, Emily, Heather Saving, and Orlanda Ward. "'Are You Tough Enough?' Performing Gender in the UK Leadership Debates 2015." *Media, Culture, and Society* 39(7) (2016): 960–75. doi:10.1177/0163443716682074.

Harris, Cheryl. "Whiteness as Property." *Harvard Law Review* 106(8) (1993): 1707–91. doi:10.2307/1341787.

Harris, Kate Lockwood. "'Compassion' and Katrina: Reasserting Violent White Masculinity after the Storm." *Women and Language* 34(1) (2011): 11–27.

Harris, Kate Lockwood, and Jenna N. Hanchey. "(De)stabilizing Sexual Violence Discourse: Masculinization of Victimhood, Organizational Blame, and Labile Imperialism." *Communication and Critical/Cultural Studies* 11(4) (2014): 322–41. doi.org/10.1080/14791420.2014.972421.

Hatewatch staff. "Identitarian Ideology." SPLC. October 12, 2015. https://www.splcenter.org/hatewatch/2015/10/12/american-racists-work-spread-%E2%80%98identitarian%E2%80%99-ideology.

Hattem, Julian. "Obama Signs NSA Bill, Renewing Patriot Act Powers." *The Hill.* June 2, 2015. https://thehill.com/policy/national-security/243850-obama-signs-nsa-bill-renewing-patriot-act-powers.

Hawley, George. *Making Sense of the Alt-right.* New York: Columbia University Press, 2017. https://www.jstor.org/stable/10.7312/haw118512.

Hayden, Michael E. "Alt-right Women Asked to 'Choose Submission' to Grow Political Movement." *Newsweek.* November 16, 2017. http://www.newsweek.com/alt-right-women-asked-choose-submission-grow-political-movement-705655.

Hayden, Michael E. "Women Shouldn't Have the Right to Vote Says 'Alt-right' Leader Richard Spencer." *Newsweek.* October 14, 2017. https://www.newsweek.com/alt-right-leader-richard-spencer-isnt-sure-if-women-should-be-allowed-vote-685048.

Heil, Emily. "'Be Kind to Each Other': Melania Trump Continues Anti-bullying Campaign." Washington Post. October 23, 2018. https://www.washingtonpost.com/arts-entertainment/2018/10/23/be-kind-each-other-melania-trump-continues-anti-bullying-campaign/?noredirect=on&utm_term=.3bddaa269ac4.

Helm, Angela. "Trump Suggests Certain Federal Financing for HBCUs May Be Unconstitutional." *The Root.* May 5, 2017. http://www.theroot.com/trump-suggests-certain-federal-financing-for-hbcus-may-1794982685?utm_source=theroot_facebook&utm_medium=socialflow. Accessed May 6, 2017.

Herbst, Philop H. *The Color of Words: An Encyclopaedic Dictionary of Ethnic Bias in the United States.* Yarmouth, ME: Intercultural Press, 1997.

Herndon, Astead W. "Elizabeth Warren Stand By Her DNA Test. But Around Her, Worries Abound." *New York Times.* December 6, 2018. https://www.nytimes.com/2018/12/06/us/politics/elizabeth-warren-dna-test-2020.html.

Hester, Scarlett L., and Catherine R. Squires. "Who Are We Working For? Recentering Black Feminism." *Communication and Critical/Cultural Studies* 15(4) (2018): 343–48. doi:10.1080/14791420.2018.1533987.

Hill, Jemele. "Donald Trump is a white supremacist who has largely surrounded himself w/ other white supremacists." Twitter. September 11, 2017. twitter.com/jemelehill/status/90739 1978194849793?lang=en.

Hill, Logan. "Beyond Access: Race, Technology, Community." In Alondra Nelson et al., eds., *Technicolor: Race, Technology, and Everyday Life,* 13–33. New York: New York Press, 2001.

Hogg, Charlotte. "Including Conservative Women's Rhetorics in an 'Ethics of Hope and Care.'" *Rhetoric Review* 34(4) (2015): 391–408. https://doi.org/10.1080/07350198.2015.1073558.

Hollander, Jocelyn, and Rachel Einwohner. "Conceptualizing Resistance." *Sociological Forum* 19(4) (2004): 533–54. http://links.jstor.org/sici?sici=0884-971%28200412%2919%3A4%3C533%3ACR%3E2.0.CO%3B2-5. Accessed February 11, 2008.

hooks, bell. *Ain't I a Woman: Black Women and Feminism.* New York: Routledge, 1981.

hooks, bell. "Eating the Other: Desire and Resistance." In *Black Looks: Race and Representation,* 21–39. Boston: South End Press, 1992.

hooks, bell. "Representing Whiteness in the Black Imagination." In Lawrence Grossberg, Cary Nelson, and Paula A. Treichler, eds., *Cultural Studies*. New York: Routledge, 1992.

hooks, bell. "Sisterhood: Political Solidarity between Women." *Feminist Review* 23, Socialist-Feminism: Out of the Blue (Summer 1986): 125–38. doi:10.2307/1394725.

hooks, bell. *Talking Back: Thinking Feminist, Thinking Black*. Boston: South End Press, 1989.

Hossain, Anushay. "Sarah Sanders and the Sexism of Women." CNN Opinion. February 1, 2018. https://www.cnn.com/2018/02/01/opinions/sarah-sanders-and-the-sexism-of-women-hossain/index.html.

Howard, Ron. "The Vernacular Web of Participatory Media." *Critical Studies in Media Communication* 25(5) (2008): 490–513. doi:10.1080/15295030802468065.

Hsu, Hua. "White Plight? In Working-class America, an Elite-resenting Identity Politics Has Emerged in which Whiteness Spells Dispossession." *The New Yorker*. July 25, 2016. http://www.newyorker.com/magazine/2016/07/25/the-new-meaning-of-whiteness.

Humprecht, Edda, and Frank Esser. "A Glass Ceiling in the Online Age? Explaining the Underrepresentation of Women in Online Political Newspapers." *European Journal of Communication* 35(5) (2017): 439–56. https://doi.org/10.1177/0267323117720343.

Hunt, Scott A., Robert D. Benford, and David A. Snow. "Identity Fields: Framing Processes and the Social Construction of Movement Identities." In E. Larana, H. Johnston, and J. R. Gusfield, eds., *New Social Movements: From Ideology to Identity*, 185–208. Philadelphia: Temple University Press, 1994.

Hutchinson, Darren L. "Critical Race Histories: In and Out." 53 *Am. U. L. Rev.* 1187 (2004). http://scholarship.law.ufl.edu/facultypub/386.

Hymowitz, Kay S. "Sarah Palin and the Battle for Feminism." *City Journal*. https://www.city-journal.org/html/sarah-palin-and-battle-feminism-13348.html. Accessed January 22, 2018.

Ibrahim, Shamira. "Once Again, Black Women Did the Work which White Women Refused To." *The Root*. November 9, 2016. http://verysmartbrothas.com/once-again-black-women-did-the-work-white-women-refused-to/. Accessed December 15, 2016.

Ignatiev, Noel. *How the Irish Became White*. New York: Routledge, 1995.

Ipsos Public Affairs. "Reuters/Ipsos/UVA Center for Politics Race Poll." September 11, 2017. http://www.centerforpolitics.org/crystalball/wp-content/uploads/2017/09/2017-Reuters-UVA-Ipsos-Race-Poll-9-11-2017.pdf.

Ivie, Robert. "The Ideology of freedom's 'fragility' in American Foreign Policy Argument." *Journal of the American Forensic Association* 24 (1987): 27–36.

Jackson, Sarah, and Sonja Banaszczyk. "Digital Standpoints: Debating Gendered Violence and Racial Exclusion in the Feminist Counterpublic." *Journal of Communication Inquiry* 40(4) (2016): 391–407. doi.org/10.1177/0196859916667731.

Jacobs, Sarah. "How Kellyanne Conway Makes and Spends Her $39 Million Fortune." *Business Insider*. April 28, 2017. http://www.businessinsider.com/how-kellyanne-conway-became-rich-2017-4.

Jacobson, Matthew Frye. *Whiteness of a Different Color: European Immigrants and the Alchemy of Race*. Cambridge, MA: Harvard University Press, 1999.

Johnson, Cathryn. "Gender, Legitimate Authority, and Leader-subordinate Conversations." *American Sociological Review* 59(1) (1994): 122–35. doi:10.2307/2096136.

Jones, Kenneth, and Tema Okun. "The Characteristics of White Supremacy Culture." In *Dismantling Racism: A Workbook for Social Change Groups*. Social up for Social Justice. 2001. https://www.showingupforracialjustice.org/white-supremacy-culture-characteristics.html..

Jones-Rogers, Stephanie E. "Epilogue: Lost Kindred, Lost Cause." In *They Were Her Property: White Women as Slave Owners in the American South*, 200–206. New Haven: Yale University Press, 2019. www.jstor.org/stable/j.ctvbnm3fz.12.

Jones-Rogers, Stephanie. "Introduction: Mistresses of the Market." In *They Were Her Property: White Women as Slave Owners in the American South*, ix–xxii. New Haven: Yale University Press, 2019. www.jstor.org/stable/j.ctvbnm3fz.3.

Kamenetz, Anya. "DeVos to Rescind Obama-Era Guidance on School Discipline." *All Things Considered*. NPR. December 18, 2018. https://www.npr.org/2018/12/18/675556455/devos-to-rescind-obama-era-guidance-on-school-discipline.

Kao, Grace. "Group Images and Possible Selves among Adolescents: Linking Stereotypes to Expectations by Race and Ethnicity." *Sociological Forum* 15(3) 2000: 407–30.

Karklis, Laris, and Emily Badger. "Every Term the Census Has Used to Describe America's Racial and Ethnic Groups since 1790." *Washington Post*. November 4, 2015. https://www.washingtonpost.com/news/wonk/wp/2015/11/04/every-term-the-census-has-used-to-describe-americas-racial-groups-since-1790/?utm_term=.12c46ce9d992. Accessed October 16, 2017.

Karolak, Hannah, and Craig T. Maier. "From 'Safe Spaces' to 'Communicative Spaces': Semiotic Labor, Authentic Civility and the Basic Communication Course." *Journal of the Association for Communication Administration* 34(2) (2015): 88–101. EbscoHost.

Kartje, Ryan. "Did Millennial Apathy Propel Trump Election?" *Orange County Register*. November 12, 2016. http://www.ocregister.com/articles/millennials-735284-election-clinton.html. Accessed December 15, 2016.

Kelly, Annie. "The Alt-right: Reactionary Rehabilitation for White Masculinity." *Soundings* 66 (Summer 2017): 68–78. doi.org/10.3898/136266217821733688.

Kelly, Casey R. "Chastity for Democracy: Surplus Repression and the Rhetoric of Sex Education." *Quarterly Journal of Speech* 102(4) (2016): 353–75. doi.org/10.1080/00335630.2016.1209548.

Kendi, Ibram X. *Stamped from the Beginning: The Definitive History of Racist Ideas in America*. New York: Nation Books, 2016.

Kendzior, Sarah. "Donald Trump and His Followers Could Destroy America Even If He Loses." *The Pied Piper*. August 5, 2016.

Kerber, Linda. "The Republican Mother: Women and the Enlightenment—An American Perspective." *American Quarterly* 28(2) (1976): 188–96. http://www.jstor.org/stable/2712349.

Kiefer, Elizabeth. "How the Women of the KKK Helped Architect a Hate Movement." *Refinery29*. October 18, 2017. http://www.refinery29.com/2017/10/176864/white-supremacy-ku-klux-klan-women.

Kinnvall, Catarina. "Globalization and Religious Nationalism: Self, Identity, and the Search for Ontological Security." *Political Psychology* 25(5) (2004): 741–67.

Kitch, Sally. *The Specter of Sex: Gendered Foundations of Racial Formation in the United States*. Albany: State University of New York Press, 2009.

Kitchener, Caroline. "The Women behind the 'Alt-right.'" *The Atlantic*. August 18, 2017. https://www.theatlantic.com/politics/archive/2017/08/the-women-behind-the-alt-right/537168/.

Knowles, Eric D., and Linda R. Tropp. "A Lot of People in the US Are Suddenly Identifying as 'White'—and a Lot of Them Support Donald Trump." Quartz. October 25, 2016. http://qz.com/816229/a-lot-of-people-in-the-us-are-suddenly-identifying-as-white/. Accessed December 15, 2016.

Koumpilova, Mila. "University of Minnesota Ramps Up Sexual Misconduct Prevention Program." *Star Tribune*. February 9, 2018. http://www.startribune.com/u-ramps-up-sexual-misconduct-program/473605633/.

Kramarae, Cheris, and Paula A. Treichler. *A Feminist Dictionary*. Champaign: University of Illinois Press, 1996.

Krolokke, Charlotte, and Anne S. Sorensen. *Gender Communication Theories and Analyses*. Thousand Oaks, CA: Sage, 2006.

Lakoff, George. *Don't Think of an Elephant: Know Your Values and Frame the Debate*. White River Junction, VT: Chelsea Green Publishing, 2004.

"Latest Trends: Usage over Time." Pew Internet and American Life Project. June 2005. http://www.pewintemet.org/trends.asp. Accessed January 12, 2006.

Legro, Michelle. "How Can Alt-right Women Exist in a Misogynistic Movement?" Longreads. 2017. https://longreads.com/2017/08/22/how-can-alt-right-women-exist-in-a-misogynistic-movement/.

Lehto, Mari. "Bad Is the New Good: Negotiating Bad Motherhood in Finnish Mommy Blogs." *Feminist Media Studies* 19(5) (2019): 1–15. doi:10.1080/14680777.2019.1642224.

Leonardo, Zeus. "The Color of Supremacy: Beyond the Discourse of 'White Privilege.'" *Educational Philosophy and Theory* 36(2) (2004): 37–52.

Lessig, Lawrence. *Code and Other Laws of Cyberspace*. New York: Basic Books, 2000.

Levmore, Saul, and Martha C. Nussbaum. *The Offensive Internet: Speech, Privacy, and Reputation*. Cambridge, MA: Harvard University Press, 2012.

Lewis, Rebecca. *Alternative Influence: Broadcasting the Reactionary Right on YouTube*. Data & Society. https://datasociety.net/wp-content/uploads/2018/09/DS_Alternative_Influence.pdf.

Light, Michael T., and Ty Miller. "Does Undocumented Immigration Increase Violent Crime?" *Criminology* 56(2) (May 2017): 370–401. https://www.ncbi.nlm.nih.gov/pmc/articles/PMC6241529/.

Lilla, Mark. "The Tea Party Jacobins." *New York Review of Books*. May 27, 2010. http://www|.nybooks.com.ezp1.1ib.umn.edu/articles/2010/05/27/tea-party-jacobins/. Accessed January 9, 2018.

Lin, Cynthia S., Alisa A. Pyketta, Constance Flanagana, and Karma R. Chávez. "Engendering the Prefigurative: Feminist Praxes That Bridge a Politics of Prefigurement and Survival." *Journal of Social and Political Psychology* 4(1) (2016): 302–17. doi:10.5964/jspp.v4i1.537.

Lipsitz, George. *The Possessive Investment in Whiteness: How White People Profit from Identity Politics*. Revised and expanded edition ed. Philadelphia: Temple University Press, 2006.

Lopéz, Haney. *White by Law: The Legal Construction of Race*. New York: New York University Press, 1996.

Lorde, Audre. "Age, Race, Class and Sex: Women Redefining Difference." Paper delivered at the Copeland Colloquium, Amherst College, April 1980. Reproduced in *Sister Outsider*. Berkeley, CA: Crossing Press, 1984. https://www.colorado.edu/odece/sites/default/files/attached-files/rba09-sb4converted_8.pdf.

Lorde, Audre. "The Master's Tools Will Never Dismantle the Master's House." 1984. In *Sister Outsider: Essays and Speeches*. Berkeley, CA: Crossing Press: 2007. Found on Collectiveliberation.org, http://collectiveliberation.org/wp-content/uploads/2013/01/Lorde_The_Masters_Tools.pdf. Accessed January 2, 2016.

Lorde, Audre. "The Uses of Anger: Women Responding to Racism." Keynote presentation at the National Women's Studies Association Conference, Storrs, Connecticut. 1981. http://www.blackpast.org/1981-audre-lorde-uses-anger-women-responding-racism.

Love, Nancy S. *Trendy Fascism: White Power Music and the Future of Democracy*. Albany: State University of New York Press, 2016.

Lozano-Reich, Nina M., and Dana L. Cloud. "The Uncivil Tongue: Invitational Rhetoric and the Problem of Inequality." *Western Journal of Communication* 73(2) (2009): 221–26. doi:10.1080/10570310902856105.

Lucaites, John L., and Celeste M. Condit. "Reconstructing <Equality>: Culturetypal and Counter-Cultural Rhetorics in the Martyred Black Vision." *Communication Monographs* 57 (1990): 5–24. EBSCOhost.

Lucaites, John L., Celeste Michelle Condit, and Sally Caudill, eds. *Contemporary Rhetorical Theory: A Reader*. New York: Guilford Press, 1999.

Luce, Edward. "Ivanka Trump's G20 Performance Puzzles World Leaders." *Irish Times*. July 1, 2019. https://www.irishtimes.com/news/world/us/ivanka-trump-s-g20-performance -puzzles-world-leaders-1.3942812.

Macedo, Donaldo. Introduction. In P. Freire, ed., *Pedagogy of the Oppressed*. New York: Continuum International Publishing, 1970.

Mackey, Nathaniel. "Other: From Noun to Verb." *Representations* 39 (1992).

Manovich, Lev. *The Language of New Media*. Cambridge, MA: MIT Press, 2000.

Marcel, Mary. *The Zapatistas and Cyberspace*. Paper presented at the National Communication Association Convention, Seattle, WA. 2000.

Martinez, Alberto A. "The Media Needs to Stop Telling This Lie about Donald Trump, I'm a Sanders Supporter—and Value Honesty." Salon. December 21, 2015. https://www.salon .com/2015/12/21/the_media_needs_to_stop_telling_this_lie_about_donald_trump_im_a _sanders_supporter_and_value_honesty/.

Martinez, Elizabeth. "Beyond Black/White: The Racisms of our Times." *Social Justice* 20(1/2) (1993): 22–34.

Martinot, Steve. *The Machinery of Whiteness: Studies in the Structure of Racialization*. Philadelphia: Temple University Press, 2010.

Massa, Jessica, Kirsten King, and Izzy Francke. "How Much of a Feminist Are You?" Buzzfeed. July 29, 2017. https://www.buzzfeed.com/jessicamassa1/how-much-of-a-feminist-are-you ?utm_term=.fx16W1ae4#.uu3Wr1wDd.

Matthews, Dylan. "Paleoconservatism, the Movement That Explains Donald Trump, Explained." Vox. May 6, 2016. https://www.vox.com/2016/5/6/11592604/donald-trump -paleoconservative-buchanan.

McAdam, Doug. 1982. *Political Process and the Development of Black Insurgency, 1930–1970*. Chicago: University of Chicago Press, 1982.

McCarthy, Niall. "U.S. Hate Crimes Rise for Third Straight Year." Statista. November 15, 2018. https://www.statista.com/chart/16100/total-number-of-hate-crime-incidents-recorded-by -the-fbi/.

McDonough, Katie. "The Silent Majority: The Quiet Racism behind the White Female Trump Voter." *Fusion*. November 17, 2016. http://fusion.net/story/370440/white-women-racism -donald-trump/. Accessed December 15, 2016.

McEvers, Kelly. "'We're Not Going Away': Alt-Right Leader on Voice in Trump Administration." *All Things Considered*. NPR. November 17, 2016. https://www.npr.org /2016/11/17/502476139/were-not-going-away-alt-right-leader-on-voice-in-trump -administration.

McGee, Michael Calvin. "The 'Ideograph': A Link Between Rhetoric and Ideology." *Quarterly Journal of Speech* 66 (1980): 1–16.

McKerrow, Raymie. "Critical Rhetoric: Theory and Praxis." *Communication Monographs* 56 (1989): 91–111.

McKinnon, Sara L., et al. "Rhetoric and Ethics Revisited: What Happens When Rhetorical Scholars Go into the Field." *Cultural Studies Critical Methodologies* 1 (2016): 1–11. doi:10.1177/1532708616659080. Accessed August 22, 2016.

McLaine, Steven. "Ethnic Online Communities: Between Profit and Purpose." In M. McCaughey and M. Ayers, eds., *Cyberactivism: Online Activism in Theory and Practice*, 233–54. New York: Routledge, 2003.

McLaren, Brian D. "The 'Alt-Right' Has Created Alt-Christianity." *Time*. August 25, 2017. http://time.com/4915161/charlottesville-alt-right-alt-christianity/.

McLaughlin, Shaymus. "YouTuber Lauren Southern's University of Minnesota Event Met with 200 Protestors." GoMN. October 26, 2017. https://www.gomn.com/news/youtuber-lauren -southerns-university-of-minnesota-event-met-with-200-protesters.

McLuhan, Marshall. *The Medium Is the Massage: An Inventory of Effects*. Corte Madera, CA: Gingko Press, 1967.

McRae, Elisabeth G. *Mothers of a Massive Resistance: White Women and the Politics of White Supremacy*. Oxford: Oxford University Press, 2018.

McVeigh, Rory. "Structured Ignorance and Organized Racism in the United States." *Social Forces* 82(3) (2004): 895–936. doi.org/10.1353/sof.2004.0047.

McVeigh, Rory, Kraig Beyerlein, Burrel Vann Jr., and Priyamvada Trivedi. "Educational Segregation, Tea Party Organizations, and Battles over Distributive Justice." *American Sociological Review* 79(4) (2014): 630–52. http://www.jstor.org/stable/43187557.

McWilliams, James. "Bryan Stevenson on What Well-meaning White People Need to Know about Race." Pacific Standard. February 6, 2018. https://psmag.com/magazine/bryan -stevenson-ps-interview.

Meeks, Lindsay, and David Domke. "When Politics Is a Woman's Game: Party and Gender Ownership in Woman-versus-Woman Elections." *Communication Research* 4(7) (2016): 895–921. doi:10.1177/0093650215581369.

Mettler, Katie, and Avi Selk. "GoDaddy—then Google—Ban Neo-nazi Site Daily Stormer for Disparaging Charlottesville Victim." Washington Post. August 14, 2017. https://www.wash ingtonpost.com/news/morning-mix/wp/2017/08/14/godaddy-bans-neo-nazi-site-daily -stormer-for-disparaging-woman-killed-at-charlottesville-rally/?utm_term=.6a902cc6be5b.

Meza, Summer. "Who Voted for Doug Jones? White Women back Roy Moore." *Newsweek*. December 13, 2017. http://www.newsweek.com/doug-jones-roy-moore-alabama-senate -race-special-election-results-demographics-746366.

Michael, George. "The Rise of the Alt-right and the Politics of Polarization in America." Skeptic. https://www.skeptic.com/reading_room/rise-of-alt-right-politics-of-polarization -in-america/. Accessed March 4, 2018.

Miller, Carolyn. "What Can Automation Tell Us about Agency?" *Rhetoric Society Quarterly* 37(2) (2007): 137–57. doi:10.1080/02773940601021197.

Mills, Charles, W. "Global White Ignorance." In *Routledge International Handbook of Ignorance Studies*, 217–27. 2015. doi:10.4324/9781315867762.

Mills, Charles W. *The Racial Contract*. Ithaca, NY: Cornell University Press, 1997.

Moeller, Kathryn. "Whiteness in an Era of Trump: Where Do We Go from Here?" Huffington Post. March 8, 2016. http://www.huffingtonpost.com/kathryn-moeller/whiteness-in-an -era-of-tr_b_9404240.html. Accessed December 15, 2016.

Montalbano, Ginny. "Feminist Snipes at Melania Are Unfair. She's a Fine First Lady." *Newsweek*. January 25, 2018. http://www.newsweek.com/feminist-snipes-melania-are -unfair-shes-fine-first-lady-790765. Accessed February 24, 2018.

Moore, Suzanne. "We Laugh at Ivanka Trump—Because to Take Her Seriously Is Frightening." *The Guardian*. July 1, 2019. https://www.theguardian.com/commentisfree/2019/jul/01 /ivanka-trump-g20-ghastly-spectacle-rise-unelected.

Moore, Suzanne. "Why Did Women Vote for Trump? Because Misogyny Is Not a Male-only Attribute." *The Guardian*. November 16, 2016. https://www.theguardian.com/lifeandstyle /commentisfree/2016/nov/16/why-did-women-vote-for-trump-because-misogyny-is-not -a-male-only-attribute. Accessed December 15, 2016.

Mukhhopadhyay, Samhita, and Kate Harding, eds. *Nasty Women: Feminism, Resistance, and Revolution in Trump's America*. New York: Picador, 2017.

"Multiracial in America. Chapter 1: Race and Multiracial Americans in the U.S. Census." Pew Internet & American Life Project. 2015. http://www.pewsocialtrends.org/2015/06/11/chapter -1-race-and-multiracial-americans-in-the-u-s-census/. Accessed June 11, 2015.

Nakamura, Lisa. *Cybertypes: Race, Ethnicity, and Identity on the Internet*. New York: Routledge, 2002.

Nakamura, Lisa. "Pregnant Sims: Avatars and the Visual Reproduction of Motherhood on the Web." In Chris Berry, Soyoung Kim, Lynn Spigel, eds., *Electronic Elsewheres: Media, Technology, and the Experience of Social Space*. Minneapolis: University of Minnesota Press, 2009.

Nakamura, Lisa. "Watching White Supremacy on Digital Video Platforms: 'Screw Your Optics, I'm Going In.'" *Film Quarterly* 72(3) (Spring 2019): 19–22. doi:10.1525/fq.2019.72.3.19.

Nakayama, Thomas K., and Robert L. Krizek. "Whiteness as a Strategic Rhetoric." *Quarterly Journal of Speech* 81 (1995): 293.

Negroponte, Nicholas. "Negroponte: Internet Is Way to World Peace." CNN Interactive. November 25, 1997. http://www.cnn.com/TECH/9711/25/internet.peace.reut/.

Neuhouser, Kevin. "If I Had Abandoned My Children: Community Mobilization and Commitment to the Identity of Mother in Northeast Brazil." *Social Forces* 77(1) (1998): 331–58; 358–59. http://www.jstor.org/stable/3006020. Accessed March 8, 2018.

"New Ban: Do Not Post in Support of Trump or His Administration." RPG.com. October 29, 2018. https://forum.rpg.net/index.php?threads/new-ban-do-not-post-in-support-of-trump -or-his-administration.835849/.

"New Policy: Do Not Post in Support of Trump or His Administration." Ravelry. June 23, 2019. https://www.ravelry.com/content/no-trump.

Newport, Frank. "U.S., Negative View of the Tea Party Rise to New High." Gallup. April 28, 2011. http://news.gallup.com/poll/147308/negative-views-tea-party-rise-new-high.aspx. Accessed January 22, 2018.

New York Times/CBS Poll. "National Poll of Tea Party Supporters." April 2010. https://www. nytimes.com/interactive/projects/documents/new-york-timescbs-news-poll-national -survey-of-tea-party-supporters.

Noble, Safiya U. *Algorithms of Oppression: How Search Engines Reinforce Racism*. New York: New York University Press, 2018.

Noble, Safiya. "Challenging the Algorithms of Oppression." YouTube. June 15, 2016. https:// www.youtube.com/watch?v=iRVZozEEWlE.

Noble, Safiya U. "Missed Connections: What Search Engines Say about Women." *Bitch* 54 (2012): 36–41. https://safiyaunoble.files.wordpress.com/2012/03/54_search_engines.pdf.

Norton, Michael I., and Samuel R. Sommers. "Whites See Racism as a Zero-Sum Game That They Are Now Losing." *Perspectives on Psychological Science* 6(3) (2011): 215–18. https:// www.jstor.org/stable/41613491.

Obama, Michelle. "TRANSCRIPT: Michelle Obama's Speech on Donald Trump's Alleged Treatment of Women." NPR. October 13, 2016. https://www.npr.org/2016/10/13/497846667 /transcript-michelle-obamas-speech-on-donald-trumps-alleged-treatment-of-women.

Olsson, Jona. "Detour-spotting for White Anti-racists." Cultural Bridges to Justice. Updated January 2011. http://www.culturalbridgestojustice.org/resources/written/detour. Accessed February 12, 2018.

Oluo, Ijeoma. "The beauty of anti-racism is that you don't have to pretend to be free of racism to be an anti-racist. Anti-racism is the commitment to fight racism wherever you find it, including in yourself. And it's the only way forward." Twitter. July 14, 2019. https://twitter .com/IjeomaOluo/status/1150565193832943617?s=20.

Oluo, Ijeoma. "The Heart of Whiteness: Ijeoma Oluo Interviews Rachel Dolezal, the White Woman Who Identifies as Black." The Stranger. April 19, 2017. https://www.thestranger .com/features/2017/04/19/25082450/the-heart-of-whiteness-ijeoma-oluo-interviews-rachel -dolezal-the-white-woman-who-identifies-as-black.

O'Neal, Lonnae. "Ibram Kendi, One of the Nation's Leading Scholars of Racism, Says Education and Love Are Not the Answer." The Undefeated. September 20, 2017. https:// theundefeated.com/features/ibram-kendi-leading-scholar-of-racism-says-education-and -love-are-not-the-answer/.

Ono, Kent, and John M. Sloop. "The Critique of Vernacular Discourse." Communication Monographs 62 (March 1995): 19–46.

Onwuka, Patrice. "Hope Brings Another Woman to Trump Leadership Circle." Independent Women's Forum. August 17, 2017. http://iwf.org/blog/2804564/Hope-Brings-Another -Woman-to-Trump-Leadership-Circle. Accessed February 23, 2018.

Oppenheimer, Maya. "Ivanka Trump's New Book on Being a Working Mother Struggling to Fit in Massages." Independent. May 2, 2017. http://www.independent.co.uk/news/world /americas/ivanka-trump-new-book-no-time-for-massages-superwoman-myth-working -mother-debunk-first-daughter-a7713546.html.

Orlov, Alex. "More White Women Voted for Donald Trump than Hillary Clinton." Mic. November 9, 2016. https://mic.com/articles/158995/more-white-women-voted-for-donald -trump-than-for-hillary-clinton#.LaNF4dN5c. Accessed December 15, 2016.

Ortega, Mariana. "Being Lovingly, Knowingly Ignorant: White Feminism and Women of Color." Hypatia 21(3) (2006): 56–74. http://www.jstor.org/stable/3810951.

Ott, Brian L., and Greg Dickinson. The Twitter Presidency: Donald J. Trump and the Politics of White Rage. New York: Routledge, 2019.

Ousey, Graham C., and Charis E. Kubrin. "Immigration and Crime: Assessing a Contentious Issue." Annual Review of Criminology 1 (2017): 63–84. doi.org/10.1146/annurev-crimnol-032317-092022.

Pallotta, Frank. "The 'P-word' Problem: Trump's Comments Pose Issue for News Outlets." CNN Media. September 7, 2016. http://money.cnn.com/2016/10/07/media/vulgar-comments -donald-trump-headlines/index.html.

Panzar, Javier. "Melania Trump's RNC Speech Is Strikingly Similar to Michelle Obama's 2008 Convention Speech." Los Angeles Times. July 18, 2016. http://www.latimes.com/nation /politics/trailguide/la-na-republican-convention-2016-live-melania-trump-s-rnc-speech -appears-to-1468901655-htmlstory.html.

Pedersen, Sarah. "Press Response to Women Politicians." Journalism Studies 19(5) (2018): 709–25. doi.org/10.1080/1461670X.2016.1200953.

Phillip, Abby. "Embassies Court Ivanka Trump to Build a Relationship with Her Father's Administration." Washington Post. May 19, 2017.

Picci, Aimee. "Kellyanne Conway on Ivanka's Brand: 'Go Buy It Today.'" Moneywatch. CBS News. February 9, 2017. https://www.cbsnews.com/news/kellyanne-conway-on-ivankas -brand-go-buy-it-today/.

Posner, Sarah. "How Donald Trump's New Campaign Chief Created an Online Haven for White Nationalists." *Mother Jones*. August 22, 2016. https://www.motherjones.com/politics /2016/08/stephen-bannon-donald-trump-alt-right-breitbart-news/.

Post, Michelle Brunetti. "Kellyanne Conway Played Key Role in Trump's Road to Presidency." *Press of Atlantic City*. November 9, 2016. http://www.pressofatlanticcity.com/news/trump -strategist-kellyanne-conway-has-deep-roots-in-south-jersey/article_59853be4–6e5a-5e9c -bdf7-cfc18fb1647e.html.

Potok, Mark. "The Year in Hate and Extremism." Southern Poverty Law Center. February 17, 2016.

Potok, Mark, and Laurie Wood. "Leaving White Nationalism." Southern Poverty Law Center. August 21, 2013. https://www.splcenter.org/fighting-hate/intelligence-report/2013/leaving -white-nationalism.

Prividera, Laura C., and John W. Howard III. "Masculinity, Whiteness, and the Warrior Hero: Perpetuating the Strategic Rhetoric of U.S. Nationalism and the Marginalization of Women." *Women and Language* 29(2) (2006): 29–37.

"Race and Ethnicity in the Midwest." Statistical Atlas. https://statisticalatlas.com/region /Midwest/Race-and-Ethnicity. Accessed February 28, 2018.

Radcliffe, Krista. *Rhetorical Listening: Identification, Gender, Whiteness*. Carbondale: Southern Illinois University Press, 2005.

Ramsey, Franchesca. "The Surprisingly Racist History of 'Caucasian.'" MTV News. April 15, 2016. https://www.youtube.com/watch?v=GKB8hXYod2w&list=PLnvZ3PbKA pGM-hHuQ91Nc50SKsusjn0Z6&index=27.

Reger, Jo. "Drawing Identity Boundaries: The Creation of Contemporary Feminism." In Jo Reger, Daniel J. Myers, and Rachel L. Einwohner, eds., *Identity Work in Social Movements*, 101–20. Minneapolis: University of Minnesota Press, 2008.

Reilly, Katie. "The Biggest Controversies in Betsy DeVos' First Year." *Time*. December 14, 2017. https://time.com/5053007/betsy-devos-education-secretary-2017-controversies/.

Reiss, Jaclyn. "Kellyanne Conway Says Anderson Cooper's Eye Roll Was 'Possibly Sexist.'" *Boston Globe*. May 14, 2017. https://www.bostonglobe.com/news/politics/2017/05/14/kellyanne -conway-says-anderson-cooper-eye-roll-was-possibly-sexist/3UsNcT24uw610AP52JylYO /story.html.

Relman, Eliza. "The Rise of Sarah Huckabee Sanders, the New Star of the Trump Administration." *Business Insider*. June 30, 2017. https://www.businessinsider.in/the-rise-of-sarah -huckabee-sanders-the-new-star-of-the-trump-administration/articleshow/59394439.cms.

Republican Party. "Restoring the American Dream." https://www.gop.com/platform/restoring -the-american-dream/.

Republican Platform 2016. Committee on Arrangements for the 2016 Republican National Convention. Accessed February 28, 2018. https://prod-cdn-static.gop.com/media/docu- ments/DRAFT_12_FINAL%5B1%5D-ben_1468872234.pdf.

"#rhetoricsowhite: Addressing Racial, Gender, Language, and Nationality Bias in Publications, Editorships, Reviews, and Citation Patterns in Rhetorical Studies." Panel at National Communication Association Convention 2018. Salt Lake City, Utah. November 9, 2018. https://www.natcom.org/sites/default/files/annual-convention/NCA_Convention _Archives_2018_Program.pdf.

Rich, Adrienne. "Disloyal to Civilization: Feminism, Racism, Gynephobia." 1978. http://chains ofblocks.com/kindle/download/id=188848&type=file.

Rickert, Thomas. "Tarrying with the <Head>: The Emergence of Control through Protocol." In Bradley Dilger and Jeff Rice, eds., *From A to A: Keywords of Markup*. Minneapolis: University of Minnesota Press, 2010.

Ridgeway, Cecilia, and Lynn Smith-Lovin. "The Gender System and Interaction." *Annual Review of Sociology* 25 (1999): 191–216. Accessed November 22, 2005.

Roff, Peter. "The Tea Party Movement Is a Women's Movement." *U.S. News*. September 23, 2010. https://www.usnews.com/opinion/blogs/peter-roff/2010/09/23/the-tea-party-movement -is-a-womens-movement. Accessed January 9, 2018.

Roberts, David. "Donald Trump and the Rise of Tribal Epistemology." Vox. May 19, 2017. https://www.vox.com/policy-and-politics/2017/3/22/14762030/donald-trump-tribal -epistemology. Accessed May 20, 2017.

Rogers, Katie. "White Women Helped Elect Donald Trump." *New York Times*. November 9, 2016. http://www.nytimes.com/2016/12/01/us/politics/white-women-helped-elect-donald -trump.html?_r=0. Accessed December 15, 2016.

Rokeach, Milton. *Beliefs, Attitudes, and Values*. San Francisco: Jossey-Bass, 1968.

Rosenberg, Alyssa. "'Politically Incorrect' Ideas Are Mostly Rude, Not Brave." *Washington Post*. August 11, 2016.

Ryan, Charlotte, Kevin M. Carragee, and William Meinhofer. "Theory into Practice: Framing, the News Media, and Collective Action." *Journal of Broadcasting and Electronic Media* 45 (2001): 175–82. doi.org/10.1207/s15506878jobem4501_11.

Ryan, Josiah. "'This Was a Whitelash': Van Jones' Take on the Election Results." CNN Politics. November 9, 2016. http://www.cnn.com/2016/11/09/politics/van-jones-results-disappoint ment-cnntv/. Accessed December 15, 2016.

Sandberg, Sheryl. *Lean In: Women, Work, and the Will to Lean*. New York: Knopf, 2013.

Saslow, Eli. "The White Flight of Derek Black." *Washington Post*. October 15, 2016. https://www .washingtonpost.com/national/the-white-flight-of-derek-black/2016/10/15/ed5f906a-8f3b -11e6-a6a3-d50061aa9fae_story.html?utm_term=.3cd769cacfc7.

Schreiber, Ronnee. "Dilemmas of Representation: Conservative and Feminist Women's Organizations React to Sarah Palin." In Kathleen M. Blee and Sandra McGee Deutsch, eds., *Women of the Right: Comparisons and Interplay across Borders*, 273–90. University Park: Pennsylvania State University Press, 2012.

Schroer, Todd. "Technical Advances in Communication: The Example of White Racialist 'Love Groups' and 'White Civil Rights Organizations.'" In Jo Reger et al., eds., *Identity Work in Social Movements*, 77–99. Minneapolis: University of Minnesota Press, 2008.

Schuetz, Janice, and Rachel Stohr. "Cyberadvocacy and the Evolution of the Tea Party Movement." Conference Proceedings, 655–63. National Communication Association/ American Forensic Association (Alta Conference on Argumentation). 2011.

Sebastian, Michael. "Who Is Kellyanne Conway? 20 Things to Know about Donald Trump's Presidential Counselor." *Cosmopolitan*. June 5, 2017. http://www.cosmopolitan.com/politics /news/a62994/kellyanne-conway-trump-new-campaign-manager/.

Shanker, Vidhya. "A Look at Language Week: Tidying Evaluation of 'Diversity' and 'Culture.'" American Evaluation Association. June 24, 2019. https://aea365.org/blog/a-look-at -language-week-tidying-evaluation-of-diversity-culture-by-vidhya-shanker/.

Shome, Raka. "'Global Motherhood': The Transnational Intimacies of White Femininity." *Critical Studies in Media Communication* 28 (2011): 388–406. doi:10.1080/15295036.2011 .589861.

Shotwell, Alexis. *Against Purity: Living Ethically in Compromised Times*. Minneapolis: University of Minnesota Press, 2016.

Singleton, Glenn Eric, and Curtis Linton. *Courageous Conversations about Race: A Field Guide for Achieving Equity in Schools*. Thousand Oaks, CA: Corwin Press, 2006.

Smith, Laura. "The KKK Might have Died in Obscurity If This Sinister, Racist Woman Didn't Come Along." Timeline. December 11, 2017. https://timeline.com/did-you-know-that -the-brains-behind-the-kkk-was-a-woman-a23d7d361d1d.

Smith, Laura. "The Truth about Women and White Supremacy." *The Cut*. New York. August 13, 2017. https://www.thecut.com/2017/08/charlottesville-attack-women-white-supremacy .html.

Smith, Paul. "Responsibilities." In Paul Smith, *Discerning the Subject*, 152–60. Minneapolis: University of Minnesota Press, 1988.

Snow, David A., E. Burke Rochford Jr., Steven K. Worden, and Robert D. Benford. "Frame Alignment Processes, Micromobilization, and Movement Participation." *American Sociological Review* 51(4) (1986): 454–81. https://www.jstor.org/stable/2095581.

Soares, Marta Alice Gabriel. *The Problem That Has a Name: On "Mama Grizzlies" and Conservative Feminism*. e-cadernos 14 (2011). http://journals.openedition.org/eces/890; doi:10.4000/eces.890. Accessed March 7, 2018.

Solotaroff, Paul. "Trump Seriously: On the Trail with the GOP's Tough Guy." *Rolling Stone*. September 9, 2015. https://www.rollingstone.com/politics/politics-news/trump-seriously -on-the-trail-with-the-gops-tough-guy-41447/. Accessed March 23, 2016.

Sonnad, Nikhil, and Tim Squirrell. "The Alt-right Is Creating Its Own Dialect. Here's a Complete Guide." Quartz. November 30, 2017. https://qz.com/1092037/the-alt-right-is -creating-its-own-dialect-heres-a-complete-g.

Southern Poverty Law Center. "Active Hate Groups in the United States in 2015." https://www .splcenter.org/fighting-hate/intelligence-report/2016/active-hate-groups-united-states-2015.

Southern Poverty Law Center. "Alt-right." Accessed March 4, 2018. https://www.splcenter.org /fighting-hate/extremist-files/ideology/alt-right.

Southern Poverty Law Center. "The Alt-right on Campus: What Students Need to Know." 2017. https://www.splcenter.org/20170810/alt-right-campus-what-students-need-know.

Southern Poverty Law Center. "Fringe racists, conspiracy theorists make bids for office." August 3, 2016. Accessed August 12, 2016.

Southern Poverty Law Center. "Ten Days After: Harassment and Intimidation in the Aftermath of the Election." November 29, 2016. Accessed December 6, 2016.

Soyez, Dietrich. "Anchored Locally—Linked Globally, Transnational Social Movement Organizations in a (Seemingly) Borderless World." *GeoJournal* 52 (2000): 7–16. doi:10.1023/A:1013191329715.

Spivak, Gayatri C. "Subaltern Studies: Deconstructing Historiography." In R. Guha and G. C. Spivak, eds., *Selected Subaltern Studies*, 3–34. New York: Oxford University Press, 1988.

Squires, Catherine. *The Post-Racial Mystique: Media and Race in the Twenty-First Century*. New York: New York University Press, 2014.

Steele, Edward, and William Redding. "The American Value System: Premises for Persuasion." *Western Speech* 26(2) (1962): 86–91.

Stephens, Maegan, Joseph Yoo, Rachel R. Mourão, Fatima Martinez Gutierrez, Brian Baresch, and Thomas J. Johnson. "The Life of the Tea Party: Differences between Tea Party and

Republican Media Use and Political Variables." *Atlantic Journal of Communication* 24(3) (2016): 157–71. doi.org/10.1080/15456870.2016.1184665.

Stevens, Jacqueline. *States without Nations: Citizenship for Mortals*. New York: Columbia University Press, 2010.

Stewart, Charles. "White Aryan Resistance on the Internet: A Rhetorical Assault on Conventional Rhetorical Wisdom." Paper presented at National Communication Association Conference. Seattle, Washington. 2000.

Stewart, Charles, and William Cash. "The Persuasive Interview: The Persuader." In Charles Stewart and William Cash, eds., *Interviewing: Principles and Practices*, 269–99. New York: McGraw-Hill, 2006.

Stewart, Charles J., Craig A. Smith, and Robert E. Denton Jr. *Persuasion and Social Movements*. 6th ed. Prospect Heights, IL: Waveland Press, 2012.

Stone, Allucquère R. *The War of Desire and Technology and the Close of the Mechanical Age*. Cambridge, MA: MIT Press, 1996.

Swain, Carol. *The New White Nationalism in America*. Cambridge: Cambridge University Press, 2002.

Szymanski, Dawn M., Arpana Gupta, Erika R. Carr, and Destin Stewart. "Internalized Misogyny as a Moderator of the Link between Sexist Events and Women's Psychological Distress." *Sex Roles* 61(1) (2009): 101–9. doi:10.1007/s11199-009-9611-y.

"Taking a Stand against Harassment, Part of the Broader Threat to Higher Education." American Association of University Professors. September 7, 2017. https://www.aaup.org/taking-stand-against-harassment-part-broader-threat-higher-education.

Taub, Amanda. "Behind 2016's Turmoil, a Crisis of White Identity." *New York Times*. November 1, 2016. http://www.nytimes.com/2016/11/02/world/americas/brexit-donald-trump-whites.html. Accessed December 15, 2016.

Taylor, Jessica. "Laptops and Playpens: 'Mommy Bloggers' and Visions of Household Work." In L. Adkins and M. Dever, eds., *The Post-Fordist Sexual Contract*, 109–28. London: Palgrave Macmillan, 2016.

Taylor, T. L. "Multiple Pleasures: Women and Online Gaming." *Convergence* 9 (2003): 21–46. doi:10.1177/135485650300900103.

Tea Party Patriots. "Mission." March 26, 2010. https://web.archive.org/web/20100326080834/http://www.teapartypatriots.org:80/Mission.aspx.

Tedford, Thomas L., and Dale A. Herbeck. *Freedom of Speech in the United States*. 8th ed. State College, PA: Strata, 2017.

Telford, Telford, and Eli Rosenberg. "A Coast Guard Officer on Florence Duty Made a Hand Gesture on TV. Some Saw a White-power Sign." *Washington Post*, September 14, 2018. https://www.washingtonpost.com/nation/2018/09/15/coast-guard-officer-ousted-florence-duty-after-viewers-claim-he-made-white-power-sign-tv/?arc404=true.

Teel, Karen. "Feeling White, Feeling Good: 'Antiracist' White Sensibilities." In George Yancy, ed., *White Self-Criticality beyond Anti-racism: How Does It Feel to Be a White Problem?*, 21–35. Lanham, MD: Lexington, 2015.

Tettegah, Sharon. "The Racial Consciousness Attitudes of White Prospective Teachers and Their Perceptions of the Teachability of Students from Different Racial/Ethnic Backgrounds: Findings from a California Study." *Journal of Negro Education* 65(2) (Spring 1996): 151–63. https://www.jstor.org/stable/2967310.

Tettegah, Sharon, Brian P. Bailey, and Kona Taylor. "Clover: Narratives and Simulations in Virtual Environments." *Journal of Negro Education* 76(1) (2007): 43–56.

Tharrington, Ali. "What Happened When I Took a 'White Women Elected Trump' Sign to the Women's March." Vox. January 24, 2017. http://www.vox.com/first-person/2017/1/24/14369914/donald-trump-womens-march-sign.

Thompson, Jason. "Magic for a People Trained in Pragmatism: Kenneth Burke, Mein Kampf, and the Early 9/11 Oratory of George W. Bush." *Rhetoric Review* 30(4) (2011): 358–59. Accessed May 20, 2016.

Trump, Ivanka. "1:2 There should be no place in society for racism, white supremacy and neo-nazis." Twitter. August 13, 2017. twitter.com/IvankaTrump/status/896705195228381187?ref_src=twsrc%5Etfw&ref_url=http%3A%2F%2Ffortune.com%2F2017%2F08%2F13%2Fivanka-trump-response-charlottesville-virginia-rally%2F.

"Trump Ends DACA, Calls on Congress to Act." National Public Radio. September 5, 2017. https://www.npr.org/2017/09/05/546423550/trump-signals-end-to-daca-calls-on-congress-to-act.

Tucker, J. B. W. "The Ultimate White Privilege Statistics and Data Post." 2015. http://www.jbwtucker.com/ultimate-white-privilege-statistics/. Accessed March 23, 2016.

"Twitter Announces New Measures to Tackle Abuse and Harassment." *The Guardian*. February 7, 2017. https://www.theguardian.com/technology/2017/feb/07/twitter-abuse-harassment-crackdown.

U.S. Department of Homeland Security. "Departments of Justice and Homeland Security Release Quarterly Alien Incarceration Report Highlighting the Negative Effects of Illegal Immigration and the Need for Border Security." June 7, 2018. https://www.dhs.gov/news/2018/06/07/departments-justice-and-homeland-security-release-quarterly-alien-incarceration.

United States District Court: Southern District Court of New York. *Knight First Amendment Institute v. Trump, Hicks, Sanders, and Scavino.* Case 1:17-cv-05205-NRB Document 72 Filed 23 May 2018. HeinOnline. https://www-heinonline-org.ezp2.lib.umn.edu/HOL/CaseLawAuth?cid=12720317&native_id=12720317&rest=1&collection=fastcasefull.

"Unity." *Concise Oxford English Dictionary*. 11th ed. 2008.

University of Minnesota. "Sexual Harassment, Sexual Assault, Stalking and Relationship Violence." Administrative Policy Statement. https://policy.umn.edu/hr/sexharassassault.

Van Aelst, Peter, and Stefaan Walgrave. "New Media, New Movements? The Role of the Internet in Shaping the 'Anti-globalization' Movement." *Information, Communication and Society* 5(4) (2002): 465–93. doi:10.1080/13691180208538801.

van Dijk, Teun A. "Discourse and the Denial of Racism." *Discourse and Society* 3(1) (1992): 87–118. https://doi.org/10.1177/0957926592003001005.

Van Natta, Don, and Jill Abramson. "The Presidential Trial: The Lawsuit; Quietly a Team of Lawyers Kept Paula Jones' Case Alive." *New York Times*. January 24, 1999. http://www.nytimes.com/1999/01/24/us/president-s-trial-lawsuit-quietly-team-lawyers-kept-paula-jones-s-case-alive.html.

Vitali, Ali. "The White House Women Who've Got Trump's Back." NBC News. September 18, 2017. https://www.nbcnews.com/politics/white-house/white-house-women-who-ve-got-trump-s-back-n799646.

Walker, Clarence. "'We're Losing Our Country': Barack Obama, Race and the Tea Party." *Daedalus* 140(1) (2011): 125–30. http://www.jstor.org/stable/25790447. Accessed January 9, 2018.

Walker, Rebecca. "Being Real: An Introduction." In Rebecca Walker, ed., *To Be Real: Telling the Truth and Changing the Face of Feminism*, xxix–xl. New York: Anchor Books, 1995.

Wallace, Nicolle. "Sarah Palin, Rage Whisperer." *New York Times*. January 25, 2016. https://www.nytimes.com/2016/01/26/opinion/sarah-palin-rage-whisperer.html.

Wallach, Phillip. "Why America's Response to the Financial Crisis Brought Us to the Edge of Political Crisis." Brookings Institution. April 21, 2015. https://www.brookings.edu/blog/fixgov/2015/04/21/why-americas-responses-to-the-financial-crisis-brought-us-to-the-edge-of-political-crisis/. Accessed February 14, 2018.

Waltman, Michael. "Stratagems and Heuristics in the Recruitment of Children into Communities of Hate: The Fabric of our Future Nightmares." *Southern Communication Journal* 69(1) (2003): 22–36. doi.org/10.1080/10417940309373276.

Walton, Douglas, and Fabrizio Macagno. "Reasoning from Classifications and Definitions." *Argumentation* 23 (2009): 81–107. doi:10.1007/s10503-008-9110-2.

Weiner, Tim, and Ginger Thompson. "Mexico Lower on Bush's List Since September 11." *New York Times*. December 29, 2001. http://www.nytimes.com/2001/12/29/world/mexico-lower-on-bush-s-list-since-sept-11.html.

Whillock, Rita K. "The Use of Hate as a Stratagem for Achieving Political and Social Goals." In Rita K. Whillock and David Slayden, eds., *Hate Speech*, 228–54. Thousand Oaks, CA: Sage, 1995.

Wideman, Stephanie L. "An American Carnival: The Tea Party and Sarah Palin." *The Forensic of Pi Kappa Delta* 96(2) (2011): 11–20.

Wilkinson, Charles A. "A Rhetorical Definition of Movements." *Central States Speech Journal* 27 (1976): 88–94. doi.org/10.1080/10510977609367873.

Williams, Sherley A. "Some Implications of Womanist Theory." *Callaloo* 27 (Spring 1986): 303–8. http://www.jstor.org/stable/2930649.

Williamson, Vanessa et al. "The Tea Party and the Remaking of Republican Conservatism." Perspectives on Politics, 9(1) (March 2011): 25–43 Stable URL: https://www.jstor.org/stable/41622724

"Women in the U.S. Congress 2018." Center for American Women and Politics. 2018. http://www.cawp.rutgers.edu/women-us-congress-2018. Accessed February 24, 2018.

"Women in the U.S. Congress 2019." Center for American Women and Politics. 2019. https://cawp.rutgers.edu/women-us-congress-2019. Accessed March 27, 2019.

"Women of Color in Elective Office 2018." Center for American Women and Politics. 2018. http://www.cawp.rutgers.edu/women-color-elective-office-2018. Accessed February 24, 2018.

Wood, Julia T. *Gendered Lives: Communication, Gender, and Culture*. 3rd ed. Belmont, CA: Wadsworth, 1999.

Wright, Jennifer. "Men Are Responsible for Mass Shootings: How Toxic Masculinity Is Killing Us." *Harper's Bazaar*. February 16, 2018. https://www.harpersbazaar.com/culture/politics/a18207600/mass-shootings-male-entitlement-toxic-masculinity/.

Yan, Holly, Kristina Sgueglia, and Kylie Walker. "'Make American White Again': Hate Speech and Crimes Post-election." CNN. November 10, 2016. https://www.cnn.com/2016/11/10/us/post-election-hate-crimes-and-fears-trnd/index.html. Accessed December 6, 2016.

Yancy, George. *Black Bodies, White Gazes: The Continuing Significance of Race*. Lanham, MD: Rowman & Littlefield, 2008.

Yancy, George. *Look, a White! Philosophical Essays on Whiteness*. Philadelphia: Temple University Press, 2012.

Yancy, George, ed. *White Self-Criticality beyond Anti-racism: How Does It Feel to Be a White Problem?* Lanham, MD: Lexington Books, 2015.

Young, Damon. "I Will Never Underestimate White People's Need to Preserve Whiteness Again." The Root. November 9, 2016. http://verysmartbrothas.com/i-will-never-underesti mate-white-peoples-need-to-preserve-whiteness-again/. Accessed December 15, 2017.

Zajicek, Anna M. "Race Discourses and Antiracist Practices in a Local Women's Movement." *Gender and Society* 16(2) (2002): 155–74. http://www.jstor.org/stable/3081859.

Zickuhr, Kathryn, and Aaron Smith. "Digital Difference." Pew Internet & American Life Project. April 13, 2012. http://pewinternet.org/Reports/2012/Digital-differences/Overview .aspx. Accessed October 3, 2012.

Index

About the Author

Wendy K. Z. Anderson is an independent researcher and instructor in the Department of Communication Studies at the University of Minnesota, Twin Cities. Her research interests lie at the intersection of critical rhetorics and digital media, where she examines how marginalized community rhetorics and critical dialogue (both in content and form) influence institutional, organizational, and infrastructural oppression to impact equity and social change. Dr. Anderson, her partner, Matthew, and their two children call the Minneapolis/St. Paul area home.